ACCLAIM FOR ROBERT J. HUTCHINSON

"*The Dawn of Christianity* is a fascinating look at the early days of the Jesus movement that became the church (from Jesus through the early days of the church). Shunning a skeptical read of this material, author Robert Hutchison works his way through the events and disputes that circulate around the origins of the Christian movement. It is a worthwhile journey with a capable guide that richly repays the reader."

—DARRELL L. BOCK. PhD, SENIOR RESEARCH PROFESSOR OF
NEW TESTAMENT STUDIES, DALLAS THEOLOGICAL SEMINARY

"Jesus was to be a 'sign of contradiction,' as Simeon prophesied in the Temple when Jesus was just an infant. History and now Robert J. Hutchinson's latest book, *The Dawn of Christianity,* continue to bear this out. It's amazing that so many books have been written about Jesus and yet there is still room for this one. *The Dawn of Christianity* will enlighten and delight those who love Jesus and maybe rile and more deeply engage those who oppose him . . . Absolutely worth reading more than once!"

—REV. EAMON KELLY, LC, PONTIFICAL INSTITUTE
NOTRE DAME OF JERUSALEM CENTER

"This entertaining book, setting its scenes with plenty of local color, demonstrates just how far the modern skepticism about Jesus has overreached itself. Questions remain, but Robert Hutchinson reminds us that we do not need to be browbeaten by those who say that only negative answers are available."

—N. T. WRIGHT, PhD, UNIVERSITY OF ST. ANDREWS

"For most of those involved in the modern 'search for the historic Jesus,' it was really a search to debunk the biblical Jesus. But, as Robert Hutchinson demonstrates in this charming book, their efforts were not up to that task—the 'new' evidence turns out to be more compatible with the biblical account."

—RODNEY STARK, PhD, AUTHOR OF *THE TRIUMPH OF
CHRISTIANITY: HOW THE JESUS MOVEMENT BECAME THE WORLD'S
LARGEST RELIGION* AND CODIRECTOR OF THE INSTITUTE
FOR STUDIES OF RELIGION, BAYLOR UNIVERSITY

"Robert Hutchinson's *Searching for Jesus* reviews the evidence, the theories, and the proposals in an informed and engaging way. Students and veteran scholars alike will profit from reading this well-written book. And don't skip the footnotes; they are a trove of famous quotations from primary and secondary literature."

—CRAIG A. EVANS, PHD, JOHN BISAGNO DISTINGUISHED
PROFESSOR OF CHRISTIAN ORIGINS, HOUSTON BAPTIST UNIVERSITY

"Robert Hutchinson's *Searching for Jesus* provides a wonderful introduction to some of the issues and debates about the Jesus of history. Hutchinson shows that the Gospels remain our best sources of information about Jesus. *Searching for Jesus* is a great place to begin learning about Jesus, the Gospels, and history."

—MICHAEL F. BIRD, PHD, LECTURER IN THEOLOGY
AT RIDLEY COLLEGE, MELBOURNE, AUSTRALIA

"Robert Hutchinson's new book—*Searching for Jesus: New Discoveries in the Quest for Jesus of Nazareth*—is a significant and very welcome contribution to the discussion about the 'historical Jesus.' In his book, Hutchinson reviews recent archaeological finds and new directions in New Testament scholarship that challenge some of the older theories. He does it with great clarity and in a lively and intriguing way."

—ISRAEL KNOHL, PHD, THE HEBREW UNIVERSITY, JERUSALEM

"*Searching for Jesus* is an excellent, informed, up-to-date review of biblical research presented in clear, engaging prose for the average reader. Robert Hutchinson shows how recent historical and archaeological investigations have overturned many of the bias-laden and unverified conclusions of biblical scholarship in the past century. I highly recommend *Searching for Jesus* to anyone who is seeking the truth—about Jesus of Nazareth and about the historical accuracy of the Gospels."

—MARK D. ROBERTS, PHD, AUTHOR OF *CAN WE TRUST THE GOSPELS?*

"*Searching for Jesus* offers the reader a readable and accessible overview to the complex field of biblical studies, archaeology, and history related to the life of Jesus. Although I do not share many of the presuppositions or conclusions of Hutchinson, he does attempt to navigate the minefield of disputes, discoveries, and controversies in the field of Jesus studies and offers, particularly in his extensive notes, a useful introductory guide for general readers who wonder what is the latest in historical Jesus research."

—JAMES D. TABOR, PhD, UNIVERSITY OF
NORTH CAROLINA AT CHARLOTTE

"*Searching for Jesus* manages to combine some of the latest (and often technical) scholarly research with a highly readable and accessible style—no mean feat! All of this is infused with relevant anecdotes, which make the book a pleasure to read. Hutchinson's book is ideal for anyone wanting to discover the controversies surrounding the historical figure of Jesus and will hopefully make more people realize why this is such a fascinating area of research."

—JAMES G. CROSSLEY, PhD, UNIVERSITY OF SHEFFIELD

"An excellent conversation starter for study groups, perfect for public and seminary library collections."

—*LIBRARY JOURNAL*

THE DAWN OF CHRISTIANITY

ALSO BY ROBERT J. HUTCHINSON

Searching for Jesus: New Discoveries in the Quest for Jesus of Nazareth—and How They Confirm the Gospel Accounts

The Politically Incorrect Guide to the Bible

When in Rome: A Journal of Life in Vatican City

The Book of Vices: A Collection of Classic Immoral Tales

THE DAWN OF CHRISTIANITY

HOW GOD USED SIMPLE FISHERMEN, SOLDIERS, AND PROSTITUTES TO TRANSFORM THE WORLD

ROBERT J. HUTCHINSON

NELSON
BOOKS

An Imprint of Thomas Nelson

Published in Nashville, Tennessee, by Nelson Books, an imprint of Thomas Nelson. Nelson Books and Thomas Nelson are registered trademarks of HarperCollins Christian Publishing, Inc.

Thomas Nelson titles may be purchased in bulk for educational, business, fund-raising, or sales promotional use. For information, please e-mail SpecialMarkets@ThomasNelson.com.

Any Internet addresses, phone numbers, or company or product information printed in this book are offered as a resource and are not intended in any way to be or to imply an endorsement by Thomas Nelson, nor does Thomas Nelson vouch for the existence, content, or services of these sites, phone numbers, companies, or products beyond the life of this book.

Unless otherwise noted, photos are from Shutterstock.

All italics in Scripture quotations are added by the author for emphasis.

Unless otherwise noted, Scripture quotations are from the ESV® Bible (The Holy Bible, English Standard Version®), copyright © 2001 by Crossway, a publishing ministry of Good News Publishers. Used by permission. All rights reserved.

Scripture quotations marked BSB are taken from the Berean Study Bible (BSB) © 2016 by Bible Hub and Berean Bible. Used by permission. All rights reserved.

Scripture quotations marked CEB are from the Common English Bible. Copyright © 2011 Common English Bible.

Scripture quotations marked CJB are taken from the Complete Jewish Bible. Copyright © 1998 by David H. Stern. All rights reserved.

Scripture quotations marked HCSB are taken from the Holman Christian Standard Bible®, copyright © 1999, 2000, 2002, 2003, 2009 by Holman Bible Publishers. Used by permission. HCSB® is a federally registered trademark of Holman Bible Publishers.

Scripture quotations marked ISV are from *The Holy Bible: International Standard Version*. Release 2.0, Build 2015.02.09. Copyright © 1995–2014 by ISV Foundation. ALL RIGHTS RESERVED INTERNATIONALLY. Used by permission of Davidson Press, LLC.

Scripture quotations marked KJV are taken from the King James Version of the Bible, public domain.

Scripture quotations marked MSG are taken from *The Message*. Copyright © 1993, 1994, 1995, 1996, 2000, 2001, 2002 by Eugene H. Peterson. Used by permission of Tyndale House Publishers, Inc.

Scripture quotations marked NABRE are from the New American Bible, revised edition © 2010, 1991, 1986, 1970 Confraternity of Christian Doctrine, Inc., Washington DC. All rights reserved.

Scripture quotations marked NASB are taken from New American Standard Bible®, copyright © 1960, 1962, 1963, 1968, 1971, 1972, 1973, 1975, 1977, 1995 by The Lockman Foundation. Used by permission. (www.Lockman.org)

Scripture quotations marked NIV are taken from the Holy Bible, New International Version®, NIV®. Copyright © 1973, 1978, 1984, 2011 by Biblica, Inc.™ Used by permission of Zondervan. All rights reserved worldwide. www.zondervan.com. *The "NIV" and "New International Version" are trademarks registered in the United States Patent and Trademark Office by Biblica, Inc.™*

Scripture quotations marked NRSV are from New Revised Standard Version Bible. Copyright © 1989 National Council of the Churches of Christ in the United States of America. Used by permission. All rights reserved.

Scripture quotations marked RSV are taken from the Revised Standard Version of the Bible, copyright 1946, 1952, and 1971 National Council of the Churches of Christ in the United States of America. Used by permission. All rights reserved.

Scripture quotations marked YLT are taken from Young's Literal Translation, public domain.

Library of Congress Cataloging-in-Publication Data

Names: Hutchinson, Robert J., author.
Title: The dawn of Christianity: how God used simple fishermen, soldiers, and prostitutes to transform the world / Robert J. Hutchinson.
Description: Nashville: Thomas Nelson, 2017. | Includes bibliographical references and index.
Identifiers: LCCN 2016044246 | ISBN 9780718079420
Subjects: LCSH: Church history—Primitive and early church, ca. 30–600. | Bible. New Testament—History of Biblical events. | Jesus Christ—Person and offices.
Classification: LCC BR165 .H84 2017 | DDC 270.1—dc23 LC record available at https://lccn.loc.gov/2016044246

Printed in the United States of America

17 18 19 20 21 LSC 6 5 4 3 2 1

For my father,
A'lan S. Hutchinson

לֹא בְחַיִל וְלֹא בְכֹחַ כִּי אִם־בְּרוּחִי אָמַר יְהוָה צְבָאוֹת

"Not by might, nor by power, but by my
Spirit, says the LORD OF HOSTS."
—ZECHARIAH 4:6

"Amen, I say to you, tax collectors and prostitutes are
entering the kingdom of God before you."
—MATTHEW 21:31 NABRE

Contents

CONTENTS

MAP OF EASTERN MEDITERRANEAN

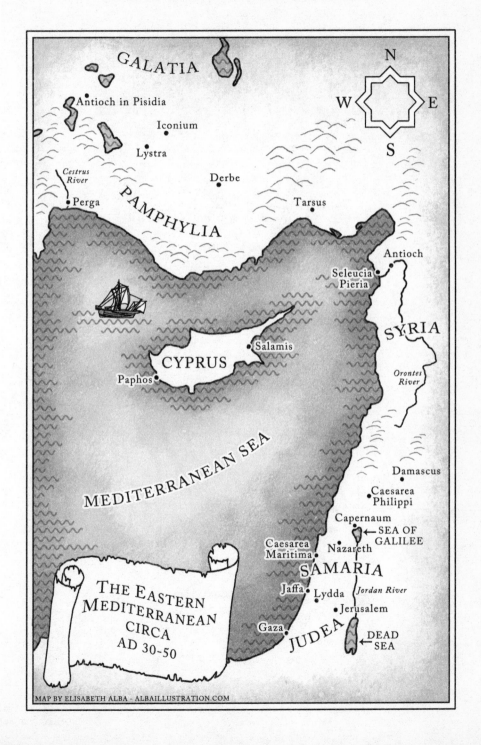

GALATIA

Antioch in Pisidia

Iconium

Lystra

Cestrus
River

Derbe

Perga

PAMPHYLIA

Tarsus

Antioch

Seleucia
Pieria

SYRIA

Orontes
River

CYPRUS

Salamis

Paphos

MEDITERRANEAN SEA

Damascus

Caesarea
Philippi

Capernaum

SEA OF
GALILEE

Caesarea
Maritima

Nazareth

SAMARIA

Jaffa

Lydda

Jordan River

Jerusalem

THE EASTERN
MEDITERRANEAN
CIRCA
AD 30-50

Gaza

JUDEA

DEAD
SEA

N
W   E
S

MAP OF JERUSALEM

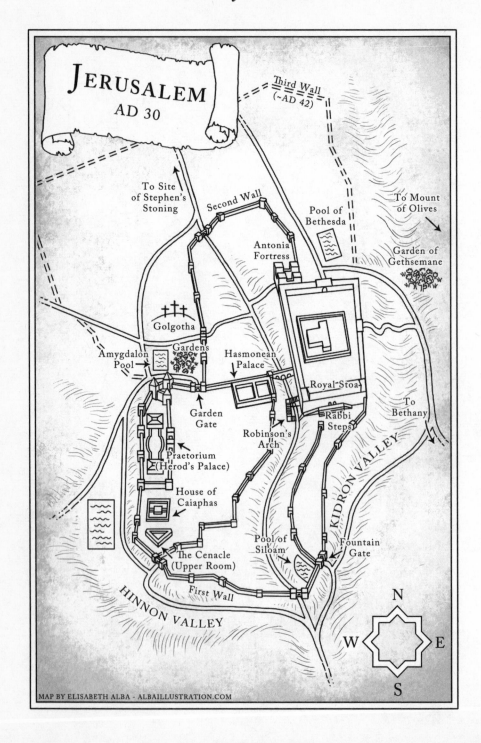

JERUSALEM
AD 30

Third Wall
(~AD 42)

To Site
of Stephen's
Stoning

Second Wall

Pool of
Bethesda

To Mount
of Olives

Antonia
Fortress

Garden of
Gethsemane

Golgotha

Gardens

Amygdalon
Pool

Hasmonean
Palace

Royal Stoa

To
Bethany

Garden
Gate

Robinson's
Arch

Rabbi
Steps

KIDRON VALLEY

Praetorium
(Herod's Palace)

House of
Caiaphas

The Cenacle
(Upper Room)

Pool of
Siloam

Fountain
Gate

First Wall

HINNON VALLEY

N
W   E
S

MAP BY ELISABETH ALBA - ALBAILLUSTRATION.COM

INTRODUCTION

"Go therefore and make disciples of all nations."
—MATTHEW 28:19

After two thousand years, historians are still trying to piece together exactly how it all happened. In a little more than two years, a mysterious Jewish rabbi from a small village in northern Israel launched an underground social and religious movement that spread like wildfire throughout the entire eastern Mediterranean. His friends would eventually call it *ha-derech* in Hebrew, *hodos* in Greek. It means simply "the Way"—short for the way of God's kingdom.

We call the rabbi who founded this new movement *Jesus*, but his real name was Yeshu'a, an Aramaic abbreviation of the Hebrew *Yehoshua* that means, coincidentally or not, "God saves." He had been raised in the tiny, isolated village of Natzara in the foothills just four miles from Sepphoris, the wealthy Jewish city that was the capital of the Galilee area. His father had been what the Greeks called a *tekton*, a builder with wood and stone. Although Jesus worked at the same trade (Mark 6:3) and had a shrewd knowledge of building and business (Luke 14:28), he had from his youth traveled all over the region, listening to what different Torah teachers had to say (Luke 2:41–52). Many learned rabbis at this time worked at trades while furthering their educations. The great rabbi Hillel, who died twenty years earlier, had worked as a woodcutter.

Jesus referred to his movement as "the kingdom of God," an unusual phrase not found in the Hebrew Scriptures but used once in the deuterocanonical or apocryphal Book of Wisdom (10:10). Jesus said he had been sent to declare the good news of the kingdom (Luke 4:43), and insisted, no fewer than three times, that it was a mission that would get him killed (Mark 8:31, 9:30–32, and 10:32–34). Jesus also warned his earliest and closest associates that they too would likely pay a high price for following in his footsteps. He predicted that many of his friends and followers would be tortured for their involvement in his crusade, and some would be executed in cold blood (Matt. 24:9). Yet despite this, many pledged their lives to his service and to the mission he dared them to undertake. In fewer than thirty months, Jesus and his friends ignited a spiritual revolution that sent shock waves far beyond the rural villages of northern Israel and into every nation and institution on earth. It would eventually change everything: politics, art, science, law, the rules of warfare, philosophy, the relations between men and women, and the family.

But the question has always been, how? Beyond the piety of believers and the doubts of skeptics lies an enduring mystery: What did Jesus do and say, in as little as one year and a maximum of three years, that could possibly have had such an impact? How did the community he somehow gathered together so quickly—made up of semiliterate fishermen, prostitutes, tax collectors, wealthy widows, day laborers, and even Roman soldiers—give birth to the spiritual revolution that became Christianity?

This book is an attempt to answer that question. It is a narrative retelling of the founding of the earliest Christian community more than two thousand years ago, based on recent discoveries in archaeology and New Testament studies. My goal is to help modern readers better appreciate how the Jesus movement began and why it succeeded—and to fill in many of the details of the story that were left out of the New Testament. My ultimate intent is to show that Christianity was not an accident. Jesus of Nazareth had a specific mission—a deliberate plan that he knew would end in the cross (Matt. 10:17–19), but which was not limited to the cross. The evidence shows that Jesus set out to create a community dedicated to carrying on his teaching and mission throughout time and across the entire world.

This book begins with an examination of the final week of Jesus' life, when he makes the fateful decision to bring his message and his movement into the very heart of Jewish society: the temple in Jerusalem. We will then observe Jesus and his followers as they confront the political and religious leaders of their time, participate in a dramatic protest within the temple precincts, and warn everyone who would listen, as the prophets had done before them, that Jerusalem and the holy temple would be destroyed if they continued on their current course. Following Jesus' sudden arrest, condemnation, and execution, this book will examine what historians know and don't know about the strange and inexplicable appearances of Jesus alive after the crucifixion— events that have been doubted, analyzed, and dismissed for millennia but never explained.

The Dawn of Christianity then follows the kingdom movement, led by one of the very first followers, Simon Peter, as it rapidly expands, despite its members being brutally persecuted and its leaders killed. Then we follow the young community as new leaders emerge, such as the Greek-speaking Jewish priest Barnabas and the brilliant and irascible Pharisee Saul of Tarsus, and as it slowly welcomes Samaritans and Jewish converts and, eventually, Roman soldiers. Finally, we will conclude with the controversy over whether pagans who wish to join the movement must first convert to Judaism. Thus, the entire narrative covers the dawn of Christianity, the first twenty years of Jesus' kingdom movement.

I write as a Christian not only for other Christians but also for people without any religious ties who are interested in learning who Jesus of Nazareth actually was. Christianity, like many communities today, is divided. Some Christians insist that Jesus' primary mission was to die as an atoning sacrifice to reconcile the human race to a just and wrathful God. Others emphasize Jesus' mission as the founder of a community of mercy and peace whose purpose is to transform the world to conform to God's original intention. Still other groups insist that only their views represent the truth about Jesus and his movement. Ultimately, I stand in the grand tradition of "mere Christianity"—beliefs that all Christians hold in common, whether Catholic, Orthodox, Anglican, or evangelical—that seeks the truth about Jesus wherever it can be found without denominational litmus tests.

WHY I'VE WRITTEN THIS BOOK

When I was young, my family owned a copy of *Life of Christ*, an illustrated life of Jesus that stitched together all the events found in all four gospels to create a coherent narrative of Jesus' life. Christians have had books like this for millennia, ever since Tatian's popular *Diatessaron* was written in the early second century. These prove perennially popular despite the disapproval of biblical scholars who prefer that each gospel be studied as an individual work. I read my family's book over and over again before I went to sleep at night.

Life of Christ used the old Douay-Rheims version of the New Testament, which transliterated, rather than translated, many of the Aramaic, Greek, and Latin words (for example, the Aramaic word *Gehenna* for hell). I was forced, therefore, to look up these words in Bible dictionaries, and this led me to works such as Henri Daniel-Rops's now-dated but wonderful *Daily Life in the Time of Jesus* and Alfred Edersheim's *The Life and Times of Jesus the Messiah*. I also read novels set in Israel during the time of Christ, and these, in turn, introduced me to the world of modern biblical scholarship and Jewish writers such as Joseph Klausner and Géza Vermes.

This strange childhood obsession eventually led me to move to Israel in my early twenties to study Hebrew and spend as much time as I could in the places mentioned in the New Testament—such as the stepped streets of Jerusalem; Cana, Mount Tabor, and the lakeside village of

Capernaum; and the ruins at Caesarea Maritima. I first attended an *ulpan,* or intensive Hebrew language school, in the Jezreel Valley near Nazareth, and I went to church every Sunday at the Basilica of the Annunciation. When I returned to the United States in the early 1980s, I covered the controversies that arose about the historical Jesus for magazines such as *Christianity Today.*[1] I interviewed famous Jewish scholars who were studying the historical Jesus, such as Talmud expert Jacob Neusner.[2] And then, in the early 2000s, I earned a graduate degree in New Testament, spending eight years trying to connect the dots between what I saw with my own eyes in Israel and what history could teach about Jesus and the kingdom.

As I've written before, all of this doesn't make me a biblical scholar: I am more a popular historian trying to bring the insights of biblical scholars and archaeologists to regular people. My heroes are New Testament scholars who accept the challenge of modern scholarship in all its complexity without abandoning their faith.[3] The truth is, academic biblical scholarship is often a "glass-half-full, glass-half-empty" type of situation. A skeptic like Bart Erhman, a former fundamentalist who lost his faith and now writes books debunking conservative Christianity, looks at the discrepancies and variations in the various gospel accounts and concludes that the Gospels are unreliable historical records. He claims that many of the incidents recounted in the Gospels, from the Palm Sunday entrance in Jerusalem to the discovery of the empty tomb, were likely made up out of thin air by the early Christians.[4] Others, myself included, look at the identical evidence and conclude not that the Gospels are unreliable, but that they contain obvious eyewitness testimonies that, as eyewitness testimonies often do, sometimes disagree on the details.[5] Rather than undermining my belief that the Gospels are accurate portrayals of who Jesus was and what he was doing in Israel in the late AD 20s, the discrepancies in the Gospels actually strengthen it. This is also the point of view of many secular historians, such as the late Michael Grant, who find the hyper-skepticism of some New Testament scholars to be, in many cases, solipsistic and not justified by the actual evidence.[6]

SOURCES

Now for a brief word about some of the sources and discoveries mentioned in this book and some of the terms we will come across. For a deeper explanation and more background on these items, refer to the Further Reading section at the back of this book.

The New Testament. Most of what historians and ordinary believers know about the life of Jesus and the first years of the movement he founded comes from the New Testament—an anthology of twenty-seven separate pieces of writing, all written in *koinē*, or common Greek, and penned between approximately AD 45 at the very earliest and AD 100 at the latest. Four of the works are mini-biographies of Jesus ranging in length from about 11,000 words (Mark) to around 19,500 words (Luke). Another work, the Acts of the Apostles, describes the early history of the Jesus movement after Jesus' death and resurrection and was written by the same author who penned the gospel of Luke. There is also a work known as an apocalypse, or account of symbolic visions, that many early Christians did not want included in the New Testament because it was not regarded as divinely inspired: the book of Revelation. All of the other twenty-one works are epistles, or public letters, written in the name of a handful of early Christian leaders. Of the twenty-one letters, thirteen are presented as written by the apostle Paul; three by the apostle John; two by the apostle Peter; and one each by an author named James (believed to be James, the brother, half brother, or cousin of Jesus); Jude, another brother or relative of Jesus; and an unnamed author who wrote the letter to the Hebrews.

Skeptics make much of the fact that historians have no independent corroboration from outside sources of most of the events described in the Gospels, but this is common with ancient history and hardly unique to Christianity.[7] For example, virtually everything historians know about the Three Hundred, the Spartan warriors who held off a Persian invasion at the mountain pass of Thermopylae in 480 BC, comes from the writings of a single Greek author, Herodotus. What's more, the earliest copy historians have of Herodotus's chronicle of this event, *The Histories*, dates to the tenth century AD—or more than 1,350 years after it was written![8] In comparison, historians have a cornucopia of historical sources and archaeological evidence about Jesus of Nazareth and the early Christian community. For example, more than fifty papyrus manuscripts of New Testament texts exist that date before AD 300. The earliest of these early manuscripts, a papyrus fragment from the gospel of John known as P[52], dates to around AD 125 or just thirty years after the original was likely written.

Works of Josephus. A first-century Jewish historian named Yosef ben Matityahu—whom historians know by his Roman name, Flavius Josephus—wrote extensively and in great detail about every aspect of the land of Israel in two enormous works, *The Antiquities of the Jews* and *The Wars of the Jews*. He provides historians with much of the cultural background and the military and economic contexts out of which Jesus and his teachings arose. Josephus fought on both sides in the tragic war that broke out in AD 66 between the Jews and the Romans—first with his countrymen and then as a captured aide to the Romans. After Jerusalem was destroyed and his family was killed, Josephus spent the rest of his life writing his voluminous histories of his conquered people. As a result, historians view some of what Josephus says with caution, especially when it comes to numbers (most experts believe he routinely exaggerates).

The Talmud. The Jewish Talmud provides an encyclopedic commentary on the Jewish laws and regulations, known collectively as *halachah*, which are contained in the first five books of the Old Testament. Compiled in its final form in the late sixth or seventh century of the Common Era, it contains sayings and traditions of Jewish rabbis who lived in the time of Jesus. The Talmud also contains a handful of references to Jesus, although a few scholars dispute that the Jesus mentioned is the same Jesus of Nazareth in the New Testament.

Deuterocanonical or Apocryphal Works. In addition to the books in the Hebrew Bible or Old Testament, a number of works dating to the centuries immediately before Jesus are included in many Christian Bibles but not in the current Jewish canon. For the Catholic and Orthodox Churches, these works are called *deuterocanonical* and are included as part of the Old Testament. These are called *Apocrypha* among Protestants and sometimes included as an appendix in some Bibles. They include 1 and 2 Maccabees, histories of the independent Jewish state that existed between 164 and 63 BC, as well as works such as Tobit, Sirach, and Baruch.

Pseudepigrapha. Historians also possess a treasure trove of Jewish writings dating to the centuries before and after Jesus' birth that were never included in Christian Bibles—written roughly between the years 300 BC and AD 300. Mostly written in Greek and Hebrew, these works include the Sibylline Oracles, 1 and 2 Enoch, Psalms of Solomon, 3 and 4 Maccabees, the book of Jubilees, and so on. By studying what Jews wrote in the century before and after Jesus, Jewish scholars in recent years have come to believe that Judaism was much more diverse than early skeptics realized—with some concluding that Jews of the time would have realistically accepted a man as a divine being.

The Dead Sea Scrolls. In 1947, a Bedouin shepherd tending goats near the Dead Sea in southern Israel discovered a cave on the side of a mountain that held clay jars containing hundreds of ancient Hebrew holy texts dating back two thousand years. Historians believe these texts were mostly written by a monastic community of scribes at Qumran near the Dead Sea and hidden around AD 70 at the end of the First Jewish War. Before this discovery, the oldest copy of the Hebrew Bible dated to just the ninth century AD. In addition to copies of various Old Testament books, the Dead Sea Scrolls also contain original works from the members of the community itself. These painted a new portrait of extreme Jewish nationalists who longed for a holy war against Rome. They also revealed that it wasn't true, as Jewish and skeptical scholars had long insisted, that the Jews had no concept of a suffering Messiah and that this idea was invented by the early Christian community to explain away the scandal of the cross.

Greek and Roman Authors. We have access to the works of numerous Greek and Roman writers who lived before, during, and after Jesus' time, such as Strabo (ca. 64 BC–AD 24) and Tacitus (ca. AD 56–117), who shed light on the cultural and political world in which Jesus lived. The Jewish philosopher known as Philo (ca. 25 BC–AD 50), who lived in Alexandria, Egypt, but who appears to have visited Jerusalem during Jesus' lifetime, wrote valuable descriptions of the Roman governor Pontius Pilate that shed light on the final week of Jesus' life.

Early Christian Writers. In addition to the writings of the New Testament, historians also have at their disposal the writings of early Christian authors known as the church fathers. The earliest of these writers, such as Ignatius of Antioch (ca. AD 35–108), Clement of Rome (d. AD 99), and Polycarp (ca. AD 69–155), are known as the apostolic fathers because they were once thought to have personally encountered Jesus' immediate disciples, the apostles. However, while some of the apostolic fathers, such as Ignatius of Antioch, did indeed meet one or more of the apostles, not all did. Yet their testimony is considered very important, especially about the writing of the New Testament.[9]

Gnostic Gospels. The Gnostic Gospels are later writings about Jesus that were not included in the New Testament. Some early copies of the texts were discovered in the Egyptian town of Nag Hammadi in 1945. They are called the Gnostic Gospels because the authors who wrote them appear to have been Gnostics, followers of Greek and Jewish theosophical philosophies that denied the goodness of earthly existence and speculated about different forms of divinity. Perhaps the most famous example of a Gnostic text with relevance to Jesus' life is the Gospel of Thomas, a collection of 114 sayings of Jesus, written in the ancient Egyptian language of Coptic probably around AD 140–180. About half of the sayings in the Gospel of Thomas echo those found in the canonical Gospels but there are many that are unique. However, these new sayings of Jesus express ideas very different from those of the canonical Gospels (for example, that women must first become males before they are allowed into heaven[10]).

Egeria and the Pilgrim of Bordeaux. Two invaluable resources come from two Christian pilgrims who visited the Holy Land in the fourth century. One, known simply as the Pilgrim of Bordeaux, is an anonymous author who penned a very brief record of his travels from Europe to Israel in AD 333–334. The account is written in Latin and called the *Itinerarium Burdigalense* ("Bordeaux Itinerary"). The second resource is a detailed narrative describing a pilgrimage to the Holy Land in the 380s, penned by an upper-class female pilgrim named Egeria who lived in Jerusalem for three years.[11] Egeria's account of fourth-century Jerusalem, and of the Christian liturgical celebrations and monuments there, has helped archaeologists reconstruct where sites mentioned in the Gospels were likely located.

In 2015, archaeologists announced the discovery of the remnants of Herod the Great's massive palace within the grounds of the City of David complex near the Jaffa Gate. Archaeologists now believe that this old palace was the *praetorium*, or Roman military headquarters, where Jesus was questioned by Pilate.

All these materials, then, round out the New Testament, allowing historians and ordinary readers alike to gain a deeper understanding about what impact Jesus' teachings had on the leaders of his society. Together, they shed new light on the trajectory of Christianity in its early years.

ARCHAEOLOGICAL DISCOVERIES

It's an amazing time for those who look to science to find out more about the life of Jesus. In just the past few years, dramatic new discoveries in archaeology and New Testament studies are forcing a reevaluation of many older ideas of what Jesus and his followers were trying to achieve. These discoveries are also shedding new light on the final week of Jesus' life on earth and on the birth of the movement he inaugurated. For example, in 2015 archaeologists in Israel announced the discovery of Herod the Great's massive palace near Jerusalem's Jaffa Gate, now widely believed to have been the *praetorium* or Roman military head-quarters where Jesus was interrogated by Pontius Pilate.[12] Until recently, archaeologists and scholars had believed that Pilate questioned Jesus in the Antonia Tower or Fortress, located on the northwest corner of the Temple Mount. This means that most of the scholarly reconstructions of Jesus' final hours, including the traditional understanding of the Via Dolorosa or Way of the Cross, are now likely obsolete.

Other recent discoveries have confirmed the existence of people, places, and events mentioned in the Gospels. One dramatic example of this was the discovery of ossuaries, or burial boxes, inscribed with the names of key gospel figures—such as the high priest Joseph Caiaphas and, perhaps, James the Just, who was the brother (or male relative) of Jesus and a leader of the Jerusalem community before being mar-tyred.[13] Almost as shocking were the twin discoveries in 2009 of stone houses in Nazareth and of a luxurious synagogue at Magdala, on the Sea of Galilee just north of Tiberias. The discovery of stone houses in Nazareth dating to the early Roman period, just steps from the Basilica of the Annunciation, proved that Nazareth was indeed settled by observant Jews during Jesus' lifetime—a fact frequently denied by those who claim Jesus never existed at all but was a myth. The synagogue at Magdala, the best preserved and most luxurious first-century synagogue ever found, confirms that there were established, lavishly decorated synagogues in Jesus' lifetime, buildings he almost certainly visited just as the Gospels claim.

Still other recent archaeological discoveries have changed historians' understanding of what Jesus' life in Galilee may have been like. The excavations in the 1980s of the city of Sepphoris, for example, have revealed that Galilee was not the simple rural backwater that scholars and everyday Christians have believed. Rather, it was a fairly multicultural, sophisticated place where the very wealthy and the very poor existed side by side. As the capital of Galilee, with a population estimated at around ten thousand, Sepphoris was a luxurious Jewish city of marble monuments, wide paved streets, Greek-style amphitheaters, enormous outdoor *cardos* or shopping malls, vast civic basilicas or government buildings, and palatial villas.[14] Sepphoris is, perhaps, what Jesus had in mind when he spoke about the "city set on a hill [that] cannot be hidden" (Matt. 5:14), located just four miles, a little less than an hour's walk, from the tiny village of Nazareth where Jesus grew up.

THE HISTORICAL RELIABILITY
OF THE NEW TESTAMENT

Finally, I would like to say a word about the historical reliability of the New Testament in general. I have written about this issue extensively in *Searching for Jesus*, but I would like to summarize a few key points here. First, I think it's fair to say that many scholars today have moved away from the hyper-skeptical attitudes that dominated New Testament studies in the twentieth century. One reason for this is that archaeological discoveries have confirmed the existence of key people and events mentioned in the New Testament—such as the high priest Joseph Caiaphas or the Roman proconsul named Sergius Paulus mentioned in Acts. But there are other factors that make a convincing case for the historical reliability of the New Testament.

CRITERIA

Secular historians have long questioned the criteria that some New Testament scholars used to evaluate whether a deed or saying of Jesus actually happened. Some of these criteria make sense. For example, the "criterion of embarrassment" says that an event described in the Gospels that was inherently embarrassing to the early Christian community likely really happened because people don't typically invent stories that make them look bad. For this reason, even skeptical historians in the past thought Peter likely did deny Jesus three times, as the Gospels say, because this is not something the early church would have made up.

Another criterion that secular historians and many New Testament scholars use is the "criterion of multiple attestation." This is the idea that if an event or saying of Jesus occurs in multiple independent sources, then it is likely authentic. This sounds reasonable at first, but upon closer examination, use of such a criterion may give rise to unnecessary suspicion. If an event or saying only occurs in the Synoptic Gospels (Matthew, Mark, and Luke), for example, but not all four gospels, does that mean it is *less* likely to have occurred? Not necessarily.

Other criteria strike some secular historians as questionable. Perhaps the most problematic is the "criterion of dissimilarity." This is based on the idea that if a saying or deed of Jesus reflects what the early Christian or Jewish community at the time believed, then Jesus likely *didn't* say or do it. This strikes many critics as absurd. It would mean that Jesus had very little in common with either his fellow Jews or with the community he founded.

ORAL TRADITION

A similar rise in "skepticism toward skepticism" involves the question of oral tradition. Historians believe Jesus traveled all over the Galilee region, speaking to larger and larger crowds of people. In the early twentieth century, New Testament scholars thought that most of what the gospel writers recorded about Jesus was passed down through oral tradition, and that, as the saying goes, the stories "grew in the telling." The mostly German scholars who pioneered this theory pointed to the way German fairy tales evolved over centuries, with the details dramatically changing over time. Later, skeptical scholars would use the analogy of the "telephone game" to explain this process—the way in which a short story is passed along in a circle of children, from one child to the next, until the final version of what happened bears little resemblance to the original account. This is how, those scholars claimed, the Gospels were composed.

But in recent years, many New Testament scholars have increasingly questioned this model—although some, such as Bart Ehrman, continue to support it.[15] One problem with the standard "oral tradition" understanding of the Gospels is that the timing is wrong. German fairy tales may have evolved over hundreds of years, but the Gospels were written no more than thirty to sixty years after Jesus' death—and possibly, in the case of Mark, just ten to thirty years. The consensus dating of the Gospels among academic scholars holds that Mark was written around AD 70, Matthew and Luke around AD 80–85, and John around AD 90–95.

The reason for this dating is largely due to Jesus' allusions to the coming destruction of Jerusalem. Skeptical scholars believe these allusions in the Gospels are "prophecies after the fact," meaning that the gospel writers put these prophecies in Jesus' mouth when they wrote the Gospels but Jesus never actually said them. However, there is nothing intrinsically implausible, even in human terms, about a prediction of Jerusalem's destruction during a war with the Romans. Jerusalem had been destroyed before when prophets were ignored and foolish wars were waged against great empires—and certainly the rising Jewish nationalism that would eventually spark the war with Rome was obvious to everyone at that time. Moreover, even many secular experts, such as the scholar James Crossley in England, reject the late dating of the

Gospels purely on internal evidence alone.[16] The Acts of the Apostles, for example, written by the same person who wrote the gospel of Luke, ends with Paul under house arrest in Rome around AD 62, and makes no mention of the destruction of Jerusalem by the Romans in AD 70. Therefore, even some very liberal scholars believe that Luke and Acts were written in the early to mid-60s.[17] If this is true, and if, as many experts believe, Luke used the gospel of Mark when writing his own account, then the gospel of Mark must have been written earlier still—perhaps in the AD 50s. In short, if the stories in the Gospels did "grow in the telling," they may not have had nearly as much time to "grow" as skeptical scholars once thought.

Still, while it may well be true that accounts of Jesus' sayings and deeds were indeed passed on by word of mouth, at least initially, it does not follow that the process was as random or haphazard as skeptics such as Ehrman claim. In fact, the New Testament presents evidence of just the opposite—that the passing along of traditions about what Jesus did and said was a very rigorous, disciplined undertaking, similar to the formal transmission of memorized teaching practiced in both rabbinical academies and pagan schools of philosophy. As British New Testament scholar Richard Bauckham points out in his seminal 2006 book *Jesus and the Eyewitnesses*, when the apostle Paul mentions "handing on" traditions regarding the resurrection in his first letter to the Corinthians, he uses the Greek technical terms *paradidomi* for "handing on" a tradition and the word *paralambano* for "receiving" a tradition: "For I handed on to you as of first importance what I also received" (1 Cor. 15:3 NABRE). As a result, even if the sayings and deeds of Jesus were communicated orally at first, it is likely they were passed on in a formal way, memorized and transmitted according to a fixed standard—the way creeds are in modern churches.

WRITTEN ACCOUNTS

The Gospels themselves reveal the use of detailed, possibly written sources in their composition. Experts have long claimed that people in the first century were largely illiterate, and that writing was especially difficult and left largely to professional scribes. Yet, in just the past few years, new evidence has surfaced that suggests people in ancient Israel may not have been as illiterate as modern skeptics allege. Notes and letters written hundreds of years before Jesus on pottery shards, known as *ostraca*, indicate that even "soldiers in the lower ranks of the . . . army, it appears, could read and write."[18] Thus, it's possible and even likely that at least some of the thousands of people who heard Jesus teach all across Israel, from southern Lebanon to Judea, took notes—as historians know occurred with the biblical prophets such as Jeremiah.[19]

In addition, critical examination of the gospel texts shows that the writers appear to have had written sources. For example, the gospels of Matthew and Luke largely follow the chronology of events in the gospel of Mark—so many scholars believe that Matthew and Luke probably used Mark as the basic outline of their gospels and then added details found in other sources.[20] These three gospels together are known as the Synoptics, from the Greek words *syn* and *optics*, which mean "to see together." They tell the story of Jesus and his followers in a similar way. Scholars call the unique material found only in Matthew "M," and the unique material found only in Luke "L." In addition to these two possible sources, scholars also believe that Matthew and Luke may have shared a collection of Jesus' sayings that they call Q (short for the German word *Quelle*, which means "source").[21] They believe this because Matthew and Luke both contain the same sayings of Jesus that are not found in Mark—and in some cases these sayings are virtually identical (with up to 98 percent agreement) in Greek. This suggests that Matthew and Luke shared a common source—and, because of the close agreement in many (but not all) of the sayings, that this "sayings source" may have been *written*. The discovery of the Gospel of Thomas in 1945, which is made up entirely of sayings of Jesus, proved that such collections existed at least at a later time.

So the scholarly consensus on the Gospels is that Mark wrote his bare-bones account first, perhaps in the late AD 60s in Rome, likely drawing upon the recollections and personal anecdotes of the apostle Peter. The writers we call Matthew (a Jew) and Luke (a Gentile) then came along and decided that Mark had left some things out of the story. Matthew, drawing upon sources unique to him as well as a collection of Jesus' sayings called Q, penned his version of Jesus' life probably around AD 80 to 90. As a Jew writing for other Jews, Matthew emphasized Jesus' Jewish roots and how he was the fulfillment of Jewish prophecies about the Messiah. Luke, a former pagan who converted to Christianity, writing around the same time but for a different audience, drew upon his own unique sources as well as Q and penned his version. As a Gentile, Luke emphasized the universal aspect of Jesus' mission to "all nations" (24:47). Thus, each of the gospel writers had his own unique points to make. By studying the individual gospels and comparing them to the other gospels—looking at what is left in one and cut out in another— New Testament scholars are able to figure out what the gospel writers were each trying to emphasize about Jesus.

Then there is the gospel of John, which adds to the complexity; it tells Jesus' life story in a very different way and with a different chronology of events. Yet the gospel of John adds details about Jerusalem and first-century Jewish practices that are found in none of the other gospels. This leads many scholars to believe that it, too, is likely based on eyewitness testimony, just as the text itself claims (John 21:24).

THE NEW TESTAMENT PUZZLE

All this means that when scholars approach the New Testament, they really want to hear the individual voice of each writer. They do the *opposite* of what screenwriters, popular historians, and authors of "gospel harmonies" do—which is to take all the events found in all the Gospels and try to make them somehow fit together. Instead, New Testament scholars study each gospel individually and then compare it to the other New Testament texts. In this book, I try to chart a middle course. I attempt to reconstruct what happened historically, based on available sources and the findings of archaeology, while also acknowledging the uniqueness of each of the New Testament authors.

The problem with harmonization is that you end up having to make unilateral decisions that may or may not be accurate. For example, in the Synoptic Gospels the cleansing of the temple occurred in the final week of Jesus' life, when he came to Jerusalem to confront the religious authorities there. In the gospel of John, it occurs at the very beginning of Jesus' ministry. A person could theoretically duck the issue by saying Jesus cleansed the temple *twice*, as conservative apologists try to do— once at the beginning of his ministry (as in John) and again at the end (as in the Synoptics). But even many conservative scholars believe this double cleansing is unlikely. The only responsible course of action is *transparency*: tell the story as best you can, but reveal your sources and the editorial decisions that lead you to prefer one version of events over another. This is what I have tried to do in this book.

There is no doubt that any attempt to reconstruct events that occurred more than two thousand years ago is an extremely difficult task. There are enormous gaps in our knowledge. For many events in the Bible, we have only a handful of sources and they don't always agree on the details. Yet there are also many intriguing clues—and archaeology and biblical scholarship are uncovering new facts that help us piece the story together, one step at a time. We are learning more about first-century Jerusalem almost every day. The more experts learn, the better historians are at figuring out what actually happened to Jesus of Nazareth during the last week of his life—and what happened to the community he founded in the years after his violent death and resurrection. I believe this search for knowledge is an undertaking that, despite its many frustrations, is well worth anyone's time. The general public never tires of trying to figure out what happened to John F. Kennedy on a fateful day in 1963; I would argue that what happened to Jesus of Nazareth and his immediate followers is at least as interesting—and ultimately far more important.

—ROBERT J. HUTCHINSON

PART I ———————————————————————————

THE ROAD TO JERUSALEM

"The Lord used to teach about those times and say: 'The days will come when vines will grow, each having ten thousand shoots, and on each shoot ten thousand branches, and on each branch ten thousand twigs, and on each twig ten thousand clusters, and in each cluster ten thousand grapes, and each grape when crushed will yield twenty-five measures of wine.'"

—A LOST SAYING OF JESUS, SUPPOSEDLY PASSED
  ON BY JOHN THE EVANGELIST[1]

CHAPTER 1

FISHERS OF MEN

"The kingdom of heaven is like a net that was thrown
into the sea and gathered fish of every kind."
—MATTHEW 13:47

Jesus of Nazareth showed up that morning by the lakeshore dressed
in a simple tunic and wearing a woolen *tallit*, a traditional Jewish
toga-like garment that covered him down to his mid-calves.[1] He was in
his early thirties—a strong and confident man with burning eyes, his
hair likely uncombed and longer than most, his skin dark and cracked
from the dry desert air.[2] He looked older than his years but strong, a
man accustomed to hard work in the hot sun. It is difficult to describe
the effect Jesus had on people, particularly on the destitute and starving
masses who lived on the fringes of society. Full of zeal and energy and
life, he was steeped in the complexities of Torah yet embraced the world
with a full heart. Jesus drew crowds—men, women, and children—to
him like moths to a flame (Mark 10:1, Matt. 27:55).

On this particular autumn day, Jesus sat on the hillside above the
large crescent bay at Tabgha, about four miles south of the fishing village
of Capernaum. Just to the south lay the town the locals called Magdala,
but that others referred to as Taricheae, or "Town of the Salt-Fish."
There, wealthy landowners from Jerusalem had set up a factory used for

exporting *salsamentum*, a popular condiment made from chopped fish, throughout the Mediterranean.[3] It was a rich town with a large synagogue where the rabbi Jesus was frequently invited to speak. It was also home to one of his most famous followers, a woman named Miriam who had been possessed by demons and who may have been a prostitute (Luke 8:2).

Large groups of people were making their way to the area from many different villages in the region. Jesus would speak here often, on the hillside covered with dazzling red poppies and bright yellow daisies. About a year later, an enormous gathering would be organized on this very spot, planned months in advance, in which tens of thousands of people showed up from all across the region, even as far south as Jerusalem and east to the Ten Cities. But on this day, the crowds were only a few hundred, perhaps a thousand. The crowd was laughing because Jesus had said something funny, which he did often.

"Therefore I tell you, do not be anxious about your life, what you will eat or what you will drink, nor about your body, what you will put on," Jesus shouted above the crowd, a large smile on his face. "Is not life more than food, and the body more than clothing?"

He then pointed to the thousands of wildflowers that covered the hillside.

"Consider the lilies of the field, how they grow: they neither toil nor spin, yet I tell you, even Solomon in all his glory was not arrayed like one of these. But if God so clothes the grass of the field, which today is alive and tomorrow is thrown into the oven, will he not much more clothe you, O you of little faith?"

Jesus paused as he let his words sink in for a moment.

"Therefore do not be anxious, saying, 'What shall we eat?' or 'What shall we drink?' or 'What shall we wear?'" he added. "For the Gentiles seek after all these things, and your heavenly Father knows that you need them all. But seek first the kingdom of God and his righteousness, and all these things will be added to you" (Matt. 6:25, 28–33).

The crowd had grown larger. Jesus stepped slowly down to the lakeshore where the well-known fisherman named Simon bar Jonah had been repairing his nets. Simon, a barrel-chested man with a big mouth but also a big heart, was famous in the area. He had a thriving business with his brother, Andrew, who had introduced Simon to Jesus. Simon lived with his wife, his brother, and his mother-in-law in an attached stone townhouse near the lakeshore there in Capernaum. Tourists today can still see the ruins of what is possibly his house. It stands just one hundred steps from the lake.

Simon had been listening attentively to everything the rabbi had said and, like most people, was transfixed by his words. When Jesus asked Simon if he could borrow his boat for a time, Simon agreed and helped him ease the boat off the pebble beach out into the lake. The boat was heavy and well built, about thirty feet long, the frames made of oak and the planking of fine Lebanese cedar. One just like it was found in 1986, stuck in the lake mud for two thousand years and only revealed after a severe drought had lowered the water levels in the lake.

Jesus stood in the bow, speaking to the crowds who had formed a large semicircle on the rocky beach. He spoke for quite some time and, by the end, had the crowds laughing and joking with one another. Jesus had been speaking about something he called the kingdom of God. He had invited his listeners to join him in a kind of crusade. He explained that the Almighty, the Creator of the universe, was taking over—in fact, had *already* taken over—and that the starving and the naked, the sick and the destitute, were his chosen people as much as the priests in the temple. More so, in fact.

This young teacher was giving these hungry people on the lakeshore something they had not had for a very long time: hope, and a new sense of purpose. The old world as everyone knew it, of might making right, was coming to an end. A new era was dawning—the time long talked about by Israel's holy prophets. The Spirit of God would now dwell not in the temple in Jerusalem but in the hearts of all who worshipped the one God in truth. The rabbi asked everyone to join him, to bring the good news of this dawning kingdom to every village in Israel.

Wooden boats of about the same size as the ones Jesus knew still operate on the Sea of Galilee between Capernaum and Tiberias. Little has changed in this area in two thousand years.

When the rabbi was finished speaking, Simon and his men pushed the boat back onto the beach. Simon was speechless. He had likely never heard anyone speak like this before. He stared at Jesus in wonder. What the rabbi was asking sounded dangerous but also thrilling—the adventure of a lifetime.

Still in the boat, Jesus told Simon he should push off and take the boat out into deeper water to catch some fish.

At that, Simon must have smiled. Clearly the rabbi knew more about the Torah than he did about fishing.

"Master, we toiled all night and took nothing," Simon said gently. "But at your word, I'll let down the nets."

Simon and his partners moved the boat out into deep water and did as the rabbi bid. When they had lowered the nets, suddenly a great shoal of tilapia, the most common fish in the lake, moved into them and filled their nets to the breaking point. Simon and his partners yelled at men in a nearby boat to come help them. Together the men hoisted the nets and filled both boats to the point that they almost began to sink. As quickly as they could, the men brought the boats back to the shore. Simon leapt out of his boat and fell at the feet of the rabbi.

"Depart from me, for I am a sinful man," he said, bowing his head.

Jesus walked away, up the hillside toward the road back to Capernaum. But then he stopped and turned back to Simon. "Come with me, Simon," he said simply. "And I will make you a fisher of men."[4]

CHAPTER 2

THE KINGDOM OF GOD

"I must preach the good news of the kingdom of God to the other towns as well; for I was sent for this purpose."
—LUKE 4:43

It started small, with three pairs of brothers and their friends: Simon bar Jonah, whom Jesus later nicknamed, perhaps somewhat ironically, *Kepha*, or the Rock; his brother Andrew; and their mutual friend Philip. There were also the brothers Ya'akov (James) and Yochanan (John), sons of a wealthy local man named Zebedee and his wife, Salome; and someone they called the "younger James" and his brother Jude (short for Thaddeus). Alongside these siblings were Shimon, nicknamed "the Zealot" for his passion for the Torah; Tau'ma (Thomas), whose name in Aramaic means "twin"; and Bar-Talmai (Bartholomew), who came from the town where Jesus turned water into wine. Then there was a Jewish tax collector named Mattityahu (Matthew), or Levi; and Yehuda (Judas), whom history remembers as the one who betrayed Jesus for thirty pieces of silver.

Yet this close-knit inner circle only represented a small fraction of Jesus' students, or *talmidim*. The kingdom movement brought together people from all walks of life—fishermen and day laborers, peasant farmers, ruffians, prostitutes, soldiers, Jewish intellectuals like Nicodemus and Joseph of Arimathea, and wealthy female patrons. Jesus also had at least one supporter among the Jewish ruling council, the Sanhedrin, and perhaps even among the Roman upper classes (Matt. 27:19). We know some of these people's names, as they are preserved in the Gospels—and remarkably for that time, even the names of the women. There were Miriam, Marta, and their brother, Eleazar (Lazarus) from the Judean village of Beit Anya; and a very wealthy woman named Susanna who contributed money to help Jesus and his students move about the country. A woman named Joanna also was one of Jesus' most important followers—a remarkable fact given that she was married to Chuza, house steward for the Jewish king Herod Antipas. These were the diverse and surprising laborers for the kingdom—and they were all part of Jesus' plan.

People often think of Jesus as a kind of early hippie who wandered aimlessly around Galilee, giving sermons and healing people at random until it was time for him to sacrifice himself on the cross. But the Gospels portray Jesus as having a very specific plan and a real urgency about his mission. "The harvest is plentiful," Jesus is quoted in one of the oldest parts of the New Testament, "but the laborers are few" (Luke 10:2). He traveled from village to village throughout Israel, announcing the good news of God's kingdom and demonstrating its power by healing the sick, feeding the hungry, giving alms to the poor, visiting the imprisoned, forgiving injuries, counseling the doubtful, comforting the sorrowful, admonishing sinners, and more.

Through his followers, he created self-perpetuating "cells" of his kingdom movement throughout Israel, each with the mission of establishing new communities. In this way, Jesus ensured that the kingdom movement grew rapidly. He had a keen understanding of human nature: when he gave his followers instructions for visiting towns and villages in his name, he told them, "If any place will not receive you and they will not listen to you, when you leave, shake off the dust that is on your feet as a testimony against them" (Mark 6:11). In other words, his followers were not to waste their valuable time in places not receptive to his message. As a result of Jesus' wise planning, demographers estimate the kingdom movement grew at a rate of about 40 percent per decade.[1] Within two years, the few dozen men and women had grown to more than five hundred, then to three thousand. Within a decade, the community could have numbered many tens of thousands. Within three hundred years, it was thirty-five million.[2] Today, it's about two billion.

The Roman army took direct control of the regions of Judea, Samaria, and Idumea in AD 6, maintaining about three thousand auxiliary (mostly non-Roman) soldiers in barracks in Caesarea Maritima on Israel's coast and in Jerusalem. Pontius Pilate became governor in AD 26.

A PEOPLE IN BONDAGE

This exponential growth was nurtured in the soil of turmoil and oppression. For six centuries before Jesus was born, the Jews had been living under brutal foreign domination—first under the Babylonians, then the Persians, then the "Greeks" (both Greco-Egyptian and Greco-Syrian), and finally the Romans. The Jews were ruled by their own people for only a brief period, between 164 and 63 BC. An independent Jewish state arose under the leadership of the priestly family known as the Maccabees, but eventually it deteriorated into internecine feuds until the Roman general Pompey was practically invited to invade the country in 63 BC.[3]

As was their custom, the Romans appointed local despots to rule in their name. The most famous and successful was Herod the Great, a half-Jewish aristocrat who lived from around 73 to 4 BC. Herod had been an active participant in the myriad intrigues of the Roman Empire, forging an alliance with the Roman general Mark Antony and even tangling with Mark Antony's famous mistress, Queen Cleopatra of Egypt.[4] Ostensibly Jewish, Herod held no scruples about adopting those aspects of Greco-Roman culture he liked, including pagan temples, nude baths and gymnasia, theaters, brothels, and other foreign innovations. During his reign, Israel became bitterly divided both religiously and socially. On the one hand, there was a vast peasant underclass loyal to the Torah and Jewish traditions, but ruling over them was a much smaller, more cosmopolitan urban elite that tried to assimilate into the dominant Greco-Roman culture, even going so far as to exercise naked in the Greek-style gymnasia. Conditions were ripe for unrest.

While many historians dismiss as mere legends the stories the Gospels tell about Jesus' birth, the accounts of the massacre of the innocents in Bethlehem and the flight into Egypt fit perfectly the political milieu of that time. Right after Jesus was born and Herod the Great died, a bloody civil war broke out. It would last for a dozen years. The rebellion was centered in Sepphoris, the affluent Greek-Jewish city located just four miles from the tiny village where Jesus was raised. Eventually, the Roman general Publius Quinctilius Varus arrived with three legions from Syria—about fifteen thousand trained soldiers—to put down the insurrection. Varus recaptured the city of Sepphoris, executed all the men, and sold the women and children into slavery. He then hunted down the Jewish nationalists who led the rebellion—two thousand men—and crucified them all.

The violence continued throughout Jesus' childhood. When Jesus was around ten years old, a Jewish revolutionary named Judah of Galilee declared the country's independence from Rome. Other Jewish rebel leaders followed suit, putting the entire country in an uproar. As a child, Jesus likely hid with his friends and family as rival armies and bandit militias marched by on the main roads just a few hundred yards from Nazareth. An archaeological discovery in 2009 supports this scenario. Among the foundations of first-century stone houses uncovered in Nazareth, archaeologists found a hidden underground chamber that looked like a kind of "safe room," an ideal place to hide when rampaging troops searched door-to-door. In 2006, Israeli archaeologists uncovered similar safe rooms and underground tunnels in Kfar Cana, the biblical Cana, dating back to the years immediately before the Jewish War against the Romans (AD 66–70). This indicated that the Jews at this time prepared for the upcoming war by fashioning underground places to hide.[5] This is the political and military background to the Gospels that is lost on most people today.

After Herod's death and the civil war that devastated the countryside, the land of Israel had been divided up into a series of despotic fiefdoms ruled by two of Herod's surviving sons or directly by the Romans.[6] Under Herodian and Roman rule, Israel became a gigantic protection racket—organized crime on a national scale. Archaeological excavations following the 1967 Six-Day War revealed that some of the homes of Jerusalem's priestly families were nothing short of palatial. One villa in Jerusalem's Upper City measured over ten thousand square feet and featured such luxuries as marble walls, mosaic floors, steam baths with built-in under-floor heating, fountains and bathing pools, and more. To finance these wonders, the temple elite had created a system of taxation, fees, and surcharges unrivaled anywhere in the ancient world.[7] A handful of wealthy families were given vast tracts of land in the fertile Galilee region and charged outrageous rents and fees to peasant farmers. Fishing rights on the Sea of Galilee were tightly controlled. According to ancient records, Herod the Great and his offspring claimed 25 to 33 percent of all grain grown within his realm and 50 percent of all fruit.[8]

And that was just the beginning. There were numerous other taxes and fees from the Herodians, the Romans, and local landowners—such as soil tax, head tax, market taxes, transit tolls on roads, and port taxes. The question posed to Jesus about whether it was lawful to pay taxes to Caesar wasn't an academic question (Mark 12:14). It was a question about survival. The temple administration in Jerusalem, too, charged taxes, such as the half-shekel tax, the tithe for priests, fees for sacrifices and vows, and more. Literally millions of silver Tyrian shekels flowed each year into the temple coffers.[9] Following King Herod the Great's death in 4 BC, the Romans looted the Jerusalem temple's treasury and removed some four hundred talents of gold—roughly $545 million in today's currency.[10] By comparison, the total annual budget for all of Israel under Herod's successor Herod Agrippa (who ruled AD 41–44) was only two thousand talents. The Jewish historian Josephus sums up what this national looting had done by saying that Herod and his successors "had indeed reduced the entire country to helpless poverty."[11]

Yet, after more than six hundred years of foreign occupation, when it seemed as though Israel's God had abandoned his people to their fate, a prophet suddenly appeared. We know him as John the Baptist.

A VOICE CRYING IN THE WILDERNESS

In contrast to the displays of excess in Israel, John the Baptist was an ascetic. He wore a tunic made of camel's hair and ate locusts and wild honey for food. According to the gospel of Luke, John's birth had been foretold by an angel named Gabriel while his father, a priest named Zechariah, was tending to the altar of incense in the temple in Jerusalem (1:5–25). Many New Testament scholars dismiss this story as a mere legend, but in 2008 Israeli archaeologists announced the discovery near the Jordan River of a first-century stone tablet, covered with oracles written in ancient Hebrew script that included sayings from an angel named Gabriel. It mentions a Messiah who would suffer and die. Known as Gabriel's Revelation, it is a dramatic archaeological confirmation that some Jews during the first century were expecting a suffering Messiah, and that an angelic figure named Gabriel was, in some way, part of this expectation.

With this background, John caused a sensation across the length and breadth of Israel. The gospel of Mark reports that "all the country of Judea and all Jerusalem" went out to hear what he had to say and were washed by him in the Jordan River (1:5). John welcomed criminals and outcasts, even the hated tax collectors and soldiers, just as Jesus would. When the tax collectors asked John what they should do to get right with God, he told them, "Collect no more than you are authorized to do" (Luke 3:13). At that time, tax collectors were given fixed monetary targets, and John was telling them they shouldn't exceed those limits as a way of adding to their profits. When soldiers asked John what they should do, he said, "Do not extort money from anyone by threats or by false accusation, and be content with your wages" (v. 14).

The site where it is believed John the Baptist washed Jesus in the Jordan River, in Judea near Jericho, was off-limits to tourists and pilgrims alike until 2011 due to the presence of land mines and military fortifications.

Because times were so desperate, the Jews had begun to wonder if God would finally send them the long-promised Messiah, a redeemer who would rescue them from the brutal Romans and the corrupt collaborators in Jerusalem who ruled in their name. It is clear that many people wondered if John himself might be the promised savior.

John shared in the messianic expectation. The Gospels portray him looking forward to an intimidating figure, someone "mightier than I" who had a "winnowing fork . . . in his hand" and was willing to gather the wheat but toss the chaff into "unquenchable fire" (Matt. 3:11–12).

When a group of Pharisees asked John why he was washing the multitudes if he was not the Messiah, he replied that there was someone coming after him who would cleanse people with the Spirit of fire and whose sandal he, John, was not worthy to untie (v. 11).

All four gospels report that Jesus, too, joined the tens of thousands of Jews who visited John at the River Jordan and heard him speak—and all agree that some dramatic supernatural event occurred that revealed Jesus' identity.

In Mark's and Luke's versions, John washed Jesus, and as he came up out of the water he saw the heavens opened and the Spirit descending on him "like a dove." Then a voice came from heaven that said, "You are my beloved Son; with you I am well pleased" (Luke 3:22, Mark 1:10–11). Matthew changes things slightly, writing that the voice said, "*This* is my beloved Son," and emphasizing that others heard it too (3:17). The gospel of John has the Baptist report that he had seen the Spirit descend like a dove on Jesus, and that God himself had told him that on whomever he saw the Spirit descend was, in fact, the Son of God, the one who would cleanse with the Spirit (1:32–34).

Historians have a good idea of when this event occurred—a crucial fact for reconstructing a time line of Jesus' life. According to the gospel of Luke, John began his ministry in the desert:

> in the fifteenth year of the reign of Tiberius Caesar;
> when Pontius Pilate was governor of Judea and Herod [Antipas] was tetrarch of Galilee and
> his brother Philip was tetrarch of the region of Ituraea and Trachonitis;
> when Lysanias was tetrarch of Abilene;
> and during the high priesthood of Annas and Caiaphas. (3:1–2)

Philip died in AD 33–34, so John must have begun his ministry *before* that. Depending upon which calendar Luke was using (the old Roman or new Julian calendar) and how he counted a year of Tiberius's reign (when Tiberius assumed office or when his predecessor died), the fifteenth year of Tiberius's reign was around the year AD 28 or 29.[12] Thus, the best guess is that Jesus began his own movement, proclaiming the kingdom of God, around this time, just a year or two after the governor Pontius Pilate arrived at the Roman city of Caesarea Maritima on Israel's central coast. It's a further reminder that Jesus' mission was very brief, just two to three years at most, and that the kingdom movement he proclaimed swept across Israel and the entire Middle East like wildfire.

The ruins of Herod the Great's hilltop fortress of Machaerus, overlooking the Dead Sea in Jordan, where Herod's son Antipas cut off the head of John the Baptist.

"THE KINGDOM OF GOD IS AT HAND"

What Jesus actually meant by "the kingdom of God" has been a source of debate among scholars across the academic and religious spectrum. For the past century or so, many have claimed that Jesus never intended to launch a movement or found a community at all. They say he was an "apocalyptic prophet" who believed that the end of the world was coming in his own lifetime. For these scholars, the "kingdom of God" that Jesus had in mind was a fiery cataclysm where God would kill all the Romans and anyone else opposed to Jesus, establishing Jesus as the ruler of all the earth. This approach permeates the international bestseller *Zealot*, written by Reza Aslan, a Muslim professor of creative writing, in 2013. The book portrays Jesus as a Jewish nationalist who at least sympathized with those elements of his society arguing for a holy war against Rome.

The idea that Jesus was an "apocalyptic prophet" was first popularized in 1906 by the medical missionary and scholar Albert Schweitzer, and it is widely taught in many seminaries and Near Eastern studies departments to this day. The most famous scholars who have argued for this increasingly challenged theory are Bart Ehrman and Dale Allison, a Christian professor of New Testament at Princeton Theological Seminary.[13] As proof that Jesus believed the world was coming to an end soon, scholars like Ehrman point to sayings of Jesus such as Mark 9:1: "Truly I tell you, some who are standing here will not taste death before they see that the kingdom of God has come with power" (NIV). This means, Ehrman says, that Jesus was a false prophet and clearly wrong about what God intended: the world did not come to an end, after all, and Jesus died on the cross a shocked and disillusioned failure.[14]

But in recent years, even many secular New Testament scholars have rejected the idea that Jesus was an end-times prophet proclaiming the imminent apocalypse. For one thing, many of the proof texts often cited, such as the one above, don't actually mention the end of the world at all. The earlier scholars assumed, rather than proved, that for Jesus the "kingdom of God" and the Last Judgment were one and the same, when in fact they are clearly distinct. The Gospels *do* show that Jesus, like many Jews, believed in a Last Judgment at the end of time; but he hints at a time before the Last Judgment when the kingdom of God would "arrive with power."

Scholars such as Ehrman speculate that the gospel writers, such as Luke and John, altered Jesus' sayings to reflect the fact that the promised apocalypse never arrived. They "de-apocalypticized" Jesus' message. Yet in the gospel of Mark, likely the *earliest* gospel to be written, Jesus insists that before the Last Judgment will occur, "the gospel must first be preached to *all* nations" (13:10 NIV). In addition, in that part of the gospels many experts believe is the very oldest of all—which scholars call Q—there is not a single mention of an imminent end of the world. Not one.[15]

So what *was* Jesus' vision of the kingdom of God? According to the records we have, when Jesus spoke about the kingdom, he said it was "good news" (Luke 4:43), "like treasure hidden in a field" (Matt. 13:44), not bad news. He compared it to *a wedding feast*, not a cosmic artillery barrage (Matt. 22:2–14). Even more to the point, Jesus said that the kingdom he was proclaiming is already "in the midst of you" (Luke 17:21) and is "not coming in ways that can be observed" (Luke 17:20). He added the kingdom is like a tiny mustard seed that, when planted, grows into an enormous tree that shelters all the birds of the air (Luke 13:19), or like yeast that when mixed with flour leavens all the dough (Luke 13:21). It is "like a net that was thrown into the sea and gathered fish of every kind" (Matt. 13:47). In other words, while the kingdom of God is plainly a supernatural event of great power and consequence, it is in no way a violent conflagration.

Thus, in recent years many New Testament scholars—even very skeptical scholars at secular universities—have come to reject the old idea that Jesus thought the world was coming to an end in his lifetime. These scholars range from Christian experts such as the Anglican bishop N. T. Wright to more skeptical, secular scholars such as John Dominic Crossan and Marcus Borg, founders of the Jesus Seminar; and Richard Horsley at the University of Massachusetts–Boston. Instead, these scholars now believe that Jesus was actually someone far more dangerous than a deluded millenarian prophet. Jesus saw himself, and was seen by others, as the long-promised Jewish Messiah, the divine Son of Man who was inaugurating a new era in human history—and whose reign would threaten and ultimately destroy all the kings and warlords of the earth. Jesus was the greatest threat to human power and arrogance ever to appear on earth. And for the authorities of his day, he had to be stopped at all costs.

CHAPTER 3

Bringing the
Dead to Life

Then he stretched himself upon the child three times and cried
to the LORD, "O LORD my God, let this child's life come into
him again." And the LORD listened to the voice of Elijah. And
the life of the child came into him again, and he revived.
—1 KINGS 17: 21–22

After three long days of walking from Galilee, Jesus and his caravan
finally reached the oasis of Jericho in the scorching flatlands south
of Jerusalem. It was a large group, made up of dozens of people, including many women followers (Matt. 27:55–56). In late March, this part
of the country would have been blistering during the day and freezing
cold at night, and many in the group would have been exhausted from
the hard travel. To add to their difficult situation, there were few places
to find water, and the hills and valleys in these years were often teeming
with bandits and cutthroats.

For two days, the caravan stayed outside of Jericho, in the region
known as Perea. On the morning of the third day, they began the ardu-
ous climb uphill into the craggy Judean foothills. Their destination

was the small village of Beit Anya, or Bethany, located about two miles southeast of Jerusalem, perhaps a forty-minute ride on horseback.[1]

As Jesus arrived on the outskirts of the village, he learned that his friend Lazarus had died and had been, according to John's gospel, "in the tomb four days" (11:17).

He entered Bethany and saw a woman named Mary, whom he knew well, running toward him. When she reached him, she fell at his feet, crying, "If you had been here, my brother would not have died" (v. 21).

Upon hearing and seeing this, Jesus immediately wept and asked, "Where have you laid him?" (v. 34).

So began a series of events that would finally tip the scales against Jesus—that would lead the authorities to begin plotting against him in earnest.

THE TOMB IN BETHANY

Interestingly, the town of Bethany was settled by Arabs who called it *el-Azariyeh* in honor of Lazarus, the word being an Arabic corruption of the Greek *Lazarion*, which means "place of Lazarus." The village of Bethany was probably located near today's Palestinian village. A small, crowded Arab town of some twenty thousand inhabitants, it has been considered the site of biblical Bethany since the early fourth century.

Some archaeologists insist the biblical village may have been located higher up on the southeastern slope of the Mount of Olives. The anonymous Pilgrim of Bordeaux (traveling ca. 333–334) and the pilgrim Egeria (traveling ca. 384) were two European pilgrims who visited Israel in the fourth century and left records of their travels. They both visited a tomb they believed to be Lazarus's. It is the spot revered today as the Tomb of Lazarus, found in the basement of a modern church that was finished in 1955 and built on top of a succession of earlier churches. Though some Israeli archaeologists doubt that this particular tomb was Lazarus's, it still provides keen evidence about what Lazarus's tomb was like.

Over the years, archaeologists have found that in the first century AD, the area surrounding this church was indeed a cemetery.[2] Numerous rock-hewn tombs from that era have been discovered.[3] These were cut from a limestone hillside with an inner chamber consisting of a number of *kokhim*, or burial niches. Large, sometimes rounded stones would be used to cover the entrances.

Israeli archaeologist Shimon Gibson believes that the ancient Jews placed their dead relatives on slabs in stone tombs because, at that time in history, they were not always sure if someone was actually dead. This led to a somewhat reasonable fear of accidentally burying someone alive in a grave. Gibson relates an account in rabbinic sources of a man being buried in a tomb and found after three days to still be alive. The man went on to live for another two and a half decades.[4]

Even today, determining whether and when someone has died can require sophisticated medical knowledge. In those times, though, medical know-how was limited and often primitive. Many were uncertain about the workings of the body, including whether or not someone had truly died. As a result, affluent Jews buried their loved ones in stone tombs and attached bells and cymbals to their bodies so that if the dead were not truly dead, they could alert the living.

Jewish burial practice was composed of two stages. First, the body was wrapped in linen and, if possible, placed in a rock-cut tomb for a period of one year. At the end of the year, the dead person's friends or family would return, gather up his or her mortal remains, and place them in a small stone box, or ossuary, for more permanent burial. This was accompanied by a special ceremony, now called *yahrzeit*, which Jews today still practice on the one-year anniversary of a person's death. In contrast, the poor were forced to bury their loved ones in the ground due to the cost of rock-cut tombs. But they also wanted to make sure their loved ones were truly dead before they were buried. Thus, a body was placed for three days in a mortuary near a cemetery before burial.

WIKIPEDIA

The traditional tomb of Lazarus in the village of Bethany.

DEAD OR SLEEPING?

This background information both clarifies and muddies the waters a bit when it comes to the three instances in the New Testament when Jesus resuscitated people who were declared dead. In two of the three instances—Jairus's daughter and Lazarus—the Gospels quote Jesus as saying the dead person in question was sleeping. In the case of Jairus's daughter, Jesus told the girl's relatives who were mourning for the girl, "Stop wailing . . . She is not dead but asleep" (Luke 8:52 NIV). Christians have traditionally understood Jesus to have been speaking ironically, not literally—that the girl really was dead and was not asleep. But that is not clear from the text itself. The gospel of Luke relates that Jesus took the girl by the hand and said, "My child, get up!" Then her "spirit returned" and she at once stood up (8:54–55 NIV). In the second case, the gospel of Luke does not say that the son of the widow of Nain was sleeping or even how long the man had been dead (7:11–17). It says that as Jesus approached the town gate of Nain, a dead man was being carried out on a bier. When Jesus saw the man's mother crying, he told her not to cry, touched the bier, and commanded the man lying on it to get up—and, to the awe of the crowd, he did.

In the case of Lazarus, Jesus is first quoted as saying that Lazarus "has fallen asleep" (John 11:11). However, John then quotes Jesus as saying that Lazarus was truly dead (v. 14). Mary told him her brother had been in the tomb for four days (v. 39). For the Jews, four days was long enough to determine that someone had truly died.

Mary, Martha, and their friends took Jesus to the tomb where Lazarus had been placed. The cave had a stone laid across the entrance, as was the custom.

"Take away the stone," Jesus commanded.

The crowd hesitated.

"Lord," Martha replied, "by this time there will be an odor, for he has been dead four days."

Jesus then stopped and prayed aloud. He thanked God for hearing him and added that he was praying for the benefit of the people there, so they might believe that God had truly sent Jesus.

Jesus then yelled out in a loud voice, "Lazarus, come out."

To the awe and probable horror of the crowd, Lazarus staggered out of the tomb like a mummy in an old Hollywood movie, his hands still wrapped with strips of linen and a cloth around his face.

A gasp must have arisen from the crowd. But John relates that Jesus said simply, "Unbind him, and let him go" (John 11:38–44).

Despite what modern skeptics claim, there is nothing inherently implausible about this event. Even in our own time, we hear accounts of people who were presumed dead but who woke in mortuaries, morgues, or even, in a few rare cases, caskets—to the shock and often terror of onlookers.[5]

Was Lazarus clinically dead? Or had he been in some form of coma, placed prematurely in a tomb? Regardless of the answer, what happened *after* Lazarus's resuscitation was crucial: Jesus' already considerable fame spread like wildfire throughout Judea. The news of the great miracle even quickly reached the authorities in Jerusalem, and a secret meeting of the chief priests and leading Pharisees was called. They could no longer suffer a miracle-worker with this much power and influence to continue to sway the people. "If we let him go on like this, everyone will believe in him," the Jewish authorities reportedly said, "and then the Romans will come and take away both our temple and our nation" (John 11:48 NIV).

THE THREAT OF RESURRECTION

Plainly, the Jewish council leaders were worried that the hundreds of thousands of people coming to Jerusalem for the Passover festival would hear the story about Lazarus and then proclaim Jesus a prophet, per-haps even the Messiah, the rightful king of Israel. That could provoke a riot, or even an outright rebellion against the Roman occupation forces, with disastrous consequences. The high priest Caiaphas lashed out at the Jewish ruling council, the Sanhedrin, because he found them too timid in their inaction against Jesus. "You know nothing at all!" he thundered at those urging caution. "You do not realize that it is better for you that one man die for the people than that the whole nation perish" (John 11:49–50 NIV).

That is why even some Jewish scholars now concede that Caiaphas could very well have wanted Jesus silenced at all costs,[6] despite claims in recent years that Jesus' arrest was ordered solely by the Roman authori-ties.[7] Given the delicate position of the temple authorities—their need to placate both the pious Jewish multitudes and the ruthless Romans—it makes sense. Earlier, other authorities had wanted Jesus killed, such as Herod Antipas (Luke 13:31–33). But now the temple authorities them-selves had spoken. The gospel of John even claims that the Jewish leaders were so worried about the impact of Jesus' latest "sign" that they made plans to kill Lazarus, for "on account of him many of the Jews were going away and believing in Jesus" (John 12:11).

For this reason, after Jesus raised Lazarus, he briefly stepped away from public view. He withdrew to a region near the wilderness, to a village called Ephraim, where he stayed with his disciples. In his absence, anticipation over Jesus' announced arrival in Jerusalem for the Passover festival reached a fever pitch. Would he or wouldn't he show up? There was a standing order that Jesus should be arrested on the spot.

Christians are so accustomed to the story of Palm Sunday—of Jesus' joyous entry into Jerusalem—that many forget what a profoundly dangerous and subversive act his arrival in Jerusalem actually was. Jesus' fame by this point was substantial. He was a well-known wonder-worker and successor to John the Baptist—a prophet who was leading a crusade as dangerous as the Maccabees' revolt against paganism in 167 BC. All of Israel was watching and wondering what Jesus would do next. "What do you think?" people asked one another. "Isn't he coming to the festival at all?" (John 11:56 NIV).

CHAPTER 4

KING OF THE JEWS

"Are you the Christ, the Son of the Blessed?" And Jesus said,
"I am, and you will see the Son of Man seated at the right
hand of Power, and coming with the clouds of heaven."
—MARK 14:61–62

The Gospels report several attempts to kill Jesus. He had been repeatedly warned that both political and religious authorities wanted him dead (Luke 13:31). Nonetheless, Jesus was determined to bring his message, and his movement, into the very heart of Jewish society: the Jerusalem temple. The Gospels relate how his closest followers, the twelve apostles, tried to dissuade him, so much that Jesus denounced Simon Peter for doing just that, even calling him Satan (Matt. 16:23). Jesus predicted three times that his upcoming visit to Jerusalem would result in his death, yet he insisted on completing his mission.[1] He announced to his followers what must have been a horrifying declaration: "The Son of Man came not to be served but to serve," Matthew records, "and to give his life as a ransom for many" (20:28).

After Jesus left Bethany, he stayed for a day in Ephraim, a village about fifteen miles northeast of Jerusalem. If Jesus thought he might be arrested after the commotion over Lazarus, this isolated spot was a good place to lie low until the Passover festival one week away. On Sunday,

Jesus arrived in a village called Bethphage, which means "house of figs." The location of Bethphage is still not exactly known, but archaeologists generally agree that it was a small village found on the eastern slope of the Mount of Olives. Near the outskirts of the village, Jesus sent two of his followers into Bethphage and told them they would find a young donkey tied to a post when they arrived. They were to bring the donkey back to him. Jesus told the pair, "If anyone says to you, 'Why are you doing this?' say, 'The Lord has need of it and will send it back here immediately'" (Mark 11:3). This incident is one of many recorded in the Gospels in which Jesus appeared to have made arrangements outside the knowledge of his inner circle, indicating that Jesus' network of associates and friends in high places may have been larger than we know.

THE ANOINTED ONE

In the first century, Jews turned to a wide array of sacred texts to understand their circumstances, why God's chosen people had been living for centuries under the domination of ruthless pagans. Many of these texts, from the Torah and the Psalms to the writings of the Prophets, contained cryptic oracles about a future ideal king, a descendent of King David, who would save Israel's people from their oppression. The word used for this figure was *mashiach* in Hebrew, or Messiah, which simply means "anointed." Israel's prophets and kings were frequently anointed with oil as a symbol of their status.

As early as the book of Deuteronomy, Israel's great lawgiver, Moses, promised that in the future God would "raise up for you a prophet like me from among yourselves, from your own kinsmen" (18:15 CJB). In many of these writings, the coming rescuer of Israel, the Messiah, the future "prophet," is described in violent, even militaristic terms as a conquering general who would vanquish Israel's enemies in battle. Many Jews came to believe that the promised Messiah would establish a government in Israel that would be the center of all world government, both for Jews and Gentiles (Isa. 2:2–4; 11:10–12; 42:1). He would rebuild the temple and reestablish its worship (Jer. 33:17–18), and the whole world would recognize the Jewish God as the only true God, and the Jewish religion as the only true religion (Isa. 2:3).

But alongside the more militaristic conceptions of the future Messiah, there were other, alternative viewpoints. The prophets also spoke of the future Messiah who, far from being a conquering general, would be a messenger of peace and would suffer indignities on behalf of the human race. Christians point to the "suffering servant" oracles in the prophet Isaiah as proof of this. Until recently, some scholars insisted that these passages did not refer to a messianic figure at all but to the Jewish people themselves. But in recent years, thanks to the discovery of the Dead Sea Scrolls and other works written around the time of Jesus, some experts have conceded that many Jews in Jesus' time did understand these texts as referring to the Messiah.[2]

It is clear that Jesus too believed in these ancient oracles. At one point Jesus sat his followers down, and, "beginning with Moses and all the Prophets, he interpreted to them in all the Scriptures the things concerning himself" (Luke 24:27). Jesus saw the Messiah of the Hebrew Scriptures as a herald of peace, not a military hero. His decision to enter Jerusalem on a lowly donkey reflected this.

The symbolism of the donkey and the Mount of Olives is often lost on modern readers, but to first-century Jews it was about as subtle as a US politician walking into a political gathering with the melody of "Hail to the Chief" blaring in the background. It was a blatant political and religious statement. A slow and plodding animal, the donkey was at that time a symbol of peace. According to the prophet Zechariah, Israel's future, ideal king, or Messiah, would arrive not on a horse—a symbol of military strength even today—but on a humble donkey:

> Rejoice greatly, O daughter of Zion!
> Shout aloud, O daughter of Jerusalem!
> Behold, your king is coming to you;

righteous and having salvation is he,

humble and mounted on a donkey,

on a colt, the foal of a donkey.

I will cut off the chariot from Ephraim

and the war horse from Jerusalem;

and the battle bow shall be cut off,

and he shall speak peace to the nations;

his rule shall be from sea to sea,

and from the River [Euphrates] to the ends of the earth. (9:9–10)

The Mount of Olives—a rocky, olive-covered hill rising up just east of Jerusalem—also loomed large in the Jewish imagination. It had been a Jewish cemetery for three thousand years and still is today. According to Zechariah, the final confrontation between the forces of evil and the God of Israel will begin on the Mount of Olives (14:4). It is there that the long-hoped-for resurrection of the dead will begin.

ARE THE ANCIENT ORACLES ACTUALLY TRUE?

Some modern New Testament scholars claim that the entire Palm Sunday narrative is an example of *midrash*, the Jewish practice of stitching together Old Testament passages to fill in the details or give a new interpretation of a biblical passage. It would be like a modern newspaper reporter saying that a current US president "could not tell a lie," deliberately alluding to an old story about George Washington while *also* describing what was actually happening in the White House. But it is just as likely that Jesus himself was using the symbolism of the donkey and the arrival from the Mount of Olives quite deliberately—in other words, to send a not-very-subtle message that he really was the peaceful Messiah proclaimed by Zechariah, not the military Messiah hoped for by the Jewish zealot underground.

THE TRIUMPHAL ENTRY

The Synoptics report that the two followers found the young donkey waiting for them, just as Jesus had described, and brought it back. Jesus' entourage then spread cloaks on the back of the donkey and Jesus rode on it beside his followers as they headed into the city. From Bethphage, Jerusalem was only about a Sabbath's day journey away (approximately half a mile). The route Jesus took has been preserved in Christian memory for centuries. Around AD 384, the Spanish pilgrim Egeria wrote an account of life in Israel that included a description of Christians retracing Jesus' steps into the city each Easter season. The pilgrims proceeded from Bethphage, likely located on the back side of the Mount of Olives, over the top of the hill, and down the other side of the Mount of Olives toward the garden of Gethsemane. These ancient paths, one to the north and one to the south, still exist and are used today.

The path from the Mount of Olives to Jerusalem crosses through the Kidron Valley just east of Jerusalem's massive eastern wall. The towering walls of Jerusalem would have been about ten feet lower in Jesus' day but just as impressive.

A large crowd lined the sides of the road as Jesus passed into the Kidron Valley and then back up again, spreading their own cloaks on the ground and waving leafy branches in the air. The crowd was yelling the Aramaic phrase *hosanna* (הושע נא), which literally means "Please save us!" Different voices in the crowd shouted out quotations from the Hebrew Psalms, such as *Baruch haba b'shem Adonai* ("Blessed is he who comes in the name of the LORD!" Ps. 118:26) and *Baruch malkut aveinu David* ("Blessed is the kingdom of our father David" Mark 11:10).[3]

Like many first-century Jews living in the land of Israel, Jesus had been to Jerusalem many times and knew it well.[4] When he first visited, the city already would have been a thousand years old and widely considered one of the wonders of the ancient world. Built high on a hill in the Judean foothills, the city was actually an enormous fortress, surrounded by walls eight feet thick that stood atop natural limestone cliffs with, according to Josephus, a hundred towers lining the perimeter.[5] Yet it was also a cosmopolitan city of tremendous wealth, full of gardens, enormous outdoor pools and fountains, and magnificent buildings, bustling energy, and great learning. Just as today, the Jewish residents in the first century shared their holy city with a bewildering array of foreigners.

Archaeologists have revealed that the city in the time of Jesus was divided in two almost equal halves running north to south—the Upper City to the west, where many wealthy priestly families lived and Herod the Great's palace was located, and the Lower City to the southeast, where foreigners and merchants had their homes. Both of these residential districts were built on a sharp incline, running north to south. In the past, archaeologists assumed that the Lower City was a poor neighborhood with small houses, but recent archaeological excavations have revealed that the Lower City too had luxurious homes and outdoor pools and fountains, such as the enormous Pool of Siloam, which was uncovered in 2004 and partially excavated.[6]

Looming above both halves of the city and situated in the northeast corner stood the Temple Mount complex, an enormous, level plaza, surrounded and buttressed by massive retaining walls, on which the temple itself stood. Herod the Great set out in 26 BC to rebuild Jerusalem in general, and the temple in particular, and turn it into a rival of Athens's famed Parthenon. He largely succeeded.

As Jesus and his followers descended the Mount of Olives and into the Kidron Valley, the massive stone ramparts of Jerusalem loomed before them. Archaeologists insist that the eastern wall of the city in Jesus' day stood just about where the eastern wall is located today, only about ten to twenty feet lower. The spot where the Muslim Dome of the Rock stands today was where the magnificent temple likely towered above the city gates in Jesus' day, its white marble walls and gold plating glistening in the sun. According to Jewish historian Josephus, the temple was like "a mountain covered with snow," and all that was not overlaid with gold was of the purest white.[7]

Forty years later, after a bitter war that lasted four years, the Romans would level the entire city, destroy the golden temple, and slaughter between three hundred thousand and one million Jews. Yet when Jesus entered the city on Palm Sunday, he paused, looked out over the valley at the magnificent city and its shining temple, and exclaimed, "O Jerusalem, Jerusalem, the city that kills the prophets and stones those who are sent to it!" (Luke 13:34). He was mourning the future destruction of the capital city of his homeland.

By this point, Jesus was a wanted man. Everyone was buzzing with anticipation about the arrival of the famous prophet and healer, wondering whether he would dare to show up. The gospel of Matthew reports that when he did arrive, the "whole city was shaken." When anyone asked, "Who is this?" the crowds replied, "This is the prophet Jesus, from Nazareth of Galilee" (21:10–11 HCSB). Thus, it is almost certain that the Jewish authorities were aware of Jesus' impending arrival. It's also likely that the Romans knew who Jesus was as well. After all, Herod Antipas, son of Herod the Great, had beheaded Jesus' colleague and relative John the Baptist for stirring up trouble among the people. Like all occupying armies, the Romans relied upon spies and informers to keep them apprised of what was happening in the city.[8]

The handful of low-ranking temple guards and Roman soldiers guarding the ramparts may have been hard-pressed to distinguish Jesus' entourage from the tens of thousands of other happy, loud, often singing Jewish pilgrims pouring into the city. Even if guards were able to spot Jesus, the Gospels tell us why he could have entered Jerusalem openly and surrounded by a large crowd of adoring fans: the authorities "feared the people" (Mark 11:32 NIV). According to the gospel of Mark, likely the first gospel to be written, "the teachers of the law and the elders looked for a way to arrest [Jesus]. . . . But they were afraid of the crowd; so they left him and went away" (12:12 NIV).

Traveling through or across the Kidron Valley, Jesus and his followers would have passed the rock-cut Tomb of Benei Hezir (left) and the Tomb of Zechariah (right).

THE GATES OF JERUSALEM

The gates of Jerusalem were significant on this day not just as points of surveillance for the reigning authorities. They had prophetic significance as well. In the first century, the main ceremonial gate of the Temple Mount complex, known as the Shushan Gate, could only be reached by climbing a large stone staircase that no longer exists. Inside the gate, pilgrims could enter directly into the temple's outer precincts. The entryway was situated in such a way that it faced the doorway of the temple itself, in a direct line with the inner sanctum, the Holy of Holies. It was said in ancient times that the Shekinah, the Divine Presence, was visible through this gate—and that it would be again when the Messiah comes.[9] According to Ezekiel, the future king or Messiah "shall enter by way of the vestibule of the gate, and shall go out by the same way" (44:3). Christian tradition says that Jesus came through this very gate on Palm Sunday.

Today there is still a gate in Jerusalem's eastern wall, but it likely was built in the sixth century AD. Christians call it the Golden Gate. It sits below a massive stone tower about fifty feet across and sixty feet high,[10] which gives tourists an idea of what the gates could have been like in Jesus' time. The Golden Gate was walled up by the Muslim ruler Saladin in 1187, and some archaeologists question whether this gate was built directly over the Shushan Gate.[11]

One of the frustrations of contemporary archaeology in the Holy Land is that archaeologists are not certain precisely where the temple stood. That is why many Orthodox Jews today refuse to walk on the Temple Mount in case they accidentally step into the "Holy of Holies," the inner sanctum of the temple, where only the high priest could enter—and only once a year, on the Day of Atonement (Yom Kippur). Most archaeologists now believe that the ancient temple likely stood close to where the Muslim Dome of the Rock now stands, but if this is true, then today's Golden Gate is likely *not* in the same location as the Shushan Gate once was. It would lie hundreds of yards north of the Dome of the Rock and, thus, not in line with the temple doorway.

What's more, the quickest way into the city, coming from Bethany, would not have been the Shushan Gate but the Fountain Gate to the south, near the large Pool of Siloam in the Lower City. For this reason, some Israeli archaeologists argue that the Fountain Gate is the one Jesus and his enthusiastic followers entered on Palm Sunday.

Jesus would have dismounted from the donkey, probably giving the animal to a trusted disciple to return as promised. At the southeastern corner of the city, Jesus and his followers would have then proceeded uphill along the main north-south street in the Lower City until they reached the Temple Mount. From there, Jesus could have entered the temple complex by climbing the massive stone steps, the so-called Rabbi Steps, into the tunnels that led upward into the outer courtyard—or he could have turned left at the southern wall of the Temple Mount and climbed the elaborate staircase above Robinson's Arch, entering directly into the Royal Stoa building that lined the entire southern wall of the Temple Mount.

Whichever route Jesus took, he did not stay long in the temple area. The gospel of Mark says simply that Jesus "looked around at everything" (11:11), but that, as it was then very late, he returned to Bethany with the twelve apostles. It's very likely that Jesus and his followers were surveying the area in anticipation of the game-changing event that would happen the next day. Jesus knew what he was about to do would seal his fate in the eyes of the Jewish authorities.

CHAPTER 5

A DEMONSTRATION ON THE TEMPLE MOUNT

Zeal for your house has consumed me.
—PSALM 69:9

Early the next morning, the man all of Jerusalem was talking about, the prophet Jesus of Nazareth, stood atop the enormous limestone staircase that abuts the southern wall of Jerusalem's Temple Mount (and which still exists today). Below him, in the large open area beneath the steps, tens of thousands of Jewish pilgrims were pushing and shoving their way toward the double gates in the southern wall. They were all eager to see and hear what Jesus had to say. Archaeologists estimate that the normal population of Jerusalem in the first century was likely between fifty thousand and one hundred thousand people. But during the three major pilgrim festivals of Passover (Pesach), Weeks (Shavuot), and Booths (Sukkot), the population swelled to a quarter million, perhaps even to a half million or more. To put that in context, Martin Luther King Jr.'s march on Washington was around 250,000 people. As anyone knows who has visited Jerusalem's walled and crowded Old City during religious holidays, the smothering effect of thousands of people pushing their way through narrow, hilly alleyways can be overwhelming.

By this time, Jesus was a superstar—a prophet and healer whose fame had reached across the eastern Mediterranean. Some were saying he was the Messiah, the long-prophesied Davidic king who would free Israel from bondage to foreign powers. For nearly three years, Jesus had been electrifying larger and larger crowds all across the length and breadth of Israel, from the hot desert of Judea in the south all the way north to Tyre in what is now southern Lebanon. We tend to think of Jesus in pastoral terms, sitting in a boat and addressing small groups by the Sea of Galilee. But the Gospels make clear that Jesus eventually led a mass movement of thousands. His followers fanned out to dozens of villages in the Galilee region and beyond, organizing his appearances in advance. In one account, Jesus sent out no fewer than seventy-two of his followers, as a kind of advance team, to spread his message "into every town and place where he himself was about to go" (Luke 10:1). We have accounts of Jesus feeding as many as five thousand people at one time (Matt. 14:13–21).

On this particular day, many of these thousands of admirers were gathered together in one place, at the base of Jerusalem's towering Temple Mount. The tension in the air was palpable, the noise from the crowds deafening. Many feared that a riot could explode at any moment. The Gospels report there had already been several attempts to kill Jesus. He had been repeatedly warned that both political and religious authorities wanted him dead (Luke 13:31).

The guards warily eyed Jesus and his thousands of noisy admirers. It was the tenth day of the Jewish month of Nissan—or, by some modern calculations, April 3—in the year AD 30. The Passover festival would begin in just four days. The city was bursting at its seams. The guards standing near the double gates almost certainly knew who Jesus was— and wondered what he was about to do. He was famous as a healer and miracle worker, someone who would even touch and cure lepers, the blind and lame, those possessed by demons. It was said he could even bring the dead back to life. According to the gospel of Mark, the teachers of the law and the elders had been looking for a way to arrest Jesus. But they were afraid of the crowd, "so they left him and went away" (12:12).

WIKIPEDIA

A massive stone staircase, known as the Rabbi Steps, leads up to the southern wall of the Temple Mount and the double gates that once took Jewish pilgrims into an underground tunnel and stairs up to the temple plaza. Rabbis such as Jesus used to address their followers at the top of these steps because they formed a natural platform.

Like the prophets before him, Jesus had decided to dramatize his message about the coming kingdom of God with a controversial but highly effective symbolic action, what we might today call an act of civil disobedience. Israel's prophets had performed similar symbolic protests throughout Israel's history. The Jerusalem prophet Isaiah walked around stark naked for three years as a warning of what the invading Assyrians were about to do to all prisoners they marched into captivity (Isa. 20:3). Jeremiah wore an ox yoke around his neck to symbolize the coming enslavement of the Babylonians (Jer. 27). Hosea went so far as to marry a notorious prostitute, Gomer, to dramatize Israel's unfaithfulness to God (Hos. 1:2–3). Jesus' kingdom message of hope and renewal also contained a sharp warning, a very public rebuke of the

39

violent Jewish nationalism beginning to sweep the country. And like the biblical prophets who proclaimed God's judgment against corrupt and lawless leaders, Jesus was about to make a lot of powerful people very angry.

PROTEST ON THE TEMPLE MOUNT

Very suddenly, Jesus and his followers began moving. Hundreds, perhaps thousands of his followers poured into the double gates of the southern wall. Others went to the left, up the enormous outdoor staircase on the southwest corner of the Temple Mount—the remains of which, now known as Robinson's Arch, are still visible. They were heading up to the Temple Mount plaza.

ARCHAEOLOGY ILLUSTRATED

This reconstruction of the Temple Mount is facing the southwestern corner with the massive stone staircase above what is called Robinson's Arch, named after the biblical scholar who identified it in the nineteenth century. A portion of the arch is still visible at the Western Wall.

The temple in Jerusalem was one of the world's oldest religious institutions. In the tenth century BC, Israel's great king Solomon built a permanent worship center for the Israelite God, also known as the first temple, high on a hill in the Judean foothills. Around 20 BC, the half-Jewish king Herod the Great set himself the task of renovating and expanding the temple and surrounding area. There had been a small natural plateau there before, fixed atop the ridge in the northeastern corner of Jerusalem; but Herod wanted something far more spectacular. He therefore enclosed this natural plateau on all sides with four immense retaining walls, some more than one hundred feet high, made up of massive rectangular ashlars, or cut stones, that weighed as much as 415 tons each.[1] These stones are so large that even modern cranes and bulldozers would have some difficulty moving them. Herod then filled in this entire quadrangle with stones and dirt, creating an artificial hilltop plaza— roughly 1,500 feet long by 1,000 feet wide—of more than thirty-five acres.[2] In modern terms, Herod's Temple Mount is so large that about twenty-six American football fields could fit in the space available. This massive engineering marvel has endured for two thousand years and still stands today, almost wholly intact.

The Temple Mount was surrounded on three sides by colonnades— single-story buildings made with columns that provided shade from the hot Judean sun. The southern wall was topped by what was known as the Royal Stoa, a 912-foot-long columned portico that housed meetings of the Jewish Sanhedrin, the highest political assembly and law court, after AD 30.[3] It was in this area, before the Royal Stoa, that the money-changers and animal salesmen had their booths. In the middle of the Temple Mount were a series of concentric rectangular courtyards, each surrounded by stone walls and gates. Each courtyard was set slightly higher than the one before it as they neared the temple building itself. The largest of the courtyards, later called the Court of the Gentiles, was open to all, including pagans.

Toward the middle of the Temple Mount was a low wall that only Jews (both men and women) were allowed to pass. In 1871, archae- ologists in Jerusalem found a warning tablet made out of limestone, about two feet by three feet, that the first-century Jewish historian

Josephus had observed attached to that dividing wall, warning Gentiles not to cross and approach closer to the temple proper.[4] This was what the apostle Paul, in his letter to the Ephesians, was referring to when he said that the Way of Jesus had "broken down the middle wall of partition between us" (2:14 KJV). For allegedly violating this ancient prohibition—that is, for bringing pagan Greeks past the partition wall into the areas reserved solely for Jews—the apostle Paul was arrested during his final trip to Jerusalem and ultimately sent to Rome as a prisoner (Acts 21). The inscription on the limestone tablet, seven lines written in Greek, reads:

NO FOREIGNER

IS TO GO BEYOND THE BALUSTRADE

AND THE PLAZA OF THE TEMPLE ZONE

WHOEVER IS CAUGHT DOING SO

WILL HAVE HIMSELF TO BLAME

FOR HIS DEATH

WHICH WILL FOLLOW

Beyond the dividing wall was the temple complex, another rectangular block of high walls and buildings that surrounded the temple itself. The main entrance to this block of buildings was a gate that faced toward the Mount of Olives. Passing through this gate, Jewish pilgrims would enter an inner courtyard two hundred feet square, later called the *Ezrat Nashim* or "Court of Women." This was where ordinary Jews would take their offerings to be sacrificed and where the business of the temple was conducted. The Court of Women was also known as the "treasury" of the temple because against its walls, under covered porticos, were thirteen locked donation boxes, called "trumpets" because they were wide at the base and narrow at the top. It was into one of these donation boxes that Jesus saw a poor widow place two small copper coins (Luke 21:1–4).

WIKIPEDIA

The inscription in Greek warning Jews not to cross the low perimeter fence separating the Court of Gentiles and the inner areas of the temple was discovered in 1871 and is now housed in a museum in Istanbul. It is the only remaining stone from the temple known to archaeologists.

THE CLEANSING OF THE TEMPLE

Within minutes, Jesus and his followers had bounded up the staircases and burst onto the main Temple Mount plaza, the Court of the Gentiles. Historians have been unable to determine exactly how large the entourage that accompanied Jesus actually was. Was it merely Jesus and a few hundred of his closest followers—or a large mob of thousands? Further, why wasn't Jesus arrested on the spot, as any troublemaker would be in a modern church or cathedral? The Gospels indicate that Jesus wasn't arrested, which supports the view that he may have had an enormous, possibly threatening group of supporters with him.

Some of these supporters saw Jesus as the Messiah, Israel's rightful king, who would lead a rebellion against the corrupt temple establishment.

43

The temple police force may not have been large enough to handle a serious disturbance involving hundreds, even thousands of determined protesters. The police force's primary mission was to ensure that Gentiles did not cross the wall into the areas reserved for Jews alone and to enforce the other purity codes—much as, in modern Jerusalem, special religious police in neon green vests patrol the plaza around the Western Wall to ensure that Torah regulations are enforced.[5] On the other hand, the Roman auxiliary forces in the nearby Antonia Fortress, which overlooked the temple complex, would have been very concerned but may not have wanted to intervene if it appeared to be merely a fracas among Jewish pilgrims.

The Synoptic Gospels describe a fairly violent scene. Whether Jesus came up to the Temple Mount by means of the underground staircase or the staircase on the southwestern corner, he entered directly in front of the Royal Stoa colonnade. There, dozens of vendors had their tables, and money-changers sat at their booths. It was a vast open market with thousands of live animals for sale, including sheep and oxen. The gospel of Matthew reports that Jesus drove out all who sold and bought in the temple area (21:12–17). Mark and Luke report that Jesus overturned the tables of the money-changers and, strangely, the seats of those who sold pigeons (Mark 11:15–19, Luke 19:45–48). Mark states that Jesus "would not allow anyone to carry *anything* through the temple" (11:16). The gospel of John coincides to a remarkable degree with the Synoptics' accounts but adds a few choice details (2:13–22). According to John, Jesus made a whip out of cords and used it to drive out not merely the buyers and sellers but also sheep and oxen. John also adds that Jesus didn't merely overturn the tables of the money-changers but also "poured out" their coins as well (v. 15). The vendors no doubt exploded in rage, screaming insults and threats.

Jesus' stated reason for this dramatic demonstration is recorded by all four gospels. Mark, whose audience included some Gentiles, quotes Jesus as saying, "Is it not written, 'My house shall be called a house of prayer for all the nations'? But you have made it a den of robbers" (11:17). Interestingly, John has Jesus address the pigeon sellers directly and records what Jesus said a little differently: "Take these things away; do not make my Father's house a house of trade" (2:16).

It is not clear from the gospel texts alone what was Jesus' actual objection to the money-changers and animal sellers. As a devout Jew, Jesus visited the Jerusalem temple regularly with his parents (Luke 2:41–52) and later in life (John 10:22–23); yet nowhere in the Gospels did Jesus object to temple worship itself, although he did insist that a time was coming when people would worship God without a temple (John 4:21). In Matthew's record of the Sermon on the Mount, Jesus alluded to temple sacrifices when he spoke about forgiveness—that a person should leave his sacrifice at the altar and seek reconciliation first (5:23–24). In Matthew 8:4, he also directed a man he cured of leprosy to go be inspected by a priest and offer the "gift," or sacrifice, as the Torah required (Lev. 14:1–9). The buying and selling of sacrificial animals for "gifts" was a necessary part of the temple worship, as were the money-changers who could exchange currencies from all over the world so pilgrims could purchase sacrificial animals.

So if Jesus was not protesting the actual buying and selling of sacrificial animals, what was the purpose behind this act of civil disobedience? He seems to have been addressing the elaborate temple system itself and, by extension, the luxurious lifestyles of the Jewish aristocracy who ran it. In this, Jesus was not alone; many Jewish groups in the first century were outraged by the corruption of the temple elite. Members of the Essene sect of Judaism, for instance, were so appalled by what they saw in the temple that they had detached from mainstream Jewish life, establishing communities in the desert with their own religious calendar and rules for living. Some of the ultranationalist and Torah-observant Essenes and their supporters likely participated in the uprising against Rome that, in AD 70, ended with the temple being destroyed and between three hundred thousand and one million Jewish inhabitants being killed.[6]

Over the years, many different hypotheses have been proposed for why Jesus overturned the tables that day. In addition to his apparent objection to the temple system, some claim that Jesus was protesting the way the holy temple had become defiled with rapacious fees and taxes—which was why he had denounced the moneylenders for making the temple a "den of robbers."[7] These outrageous charges and levies exploited the people who could least afford them. Another view is that, as a prophet, Jesus was symbolically enacting the coming destruction of the temple.[8] Part of Jesus' message was that if the Jewish people ignored his call for a new covenant of forgiveness, if they took the path of violence, then Jerusalem and the temple would be utterly destroyed. Luke quotes Jesus, saying:

> If you, even you, had only known on this day what would bring you peace—but now it is hidden from your eyes. The days will come upon you when your enemies will build an embankment against you and encircle you and hem you in on every side. They will dash you to the ground, you and the children within your walls. They will not leave one stone on another, because you did not recognize the time of God's coming to you. (19:42–44 NIV)

Fortunately, Jesus' purpose in chasing the money-changers from the temple became clearer over the following days as he engaged in increasingly heated disputes with Jewish leaders in Jerusalem. The Gospels record these disputes in detail (e.g., Matt. 21–22)—and they reveal, at least partially, what was at the heart of Jesus' revolutionary religious and social movement. Jesus' action in the temple was a prophetic act—a protest against the injustice, corruption, and violence of some Jewish political leaders. And it would end for Jesus in the same way it had ended for the prophets. Jesus acknowledged that fact when he said, "See, we are going up to Jerusalem, and everything that is written about the Son of Man by the prophets will be accomplished" (Luke 18:31). He knew it would end badly for him. Yet Jesus was determined to finish what he had started just a few years earlier: to proclaim in the very heart of the world, the Jerusalem temple, what the kingdom of God was all about. The world would change irreversibly as the kingdom of God came in power.

CHAPTER 6

PROCLAIMING LIBERTY TO THE CAPTIVES

The Spirit of the Lord GOD is upon me,
because the LORD has anointed me
to bring good news to the poor;
he has sent me to bind up the brokenhearted,
to proclaim liberty to the captives,
and the opening of the prison to those who are bound.
—ISAIAH 61:1

The demonstration on the Temple Mount was only the beginning. Over the next two days, Jesus engaged in a series of increasingly angry confrontations with the religious and civil authorities of his society. There is no way to minimize this conflict. Jesus denounced not only what he saw happening on the Temple Mount but also some of the key religious ideals and practices of his age. His message of the new covenant, the kingdom of God, was an attack on many of the central beliefs of the leaders in Jerusalem—and the three days Jesus spent announcing the kingdom in the holy city were filled with debates, angry arguments, and even violent scuffles.

Jesus moved all around Jerusalem during the next two days, speaking at many different places. The gospel of John mentions the recently rediscovered Pool of Siloam (9:7), an enormous outdoor pool located in the southeastern corner of the Lower City. From the top step, Jesus could have addressed thousands of pilgrims gathered around the deck of the pool and on the steps leading down into it. From the Pool of Siloam, it was a short walk uphill to the southern wall of the Temple Mount and the Rabbi Steps. Here, Jesus likely encountered the angry questions of Jewish leaders—not merely the Sadducean aristocrats who ran the temple establishment but also questions from sympathetic and curious teachers, such as the Pharisees.

THE KINGDOM OF GOD IS OPEN TO ALL

Perhaps the most shocking aspect of what Jesus proclaimed at this time was his insistence that God was calling *everyone* into his kingdom— sinners, prostitutes, even tax collectors—not merely those who kept every rule and regulation to the letter. It was one of the central aspects of Jesus' teaching, and it frequently brought him into conflict with religious authorities. Once Jesus overheard some Pharisees asking Jesus' followers why their rabbi ate with tax collectors and sinners: "Those who are well have no need of a physician, but those who are sick," Jesus told them. "Go and learn what this means: 'I desire mercy, and not sacrifice.' For I came not to call the righteous, but sinners" (Matt. 9:12–13). In Jerusalem, he explained what he meant in a series of parables that he delivered on what the kingdom of God was all about. One parable, reported only by Matthew in chapter 20, is about a vineyard with a very generous owner.

"The kingdom of heaven is like a landowner who went out at dawn to hire laborers for his vineyard," Jesus began, settling down to one of his famous stories. He added that the landowner agreed to pay the laborers the customary wage for a day's work, the silver Roman coin called a *denarius*. After an hour or two, the landowner saw other day laborers standing around idle in the marketplace, so he told them that they, too, had jobs if they wanted them, and sent them out to work in the fields. He did the same thing again around noon and then again at three in the afternoon. Around five o'clock, he saw another group of men standing around and asked them why they sat around all day instead of working. The men replied that it was because no one had hired them to work. At that the landowner told them that they, too, could go out into his fields and work.

The Roman silver coin known as a denarius was considered a day's wage in the first century. The coin bore the image of the current emperor.

Finally, in the evening, the owner of the vineyard told his foreman to summon all the workers and pay them, beginning with those who had started last. The men who had started work at five o'clock in the evening received a *denarius*—in other words, a full day's pay. Seeing this, the men who began working early in the morning assumed they would get more than a usual day's wage; it would only be fair. So they were shocked when they stepped up to receive their pay and got a single *denarius*. And here is where Jesus' psychological acuity is revealed—and where the key to understanding his kingdom movement can be found.

The workers who worked all day in the fields were furious and complained. "These last ones worked only one hour, and you have made them equal to us, who bore the day's burden and the heat," they said to the landowner.

"My friend, I am not cheating you," the landowner in Jesus' story replied. "Did you not agree with me for the usual daily wage? Take what is yours and go. What if I wish to give this last one the same as you? Am I not free to do as I wish with my own money? Are you envious because I am generous?" (Matt. 20:1–15 NABRE).

This was a shocking message, guaranteed to thrill many but anger more than a few. As Jesus had done throughout his time in Galilee, he insisted that God's work on earth would not be limited to the pious guardians of the Law—the righteous and the good. It was not just for those who worked hard all day in the vineyard, but also for those who were, to put it metaphorically, very late to the party. In fact, it's for those who only started to work a few *minutes* before everyone else was paid.

"What is your opinion?" Jesus asked the assembled Jewish nobles and intellectuals lingering on the Rabbi Steps, pressing home his point.[1] "A man had two sons. He came to the first and said, 'Son, go out and work in the vineyard today.' He said in reply, 'I will not,' but afterwards he changed his mind and went. The man came to the other son and gave the same order. He said in reply, 'Yes, sir,' but did not go. Which of the two did his father's will?"

The Jewish teachers and rabbis thought for a moment, then answered, "The first."

And then Jesus said to them, "Amen, I say to you, tax collectors and prostitutes are entering the kingdom of God before you. When John came to you in the way of righteousness, you did not believe him; but tax collectors and prostitutes did. Yet even when you saw that, you did not later change your minds and believe him" (Matt. 21:28–32 NABRE).

This story certainly caused an uproar among Jesus' listeners. Tax collectors and prostitutes were among the most hated members of Jesus' society, as in many societies today. Tax collectors were considered traitors, collaborators with the Roman occupation forces. Prostitutes were tolerated but despised, "unclean" in both a moral and a ritual sense. Yet Jesus was telling learned rabbis and temple officials that these sinful wretches were entering the kingdom of God *before* them. This was, of course, true in the sense that tax collectors and prostitutes were joining Jesus in his proclamation of the kingdom while the temple officials were not.

It is easy to imagine a crowd of thousands gathered before the southern steps of the temple, with a large group clapping and shouting out their support for what Jesus was saying, and another group guffawing and jeering. Like the prophets before him, Jesus was a divisive figure, wildly popular with the poor pilgrims who pushed and shoved their way into the city but hated by many (though not all) of the wealthy and respectable.

YOAV DOTHAN (PUBLIC DOMAIN)

A mural in Jerusalem depicts what the Pool of Siloam likely looked like in the time of Jesus.

CONFRONTATION WITH THE PHARISEES

At some point, the debate escalated. It appears that Jesus' teaching on the kingdom aroused the ire of the Pharisees—the self-appointed guardians of Jewish law. In some ways, this is surprising. Jesus had good relations with many Pharisees and shared common ground with them. In the gospel of Luke, Jesus dined with Pharisees three times (7:36, 11:37, 14:1). The book of Acts mentions Pharisees who actually became believers in Jesus and the Way (15:5). (Later, these same Pharisees in the Jesus movement would insist on ritual circumcision for all Gentile males who wished to join the community.) Some Jewish authors have even claimed that Jesus was a Pharisee himself.[2] Yet the fact that Jesus openly flouted one of the Pharisee movement's most characteristic and beloved practices, the ritual purification of the hands (*netilat yadaim*) before eating food, is evidence to the contrary.[3] The Torah only commands *priests* to wash before approaching the altar (Ex. 30:20), but the Pharisees wanted to be in a state of ritual purity at all times. So they encouraged everyone to follow this priestly practice in their daily lives as well.

The word *Pharisee* comes from the Hebrew verb *parash*, which means to set apart or separate. Pharisees were in a sense Jewish separatists, pious Jews who believed in separating themselves—somewhat like the Amish today—from the corrupting influences of the masses, especially pagan Gentiles. At that time, they were a relatively small, elite group. The first-century Jewish historian Josephus, himself a Pharisee, estimates that in the entire land of Israel only about six thousand people called themselves members of the group.[4] This is out of a total population of what modern experts gauge to be between three hundred thousand and two million.[5]

In the past, some New Testament scholars thought that Jesus' disputes with the scribes and Pharisees, as recorded in the Gospels, were likely *not* historical—or at least, that Jesus did not engage in them. These early scholars believed Jesus primarily lived in harmony with the Pharisees and that the disputes recorded in the Gospels were really between Jesus' followers and Jewish leaders in the AD 80s and 90s, not between Jesus and the Jewish leaders in the late 20s. However, in recent years, in part due to the discovery of the Dead Sea Scrolls, some Jewish scholars have changed their minds. They now recognize that Jerusalem was a cauldron of religious and ethnic animosities. Jesus did have legitimate objections to the Pharisee movement, the corrupt temple establishment, and the Jewish nationalists secretly plotting a rebellion against Rome.

The Dead Sea Scrolls revealed that many pious Jews looked upon the temple with hostility. In one of their biblical commentaries, the members of the Dead Sea community describe the high priests in Jerusalem as "wicked" and accuse them of robbing the poor and amassing great wealth—a fact largely confirmed by recent archaeological findings.[6] Yet Jesus' followers were less hostile toward the temple cult than other Jewish groups. We know this because they continued to meet and pray in the temple precincts even after Jesus was executed. In contrast, the ultra-observant Essenes at Qumran believed the temple authorities were incurably corrupt; they wanted nothing to do with them and established alternative forms of Judaism outside of the temple system altogether.

The Pharisees believed that the Torah given by God at Sinai actually came in two parts—the written Torah, recorded in the first five books of the Hebrew Bible; and an oral Torah, or oral tradition, that was passed on by the elders of Israel and that supplemented, or interpreted, the written Torah. This oral tradition created what the later rabbinic sages called a "fence for the Torah," a series of extra rules and regulations that make it very difficult to violate any of the 613 written commandments.[7] For example, the written Torah commands that on the seventh day of the week Jews should "cease from labor" (Ex. 23:12 NASB) but does not define what "labor" actually entails. The oral Torah of the Pharisees includes myriad rules and definitions that made it clear what "labor" is and how to avoid violating the commandment against it on the Sabbath.[8] In essence, the Pharisees were attempting to make Jewish tradition practical in daily life and to give ordinary people a way to actively resist, without taking up arms, the corrupting influence of pagan Roman culture. And they were aligned with Jesus and his followers in advocating peaceful coexistence with the Romans.[9]

Of course, Jesus also believed in following the commandments of the Torah. Matthew quotes him as saying that "whoever relaxes one of the least of these commandments and teaches others to do the same will be called least in the kingdom of heaven" (5:19). But Jesus was openly skeptical of the extra rules that the Pharisees insisted came from the oral Torah. It is clear from the Gospels that Jesus objected to the tendency among some Pharisees to exclude and look down upon the poorest and most vulnerable. "They tie up heavy burdens, hard to bear, and lay them on people's shoulders, but they themselves are not willing to move them with their finger," Matthew records Jesus saying. "They do all their deeds to be seen by others. For they make their phylacteries broad and their fringes long, and they love the place of honor at feasts and the best seats in the synagogues and greetings in the marketplaces and being called rabbi by others" (23:4–7).

Harsh words indeed. But Jesus was just warming up. In Matthew's account, especially, Jesus displays a sharp tongue and a talent for polemics. The Greek word *phylacteries* refers to what is called in Hebrew *tefillin*, which were the small leather boxes attached to the forehead and upper arms with leather straps. The boxes contained scraps of parchment with Torah commands for their use.[10] The "fringes" Jesus refers to are the *tzitzit* on Jewish prayer cloaks, or *tallitot*, that many observant Jewish males wear to this day and which Matthew reports Jesus also wore (9:20).

In this model of ancient Jerusalem, the southern wall can be seen with the Rabbi Steps at the base where Jesus likely debated the Pharisees during the last week of his life on earth.

At this point, many of the pilgrims listening to Jesus were likely very excited by what they heard—and perhaps openly wondering whether Jesus could be the Messiah. Who else could speak with such authority? But others were enraged, furious at the apparent presumption in Jesus' words. Jesus knew that he and his followers would soon suffer at the hands of pious men with what seemed like the best of intentions. Jesus repeatedly called his opponents "blind guides" and said they were like "whitewashed tombs" (Matt. 23:27); tombs were painted white so Jews could see them and avoid the ritual impurity that comes from contact with a corpse.[11] They looked beautiful on the outside but inside were "full of dead men's bones and every kind of filth." On the outside, he added, they appeared righteous but inside they were filled with "hypocrisy and evildoing" (Matt. 23:27–28 NABRE).

In other words: it was getting personal. We can imagine the reactions of Jesus' opponents when they were openly denounced in front of throngs of pilgrims. Toward the end of the debate, Jesus raised the issue of what the pious residents of Jerusalem had done to earlier prophets sent by God. "You say, 'If we had lived in the days of our ancestors, we would not have joined them in shedding the prophets' blood,'" Jesus said. "Thus you bear witness against yourselves that you are the children of those who murdered the prophets" (Matt. 23:30–31 NABRE).

Jesus then issued a prophecy of his own—one that came true within months. Looking at his closest followers nearby, Jesus told the crowd that God would soon "send to you prophets and wise men and scribes" but that "some of them you will kill and crucify, some of them you will scourge in your synagogues and pursue from town to town"—as the pious had done to the prophet Zechariah. "Amen, I say to you, all these things will come upon this generation," Jesus concluded (Matt. 23:34, 36 NABRE).

By this time, it was pandemonium. It's very possible that pushing and shoving between the pro-and anti-Jesus groups quickly escalated into outright fistfights—and that temple guards descended upon the scene, weapons drawn. The city was already on edge. Less than a year earlier, after the Roman governor Pilate had seized hundreds of talents of gold from the temple treasury to build a new aqueduct for Jerusalem, mobs of pious Jews had rampaged through the city, beating up anyone they suspected of being a Roman collaborator. Josephus reports that "tens of thousands" of rioting Jews surrounded the Roman *praetorium* in the Upper City when Pilate was in town, attempting to force their way in. Pilate responded by dispatching Roman auxiliary forces dressed like Jews, and then had them attack the rioters all at once.[12] Many were killed. All this makes the observation of the high priest Joseph Caiaphas seem plausible—that it "is better for you that one man die for the people than that the whole nation perish" (John 11:50 NIV).

CHAPTER 7

An Anointing
in Bethany

Samuel took a flask of oil and poured it on his head
and kissed him and said, "Has not the LORD anointed
you to be prince over his people Israel?"
—1 SAMUEL 10:1

The evening after Jesus' confrontations with Jewish leaders, on
Wednesday, Jesus and his closest followers left the city. They
crossed the Kidron Valley, and again made their way up the Mount
of Olives toward the village of Bethany, where Jesus and his followers
had been staying since they arrived in the area. The group sat down to
rest. They could see the eastern wall of the city and the magnificent
golden temple in all its glory. According to Mark, four of Jesus' closest
followers—Peter, James, John, and Andrew—took Jesus aside and asked
him something privately. They were obviously disturbed by the near
riot that had occurred—and by what Jesus had said would happen to his
followers after he was gone. "Tell us, when will this be, and what will be
the sign when these things are all to be accomplished?" they asked (13:4
RSV). They were asking about the predicted destruction of Jerusalem
and the temple.

Contrary to what many say today, Jesus explicitly told these followers that the end of the world was not coming soon. Rather, he described the start of their own work. "When you hear of wars and rumors of wars, do not be alarmed," Mark records Jesus saying. "This must take place, but the end is not yet. For nation will rise against nation, and kingdom against kingdom; there will be earthquakes in various places, there will be famines; *this is but the beginning of the birth-pangs*" (13:7–8 RSV).

The Synoptics don't beat around the bush. They all insist that Jesus was predicting not the end of the world but the end of Jerusalem—the end of an era that had lasted a thousand years. "When you see the desolating sacrilege set up where it ought not to be . . . then let those who are in Judea flee to the mountains," Jesus added. "Alas for those who are with child and for those who give suck in those days! Pray that it may not happen in winter" (Mark 13:14, 17–18 RSV).

Jesus, like many Jews in his time, did indeed proclaim a final judgment at the end of time. He spoke of his return, as part of this final accounting, as the triumphant divine Son of Man depicted in the book of Daniel (7:12–14). At some unforeseen time in the distant future, there will come a time of cosmic catastrophe when even the moon grows dark and "the stars will be falling from heaven" (Mark 13:25). Yet Jesus told his followers that even he did not know when this would happen (v. 32). It is "*then* they will see the Son of man coming in clouds with great power and glory," Mark records Jesus saying. "And *then* he will send out the angels, and gather his elect from the four winds, from the ends of the earth to the ends of heaven" (vv. 26–27 RSV).

It's clear that Jesus foresaw a very long period of time when his followers would spread the news about the kingdom he was announcing. They would suffer the same injustices and ridicule that he was about to suffer. Yet they would also do, incredibly, even greater works than he had done (John 14:12). "Take heed," Jesus told his followers. "They will deliver you up to councils; and you will be beaten in synagogues; and you will stand before governors and kings for my sake, to bear testimony before them" (Mark 13:9 RSV).

Before any final judgment would occur, Jesus said, "The gospel must first be proclaimed to *all* nations" (Mark 13:10). Given the limitations of first-century transportation and communications, Jesus must have foreseen a prolonged period before any final consummation of history. It's debatable whether the gospel has been preached to "all" nations even today, after two thousand years. So it is by no means self-evident that Jesus believed he would return very soon—or even that his followers, after his crucifixion, believed he would return in glory soon.

To drive the point home, Jesus added, "Concerning that day or that hour, no one knows, not even the angels in heaven, nor the Son, but only the Father" (v. 32). Jesus' final admonition on the topic was that his followers were to act *as if* the judgment day were just around the corner. "Stay awake at all times," Luke quotes Jesus as saying, "praying that you may have strength to escape all these things that are going to take place, and to stand before the Son of Man" (21:36).

MARY'S SACRIFICE

After watching the sun set behind the dazzling white and gold temple ablaze with light, the group continued up the Mount of Olives and along the northern ridge path back to the village of Bethany. Jesus had been invited to the home of a leper, a Pharisee named Simon, for dinner. Also present were Martha, Mary, and their brother, Lazarus, whom Jesus had restored to life just a week earlier. What happened at this dinner party was reported in all four of the gospels—a good sign that, even for skeptical modern scholars, it actually happened.[1] At this dinner Mary, Lazarus's sister, poured an expensive bottle of aromatic perfume on Jesus' head. The depiction of Mary is less than flattering. Luke describes her as a "sinner" so overwhelmed with gratitude to Jesus—for his compassion to her or for saving her brother, we don't know which—that she washed his feet with her tears and dried them with her hair (7:37–38). Mary must have had a less-than-positive reputation because the owner of the house, Simon the Pharisee, was secretly scornful that Jesus would allow such a woman even to touch him. He said to himself that if Jesus really were a prophet, he would know what sort of woman she was (Luke 7:39). But Jesus, possessing the psychological insight that makes his parables so interesting, could see what was in his host's heart.

"Simon, I have something to say to you," Jesus finally declared.

"What is it, Teacher?"

"A certain creditor had two debtors," Jesus continued. "One owed five hundred denarii, and the other fifty. When they could not pay, he forgave them both. Now which of them will love him more?" (Luke 7:40–42 RSV).

As we've seen, a *denarius* was a Roman silver coin that was widely considered worth a single day's pay for a laborer. In Jesus' example, then, one man owed fifty days' worth of pay and another nearly a year and a half's.

The Pharisee thought the question over. "The one, I suppose, to whom he forgave more."

"You have judged rightly," Jesus exclaimed. Then he turned to the woman at his feet, Lazarus's sister Mary and his good friend.

"[Simon,] do you see this woman? I entered your house, you gave me no water for my feet, but she has wet my feet with her tears and wiped them with her hair. You gave me no kiss, but from the time I came in she has not ceased to kiss my feet. You did not anoint my head with oil, but she has anointed my feet with ointment."

Jesus paused for a moment, and the man lowered his eyes.

"Therefore I tell you, her sins, which are many, are forgiven, for she loved much," Jesus concluded. "He who is forgiven little, loves little" (Luke 7:43–47 RSV).

Jesus then turned to Mary, who cried at his feet. "Your sins are forgiven," he said to her. "Your faith has saved you; go in peace" (vv. 48, 50).

The rest of the dinner guests were shocked. They said to one another, "Who does he think he is, forgiving sins!" (v. 49 MSG)—because, of course, only God can forgive sins. Interestingly, all four gospels relate outrage among some of Jesus' own followers that the expensive ointment Mary poured on Jesus' head or feet would be used to anoint him.

According to Mark, there were "some" present who said the ointment could have been sold for three hundred *denarii* and the money given to the poor (14:4–5). So, we're talking about a bottle of rare perfume—an alabaster flask of nard, an amber-colored oil used to this day in the Middle East— that would cost around $50,000 in today's currency.[2]

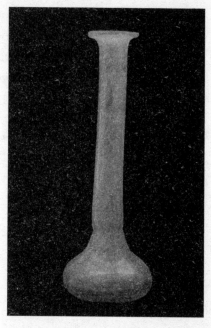

A Roman perfume flask from the first century. Mary of Bethany would have kept the aromatic nard she poured on Jesus' head in such a bottle.

The gospel of John agrees to the penny on the value of the ointment, three hundred *denarii*, but insists it was Judas Iscariot who challenged Jesus, adding that he did so not because he cared about the poor but because he was a thief (12:4–6).

In all four gospel accounts, Jesus angrily defended Mary. "Leave her alone," Jesus snapped at Judas (Mark 14:6 NIV). "She did what she could. She poured perfume on my body beforehand to prepare for my burial. Truly I tell you, wherever the gospel is preached throughout the world, what she has done will also be told, in memory of her" (vv. 8–9 NIV).

And then Jesus said something that is reported in Mark's, Matthew's, and John's gospels: "The poor you will always have with you," Jesus said, "but you will not always have me" (Matt. 26:11 NIV).[3]

The argument must have been vehement because, according to Mark, Judas stormed out of the dinner party in a huff and then went directly to the Jewish authorities to betray Jesus. The authorities promised to give Judas money, and he returned to Jesus' followers, watching for an opportunity to hand him over (14:10–11). We don't know the details of where Judas went or with whom he spoke, but it is possible that some of Jesus' other followers tailed him and reported back on what he had done. In any case, the Gospels contain hints that, from that time onward, Jesus knew what Judas had done, and that the group had a traitor in their midst.

CHAPTER 8

"Do This in Memory of Me"

"Behold, the days are coming, declares the LORD, when I will make a new covenant with the house of Israel and the house of Judah."
—JEREMIAH 31:31

The Jewish festival of Pesach, or Passover, had almost arrived. It was and still is a national holiday in Israel, a time when Jews give thanks to God for delivering them out of bondage in Egypt. The book of Exodus tells us how Moses, who had been raised in the Egyptian Pharaoh's household, was called by God to lead the Israelite people out of slavery. Though he repeatedly told the Pharaoh that God demanded that he "let my people go," Pharaoh adamantly refused. Then God sent ten plagues upon Egypt. With the last plague, the angel of death was to strike the firstborn sons of all the people. To protect the Israelites, God told Moses to have the people prepare for a journey, to bake unleavened bread suitable for carrying and to sacrifice a lamb. They were to put the blood of a sacrificed lamb on the doorposts outside of each Israelite house. Then, when the angel of death came, he would "pass over" (*pasach*) the homes of the Israelites and spare the lives of their firstborn sons.

For more than a thousand years before Jesus, the Jewish people had reenacted this ancient event in a special meal during the Passover festival in Jerusalem. Unleavened bread, called *matzot*, was baked, and a lamb was sacrificed. The blood of the lamb was no longer placed on the doorposts of homes but poured out on the high altar in the temple.

Spice dealers in the Old City of Jerusalem today offer the same exotic Mediterranean spices that were almost certainly on sale when Jesus' followers prepared his final Passover meal.

It was not lost on the Romans of Jesus' time that Passover was a festival of freedom, celebrating the Jewish people's liberation from slavery to an empire. This was why every year at this time a large detachment of Roman auxiliary forces left their main quarters in Caesarea Maritima on Israel's central coast and traveled to Jerusalem. Their job was to maintain order, to make sure that the hundreds of thousands of Jewish pilgrims who crowded into Jerusalem did not take the message of Passover *too* literally or develop any idealistic notions about freeing themselves once again from bondage.

THE UPPER ROOM

On Thursday morning, Jesus and his followers lingered in Bethany and did not go early into Jerusalem, as they had the past few days.

Some of Jesus' followers wondered what they were going to do about Passover. "Where do you want us to make preparations for you to eat the Passover?" they asked (Matt. 26:17 NIV). According to the Synoptics, Jesus responded by sending two of his followers into the city to get things ready.[1] "Go into the city, and a man carrying a jar of water will meet you," he told the pair. The implication was that this man would be easy to spot. Women usually carried the water jars, not men. "Follow him, and wherever he enters, say to the householder, 'The Teacher says, "Where is my guest room, where I am to eat the passover with my disciples?"' And he will show you a large upper room furnished and ready; there prepare for us" (Mark 14:13–15 RSV).

This is another example of Jesus' apparent substantial network of contacts—and how he repeatedly made plans without informing even his closest followers.[2] As Jewish pilgrims often did for Passover, Jesus likely leased or arranged for a room in Jerusalem for his use during the festival. In the hot climate of the Middle East, families would often build an addition on the roof of their homes, a guest parlor, reserved for use when visitors came.[3] This "upper room" could be accessed by outside stairs or a ladder so guests would not have to enter the main living quarters of the home. This particular location was a center for Jesus' followers because they stayed there for weeks, months, and perhaps years after Jesus' arrest and execution.[4] The security precautions are also obvious. Jesus sent only two disciples, Peter and John, so that each could keep watch on the other to ensure that no one else knew the location of this upper room.

Archaeologists have been unable to establish with certainty where this upper room was located. The traditional site in Jerusalem, a second-story room above the site revered as King David's tomb, is located near the current Zion Gate. This spot would have been at the southwestern corner of the Upper City, near the wall. The building in its present form dates only to the 1300s.[5] However, the foundations beneath go back all the way to the second century and may be from one of the earliest churches in the Holy Land, said to have been built in AD 130.[6]

Luke reports that Peter and John, at Jesus' bidding, went into the city in the morning and, just as Jesus had said, found a man carrying a jar of water (Luke 22:13). They likely followed him from the Pool of Siloam through the Lower City to a large house, went up the outdoor steps to the second story, and entered a sizable room, just as Jesus had said. It was furnished, likely with a long, low table surrounded by couches and pillows on which Jesus and his followers could recline while eating. After making arrangements with the owner of the house, the two disciples then likely went back to the main north-south street ascending the Tyropoeon Valley, climbed the huge stone steps that made up the street, and went in search of Jerusalem's many outdoor markets. There they purchased food for the coming meal—an unblemished lamb and also bitter herbs, matzo, and other ingredients. They brought the herbs and other foods to the upper room.

The Cenacle, or upper room, where tradition claims Jesus had his Last Supper with his followers, is found near the Zion Gate. Rebuilt in the thirteenth or fourteenth century, it stands atop the foundations of a synagogue church that dates back to AD 130.

PREPARING THE MEAL

Here is where it gets tricky. Though Jesus almost certainly saw this meal as being in some way a Passover meal, it is unclear whether Jesus' final banquet with his followers was celebrated on the same day the people of Jerusalem celebrated Passover or, as an alternative, a day early. This confusion is one of the central historical mysteries of the Gospels. Because the Synoptic Gospels and the gospel of John appear to disagree on which day Jesus was crucified, the day Jesus and his twelve apostles ate their final meal is also unclear. The Synoptics state that Jesus ate the Last Supper with his followers on the Day of Preparation, when the Passover lambs were sacrificed in the temple, and was crucified the following day—that is, on the first official day of Passover.[7] On the other hand, John says explicitly that Jesus was *crucified* on the Day of Preparation *before* the Passover, when all the lambs were ritually slaughtered within the Court of the Priests, between noon and three o'clock in the temple and before the Passover meal was eaten (John 19:14, 31, 42). If John is correct, then Jesus and his disciples ate their final meal together before the official Passover festival had begun.

One attempt to reconcile this apparent discrepancy is to note that John, who explicitly calls Jesus the "Lamb of God," may have tinkered with the chronology just for the symbolism involved (John 1:29).[8] However, John also meticulously records most details involving Jerusalem and Jewish customs and claims to have been an eyewitness (21:24). He may well have known the chronology of events better than the authors of the Synoptics. Adding to the confusion is the fact that John nowhere alludes to Jesus' final meal with his followers being a Passover meal, although he also doesn't say it wasn't. Perhaps John has the chronology correct but the Synoptics are also right in that Jesus treated this final meal as a Passover meal eaten a day early.[9] It seems implausible that Jewish authorities would press for an execution on the first day of the holy festival.[10]

The Synoptic Gospels state that Jesus' farewell meal with his closest followers occurred on a Thursday. The confrontation with temple authorities, the outrage of many in the crowds he was addressing, and the angry dispute he had with Judas Iscariot likely convinced Jesus that he was running out of time. Jesus knew that he could be arrested at any moment. That was probably why he had elected to stay that entire week in Bethany, outside the city; and that is also why he appears to have kept the location of the upper room a secret even from his closest followers.

PREPARING A PASCHAL LAMB

If John's chronology is correct, then, Peter and John could not have taken a lamb to the temple to be ritually slaughtered on the Day of Preparation because that wouldn't occur until the next day. This special ceremony in the Court of the Priests involved bringing in the Passover lambs after the daily afternoon burnt offering sacrifice, which was around three o'clock in the afternoon. Only Jews who had been ritually cleansed in a *mikveh* pool, or ritual bath, were allowed to enter the Court of the Priests for this ritual.

Jews came to the Court of Priests to make "offerings" (*korbanot*) to God, usually domesticated animals and flour. There were two types of *korbanot*—sacrifices in which the offering was totally destroyed (*olah*) and ones in which the meat was merely cooked but eaten later by either the priests or by the people making the offering. Dressed in white garments, the priests would ritually kill sacrificial animals—pigeons, lambs, and sometimes bulls—and then prepare them to be roasted on the high altar.

The lambs were brought into the courtyard in large groups and placed on tables, and their throats were cut in a prescribed manner. Priests caught the blood in special rounded silver and gold cups—rounded so they could not be set down on a table—and then passed them, from one priest to another in a long line to the high altar, where the blood was poured out onto the surface. While all this was going on, Jewish priests were chanting the Hallel ("praise") songs (Ps. 113–118) accompanied by brass instruments. The lambs were then flayed, their skins peeled off their bodies and allowed to hang on special hooks for a brief period. The pilgrims then took their paschal lambs home, where they were cooked and eaten for the Passover meal that evening. Whether or not Jesus' Last Supper occurred on the evening of the Day of Preparation—that is, in the evening after the Passover lambs were slaughtered in the temple— Jesus emphasized the symbolism of this rite as he gathered his followers around him.

THE WASHING OF FEET

Before sunset, Jesus and his group of followers made their way back to Jerusalem from Bethany to join Peter and John. As usual, they likely entered the city through the Fountain Gate, near the Pool of Siloam, and then probably turned left and made their way west toward the Upper City. When they arrived at the house where Jesus had arranged for this meal, they found everything ready. Touching the doorway as they entered, the way observant Jews still do today, the disciples greeted one another. "*Shelama*," they said to one another in Galilean Aramaic, which means "peace."

Many people at this time, especially poor people, would normally walk about barefoot. Thus, it was customary when entering a home to wash your feet—just as today some people remove their shoes before entering a private home. Archaeologists have uncovered little stone foot-baths located outside of buildings used for just this purpose. In a larger home, a slave or servant would often wash the feet of arriving guests as a courtesy.

This explains why Jesus' next act was so shocking. This incident is reported only in the gospel of John, which many skeptics believe to be almost entirely fictional, but there is no reason to think it didn't happen (13:1–17). After greeting his friends and followers, Jesus proceeded to take off his *tallit* and the long woolen cloak or blanket, a *himation*, that reached almost to the ground. Dressed in a knee-length tunic called a *chiton*, Jesus proceeded to wrap a large towel around his waist, pour water in a basin, and then kneel down in front of Simon Peter. Jesus then took Simon's bare, calloused, probably smelly foot in his hand and began to wash it. According to John's account, Simon was understandably horrified. You can almost hear the incredulity in the big fisherman's voice as he said out loud, in disbelief, what he was seeing.

"*Marya*," he began, using the Aramaic word for Master. "Are you *washing my feet?*"

Jesus nodded. "You will understand later," he said simply.

Simon protested. "You will *never* wash my feet!"

"Well, if that is true," Jesus replied, no doubt with a smile, "you will have no part of me."

Simon Peter thought about that reply for a moment.

"If that's the case, then don't stop with my feet. Wash my hands and my head!"

Jesus tempered Simon Peter's enthusiasm. "Anyone who has already bathed does not need to wash, only his feet," he said. "You are clean, but not every one of you." The latter comment was almost certainly a reference to Judas, a none-too-subtle hint that Jesus knew there was treachery in their midst.

Jesus then proceeded to move from one apostle to the next, carefully washing each person's dirty feet. The group no doubt gaped in astonishment at this act of humility.

Finished, Jesus then stood up, picked up his clothes, got dressed, and then sat at the table.

"Do you know what I have done?" Jesus finally asked the group. "You call me Teacher and *Marya*, Lord, and you are right to do so, for that is what I am. If I, then, your Lord and Teacher, have washed your feet, you also ought to wash one another's feet. I have given you an example that you also should do as I have done to you" (John 13:13–14, paraphrased). Jesus looked around the table. John reports that Jesus then said something that both Matthew and Luke, with minor variations, also describe. "Truly, truly, I say to you, a servant is not greater than his master, nor is a messenger greater than the one who sent him" (13:16).

THE PASSOVER MEAL

Their subsequent Passover meal would follow a prescribed menu and ritual that had been practiced for a thousand years.[11] It reenacts God's rescue of the Jewish people from bondage in Egypt. The meal is divided into four basic parts, each with a cup of wine to be drunk. There are four cups of wine with special blessings associated with each.

First, the host, in this case Jesus, would likely say the *kiddush*, a blessing over the first of the cups. He would say the prayer in Hebrew: *Baruch ata Adonai Eleheinu melech ha-olam borei pri ha-gafen.* "Blessed are you, Adonai Our God, King of the Universe, creator of the fruit of the vine." It was customary to drop three drops of water into the wine—a custom that many churches today, when celebrating the Eucharistic rite, maintain.

In every Passover meal, there are typically three pieces of matzo. Jesus picked up the middle piece, broke it in two—as was the custom then and still today during the Eucharist—and said the blessing over it.

But then Jesus said something else—something so strange that it has been repeated thousands of times a day, every day, for two thousand years. The words are repeated in the Synoptic Gospels and repeated by Paul in his first letter to the Corinthians:[12] "This is my body, which is for you," Jesus said solemnly, no doubt looking at the shocked faces of his friends. "Do this in remembrance of me" (1 Cor. 11:24).

This is my body? What could *that* possibly mean?

And then Jesus did something far more shocking, the symbolism of which was not lost on anyone present.

Jesus picked up the third cup of wine, the cup of redemption. Instead of the traditional blessing, Jesus said something else.

"This is my blood," he continued, looking at each of his followers in turn, "[the blood] of the covenant, which is poured out for many for the forgiveness of sins. . . . I shall not drink again of this fruit of the vine until that day when I drink it new with you in my Father's kingdom" (Matt. 26:28–29 RSV). Jesus then handed this cup around the table.

His followers likely hesitated—and then, very slowly, each one in turn drank from it.

There is probably nothing Jesus could have said that would have been more shocking to Jewish sensibilities.

Some experts believe the Last Supper was a Passover meal, perhaps celebrated a day early, during which Jesus identified himself with the slain Passover lamb sacrificed for the redemption of the Jewish people.

Everyone present was familiar with the cups of lambs' blood that were passed from priest to priest in the temple and poured out on the altar.

But no one *drank* this blood! Drinking blood was condemned in no uncertain terms by the Torah, and was considered one of the abominations of the pagans (Gen 9:4). Yet here Jesus was saying this wine was his blood and his followers were to . . . drink it? Why?

Before the disciples could absorb any of this or figure out what it could possibly mean, the meal continued. Finally, Jesus said, "Amen, I say to you, one of you will betray me" (Matt. 26:21 NABRE).

This sparked an uproar as each of Jesus' closest friends and followers protested, then asked, "Is it I?" (v. 22).

When everyone asked, "Is it I?" Jesus replied that it was the one who was dipping his bread in the dish with him. Matthew reports that Judas, too, asked the question, and Jesus replied with a response he would soon give to Pilate: "You have said so" (26:25).

This incident, too, is reported in Matthew, Mark, and, unusually, John.[13] John records what happened slightly differently. In his version, Jesus replied, "It is he to whom I will give this morsel of bread when I have dipped it"—and handed the piece of matzo directly to Judas, son of Simon Iscariot. Then Jesus whispered to Judas, "What you are going to do, do quickly" (13:26–27). Judas promptly jumped up from the table and dashed out. Jesus must have lowered his voice when he spoke to Judas because John reports that the other followers thought that Jesus had asked Judas, who was in charge of their money, to go buy something else for the feast (vv. 28–30).

After Judas left, the disciples began arguing about who would betray Jesus and who was the greatest among them. Mark reports a similar argument occurring earlier, on their way to Jerusalem (9:34). But in Luke's telling, the argument was at this final meal between Jesus and his closest followers (22:24).

The evening probably ended with the singing of the last three Hallel psalms, the ancient Hebrew songs about God's rescue of his people from Egypt and how the lowly shall be raised up. These songs, still sung today, contain phrases that were burned into Jesus' followers' minds, and which have been used by Christians ever since as interpretive keys for what Jesus was all about. For Jesus the last Hallel psalm was poignant for another reason: it is a plea to God to save the petitioner's life! This is the psalm Jesus and his followers likely sang as they left the upper room, proceeded down the long stone steps to the Pool of Siloam, out the Fountain Gate, and across the Kidron Valley to the olive groves we remember as the garden of Gethsemane:

> The LORD is on my side; I will not fear.
> What can man do to me?
> The LORD is on my side as my helper;
> I shall look in triumph on those who hate me. . . .
> The stone that the builders rejected
> has become the cornerstone.
> (Ps. 118:6–7, 22)

CHAPTER 9

BETRAYAL

Even my close friend in whom I trusted,
who ate my bread, has lifted his heel against me.
—PSALM 41:9

Jesus knew what was about to happen to him. Christian theology has long asserted that it was Jesus' destiny to die in an act of atonement for the human race, but the New Testament makes clear that, up until the very end, Jesus hoped that he could somehow escape this fate. He knew that both the temple authorities and Herod Antipas wanted him dead; and, following the angry dispute with Judas, he knew there was a traitor in their midst who could lead the authorities to him. Yet he prayed to God, in poignant desperation, that somehow he would be spared what was to come.

It must have been a brief but lonely walk from the upper room to the garden of Gethsemane. The road through the Fountain Gate, in Jerusalem's southern wall, passed by an ancient Jewish cemetery on the hillside above, which still exists; the small group would have walked by numerous "whitewashed tombs" as they sang the ancient songs of deliverance from death. All four gospels mention that, on the group's way toward the Mount of Olives, Jesus predicted that his closest friends and followers would soon abandon him. The gospel of John expresses Jesus' thoughts with characteristic bluntness: "The hour is coming, indeed it has come, when you will be scattered, each to his own home, and will leave me alone," Jesus said (16:32). Matthew and Mark agree. "You will all fall away," Mark records Jesus saying, "for it is written, 'I will strike the shepherd, and the sheep will be scattered'" (14:27).

The Synpotics recall that Simon "Petros," the so-called Rock, protested his loyalty. "Even though *they* all fall away," he boasted, referring to his fellow disciples, "I will not" (Mark 14:29).[1] And then Jesus made one of the eeriest predictions in history. "Amen, I say to you, this very night before the cock crows twice you will deny me three times" (v. 30 NABRE). Simon the Rock continued to loudly protest that he was willing to die, if need be, but would *never* deny Jesus. The other disciples said the same. This is one of those incidents that even many skeptics believe must be historical under the "criterion of embarrassment," which means that the Christian community was unlikely to invent a story that cast such a bad light on its leaders; therefore, it must have actually happened.

The general location of the garden of Gethsemane, at the foot of the Mount of Olives, has been known for two thousand years. It is still there today.

THE GARDEN OF GETHSEMANE

Both archaeologists and Christian pilgrims have long known the general location of the garden of Gethsemane at the base of the Mount of Olives. It is one of the most easily identified locations associated with Jesus' life. The entire area is, still today, terraced and covered with ancient olive trees. *Gethsemane* means "oil press" in Hebrew and Aramaic, and it was undoubtedly an olive orchard that had olive-pressing equipment in it, typically the large round rock-wheels found in various locations throughout Israel. No one knows the precise location where Jesus came to pray, of course. However, the garden itself has been preserved in Christian memory for millennia.[2]

When the group reached the garden that faces the eastern wall of Jerusalem, Jesus told his disciples to sit while he went to pray.[3] He took with him his closest followers—Peter and James and John, the sons of Zebedee—and went a little further up the slope. Mark reports that Jesus "began to be greatly distressed and troubled," and told the trio that he was sorrowful, "even to death," and he asked them to remain where they were and keep watch (14:33–34). Jesus then walked on a few steps, up the Mount of Olives, fell on his face, and begged God for his life. Mark, possibly the companion of Peter, adds the detail that Jesus addressed God as *Abba*, the ordinary Aramaic word (still used in Israel today) for father. "Abba, Father, all things are possible for you," Mark records Jesus praying. "Remove this cup from me. Yet not what I will, but what you will" (v. 36). Luke reports that Jesus was in such agony and he prayed so fervently that his sweat became "like great drops of blood falling down to the ground" (22:44). This rare but documented condition is known as *hematohidrosis* and is known to occur in persons suffering from highly emotional states.[4]

Jesus must have remained in the garden for quite some time, trying to decide what to do and asking God to spare him the ordeal. Three times he checked on Peter, James, and John and, each time, found them sleeping rather than keeping watch as he had asked.[5] "Simon, are you asleep?"

Jesus asked incredulously, according to both Mark and Matthew. "Could you not watch one hour?" (Mark 14:37).

Jesus must have been tempted to run for it. Even at this late stage, he could have gotten away. A quick walk up the Mount of Olives and, under cover of darkness, he could have slipped away to the wild country to the east. Once across the Jordan River, an area Jesus knew well, he would have been home free. He could have traveled north to Damascus in Syria, to Tyre on the Lebanese coast, or to anywhere. In an age without fingerprinting or DNA testing, Jesus could have shaved his beard, cut his hair, wrapped a Bedouin cloak around his head, and easily assumed a new identity. Yet according to the Gospels, Jesus agonized over what to do.[6] In the end, he chose not to run. He decided to allow the authorities to do to him what they would, to sacrifice himself.

On the third occasion when Jesus checked on Peter and the snoring "sons of thunder," he knew his time was up. "The hour has come," he said to the dazed men. "The Son of Man is to be handed over to sinners. Get up, let us go. See, my betrayer is at hand" (Mark 14:41–42 NABRE).

All four gospels report that Judas led a large mob to arrest Jesus.[7] According to John, Judas knew where they were likely to be, "for Jesus often met there with his disciples" (18:2). According to Mark and the other Synoptics, Jesus' arrest was planned in advance. Two days before the start of Passover, the "chief priests and the scribes" were seeking a way to arrest Jesus "by stealth" in order to put him to death (14:1).[8] But they feared the people, according to the texts, and did not want to arrest Jesus during the Passover festival lest they accidentally spark a riot. All four gospels describe how Judas left Jesus and the other disciples as they were coming into Jerusalem, and then again after the argument over Mary anointing Jesus with expensive nard in Bethany, and how Judas met with the chief priests and agreed to betray Jesus for money.[9] Only Matthew adds the detail that it was for thirty pieces of silver (27:9).

The arrest party appears to have been a very large group, including soldiers, officers, and "priests and the elders of the people," armed with swords and clubs and carrying lanterns and torches (Matt. 27:1). Judas identified who Jesus was with a kiss.[10] Luke adds that Jesus remarked sadly, "Judas, would you betray the Son of Man with a kiss?" (Luke 22:48).

ROBERT HUTCHINSON

The steps leading up to the Church of St. Peter in Gallicantu in Jerusalem date back to the first century and could well have been used by Jesus when he was taken to the house of Caiaphas on the night of his arrest.

Apparently, "one of the bystanders" leapt to Jesus' defense with a sword, managing to cut off the ear of the high priest's slave (Mark 14:47 BSB).

The gospel of John, as usual, names names: it was the impetuous Simon Peter who drew his sword, and the name of the slave was Malchus (18:10).

"Have you come out as against a robber, with swords and clubs to seize me?" Jesus asked the crowd (Matt. 26:55 NABRE). "Day after day I was with you in the temple teaching, and you did not seize me" (Mark 14:49). Just as Jesus predicted they would, all of his followers ran for their lives. Mark records that one young man (whom Christian tradition has claimed may have been the evangelist himself) tried to follow the arresting party as they led Jesus away, and that he was dressed only in a linen cloth. Some of the soldiers tried to grab the boy, seizing the cloth, but he somehow managed to slip from their grasp and ran off, stark naked (14:51–52).

The group likely retraced the steps Jesus and his followers had taken just an hour or two earlier, marching back across the Kidron Valley. Their destination was likely the palatial home of the former high priest Annas and his son-in-law, the current high priest, Joseph Caiaphas. According to the gospel of John, the high priest worried that the charismatic prophet Jesus could accidentally or deliberately spark an uprising against Rome (18:14). Jesus could be, he feared, the match that lit the entire house of Israel on fire and brought the full wrath of the Roman legions down on Jerusalem.

THE HISTORICAL CAIAPHAS

According to Josephus, Caiaphas was appointed high priest in AD 18 by the Roman prefect Valerius Gratus, Pontius Pilate's immediate predecessor.[11] He ruled for eighteen years until AD 36, longer than any high priest before him. In 1990, road workers in the Abu Tor neighborhood of Jerusalem accidentally uncovered an ancient first-century tomb in which was found an ossuary, or "bone box," that contained human remains. On the ossuary was written the Hebrew words *Yehosef bar Qafa*, Joseph son of Caiaphas. The ossuary contained the remains of six people—two infants, a child aged two to five, a boy aged thirteen to eighteen, an adult female, and a man about sixty years old. Although some scholars have recently disputed its authenticity, the Caiaphas ossuary is widely considered to be authentic; Israeli archaeologists believe it came from Caiaphas's family tomb.[12]

In 2011, another ossuary was uncovered that purported to be that of Caiaphas's granddaughter, Miriam. It revealed from which priestly "course," or division, Caiaphas came. The ossuary's inscription read: "Miriam, daughter of Yeshua, son of Caiaphas, Priest of Ma'aziah from Beth 'Imri."[13] This told archaeologists and historians that Caiaphas was from the priestly course of Ma'aziah, one of the twenty-four divisions of priests that took turns making offerings at the temple in Jerusalem (1 Chron. 24:1, 18). Beth 'Imri, or the House of Immer, refers to a priestly family in Israel after the Babylonian Exile, mentioned in Ezra 2:36–37 and Nehemiah 7:39–42. Once again, recent archaeological discoveries are showing that the New Testament in general, and the Gospels in particular, are far more reliable historical sources than previous generations of New Testament experts realized.

WIKIPEDIA

The ossuary, or burial box, of the high priest Joseph Caiaphas was discovered in an underground tomb in 1990 and is widely believed to be authentic. It is now found in the Israel Museum in Jerusalem.

Archaeologists are not sure precisely where Caiaphas's home was located, yet they have come across some exciting clues. Some Israeli archaeologists believe that both Caiaphas and his father-in-law, Annas, lived in the same mansion, albeit in different wings. The building would have been palatial since Caiaphas held the highest non-Roman office in the country and, in effect, functioned as much as a prime minister as the chief religious figure. In 1967, after the Six-Day War, Israeli archaeologists were able for the first time to excavate homes in the former Upper City that had been destroyed in the Jewish War of AD 66–70. As noted earlier, one of the homes, dubbed the Palatial Mansion, was over ten thousand square feet and had marble walls, mosaic floors, steam baths with under-floor heating, and a *mikveh*, or ritual bath, in the basement.[14] It is very likely that the home of the high priest Caiaphas was similar. These excavations have shown us, in a dramatic way, just what life was like in first-century Jerusalem—in which some priestly aristocrats lived a life of luxury that rivaled that of kings.

There are two possible candidates for Caiaphas's house, both of which have plausible dungeons beneath the existing structures. The first, the Armenian Church of the Savior in the Armenian Quarter, was excavated by Israeli archaeologists in 1971 and 1972. Beneath and at the side of the church, the archaeologists discovered evidence of lavish buildings from the Herodian period, including frescoes.[15] The second candidate is the Church of Saint Peter in Gallicantu (Cock Crowing), a modern building erected in the 1930s on top of a Byzantine shrine built in AD 457. Beneath it is a series of underground caves, dating to the Second Temple period, which have been revered for centuries as the dungeon in which Jesus was held before his arraignment before Pilate.[16] Next to this structure is a stone staircase that could date back to the first century. While the stones themselves have likely been replaced over the centuries, it is quite possible that the street stairway was the same path used by the arresting party as they marched Jesus up toward Caiaphas's house.[17]

JESUS' INTERROGATION

There is remarkable agreement between the Synoptic Gospels and the gospel of John about the interrogation and "trial" of Jesus, such as it was. Both the Synoptics and John agree that Jesus was taken first to the home of Caiaphas and only later to the Roman prefect Pilate.[18] According to the gospel of John, Jesus was taken first to Annas and then, only later, to Caiaphas, but this could have simply been to different areas of the same large house (18:13). John reports that Peter and another unnamed disciple of Jesus were secretly following the arresting party from a distance, and that they were able to gain entrance to the house's inner courtyard through an outer door or gateway (18:16). The other disciple was allowed into the courtyard and he quickly returned and spoke to the maid guarding the doorway. She let Peter in as well. But in doing so, the maid recognized Peter and asked if he wasn't one of Jesus' disciples—and Peter promptly denied it (18:17).

This inner courtyard must have been substantial because a fairly large group was gathered inside it and, according to John, the servants and officers had made a charcoal fire because it was cold. It was while he was standing there, warming himself, that one of Caiaphas's servants—a relative of Malchus, the man whose ear Peter had cut off—also recognized Peter. He too challenged him, asking if he knew Jesus. Once again, Peter denied it (John 18:25–27).

At this point, Jesus was brought before Annas, the former high priest, and interrogated about his teaching. Jesus gave what the temple officials interpreted as a fairly impertinent response. "I have spoken publicly to the world," Jesus told the officials. "I have always taught in a synagogue or in the temple area where all the Jews gather, and in secret I have said nothing. Why ask me? Ask those who heard me what I said to them. They know what I said" (John 18:20–21 NABRE).

It didn't go over very well. John reports that one of the temple guards standing there struck Jesus and said, "Is this the way you answer the high priest?" (v. 22 NABRE).

Whatever Jesus meant by his saying about turning the other cheek, it didn't mean that a wrong should go unchallenged. "If I have spoken wrongly, testify to the wrong," he answered the guard who hit him, no doubt looking him squarely in the eye, "but if I have spoken rightly, why do you strike me?" (v. 23 NABRE).

In the version in the Synoptics, this initial interrogation does occur at the home of Caiaphas, but many more people were present.[19] Matthew reports it was the "entire Sanhedrin," but a number of experts believe this must be a literary exaggeration (26:59 NABRE). It was the middle of the night, right before Passover, and it seems unlikely that the highest legal body in the land could have been gathered together at such short notice—and at such a late hour. Perhaps Caiaphas gathered together in his own home key members of the Sanhedrin who happened to live close by, to figure out what they should do with this troublemaker.

Mark and Matthew report that these judicial officials kept trying to obtain testimony from Jesus so they could put him to death but were not successful.[20] They brought in witnesses who testified against Jesus, but their statements did not agree. Some witnesses even testified that they had heard Jesus make *threats* against the temple. "We heard him say, 'I will destroy this temple that is made with hands, and in three days I will build another, not made with hands,'" one witness testified (Mark 14:58). Plainly frustrated, the high priest himself stood before the officials present and asked Jesus if he did not have anything to say, but Jesus remained silent. Finally, Caiaphas decided to be direct. He asked Jesus point-blank if he was, in fact, the Messiah, the "Son of the Blessed" (v. 61).

In all likelihood, a great silence fell over the room. The Synoptics all agree that Jesus finally answered.[21]

"I am," he replied forcefully, no doubt to astonished gasps from his interrogators. Then, quoting Daniel 7:13, Jesus added, "You will see the Son of Man seated at the right hand of Power, and coming with the clouds of heaven" (v. 62).

With that, Caiaphas tore his garments (the ancient custom when blasphemy is heard) and asked out loud, "What further witnesses do we need? You have heard his blasphemy. What is your decision?" (vv. 63–64).

The Mount of Olives as seen from Jerusalem's eastern wall with the Church of All Nations below and the Russian Orthodox Church of St. Mary Magdalene halfway up. Jesus could have easily slipped away by climbing this hill on Holy Thursday night.

JESUS TRANSFERRED

By this time, dawn had arrived. The officials had been meeting all night. The high priest gathered other officials and held an emergency council.[22]

One theory for why the temple authorities handed Jesus over to Pilate rather than execute him themselves was that Jesus was, in fact, a highly popular figure. He was hated by some but adored by many more, especially by the masses of impoverished rural people who flooded Jerusalem during the Passover festival. By handing Jesus over to the Romans on trumped-up charges of sedition, Caiaphas and the temple elite solved two problems in one neat stroke: Jesus and his talk of a new "kingdom of God"—one that didn't require millions of Tyrian shekels flowing through the temple treasury—would be silenced once and for all. At the same time, the blame would ultimately be placed on the brutal Romans, whom the common people already and quite understandably detested. The maneuver was beautiful in its elegant simplicity.

The only problem was convincing the stubborn, suspicious Romans that Jesus was a real political threat. By this time, Jesus was famous, and his teaching was, just as Jesus said when questioned by Annas, well-known among the people.[23] Everyone *knew* what Jesus taught—and that he was in no way a zealous Jewish nationalist advocating rebellion against Rome. What's more, Pilate hated the Jews as much as the Jews hated him. As a result, the plot to get Pilate to execute Jesus would have had to be handled carefully. But there was a way. Many of Jesus' followers publicly proclaimed him the *mashiach* . . . and what was the *Messiah*, after all? Why, he was the long promised King of the Jews! Claiming to be king was a charge the paranoid Romans could understand—and act on.

CHAPTER 10

ON TRIAL

He was oppressed and afflicted,
yet he did not open his mouth;
he was led like a lamb to the slaughter,
and as a sheep before its shearers is silent,
so he did not open his mouth.

—ISAIAH 53:7 NIV

S hortly after dawn on Friday, the fourteenth day of the Jewish month
of Nissan, probably the Day of Preparation that year for both the
Passover and the Sabbath, Jesus was marched from Caiaphas's home in
the southern part of the Upper City uphill to the old palace of King
Herod the Great—what the Romans then called the *praetorium*.[1] The
praetorium was simply the Roman term for military headquarters and
could be a tent, a house, or a palace. For centuries and until very recently,
Christian pilgrims and New Testament scholars believed that Jesus was
almost certainly interrogated by Pilate in the Antonia Tower, sometimes
called the Antonia Fortress. It was a small but formidable structure built
by Herod the Great on the northwestern corner of the Temple Mount. It
was something akin to a lookout tower; Josephus describes it as "a tower
with other towers at each of the four corners."[2] Roman soldiers used it to
observe the sprawling stone plaza where the temple stood.

Very little of the fortress's foundations still exists, and most of it is beneath the Convent of the Sisters of Zion in the Old City of Jerusalem. Among its foundations is an ancient stone pavement that archaeologists once believed was the *lithostratos*, or Roman flagstones, located in front of Pilate's judgment seat as described in John 19:13. However, recent archaeological research now indicates that this stone pavement actually dates to second century AD when Hadrian built the new Roman city of Aelia Capitolina on the ruins of vanquished Jerusalem.[3] This new information means that it is unlikely that the *praetorium* described in the Gospels was located in the cramped, narrow spaces of the Antonia Tower; instead, it aligns with the verse in the gospel of Mark that describes the *praetorium* as a "palace" (*aule*).[4]

In 2015, the gospel accounts were further verified when the ruins of Herod the Great's massive palace were discovered near the Tower of David and the current Jaffa Gate, across the city from where the Antonia Tower was located. In the first century, this palace abutted the western wall of the city, just south of a massive outdoor pool and lush gardens. Now many scholars believe that the Romans likely used *this* lavish building as the official residence of the Roman governor, not the cramped barracks of the Antonia Fortress or Tower.[5]

The palace was located in the northwestern corner of Jerusalem's First Wall,[6] fortified by the three massive towers of Hippicus, Phasael, and Mariamne (named after two of Herod's good friends and the wife he had executed). Such a fortified palace would have appealed to the security-conscious Romans. Unlike the Antonia Tower, Herod's palace had a large inner courtyard that was almost certainly paved. It was big enough that crowds could stand outside of it while Pilate appeared to them from a balcony in the palace wall.

The gospel of John states that Pilate "went outside" to meet the Jewish leaders and asked them what their accusation was against Jesus (18:29). The leaders said Jesus was a criminal so they had to bring him before the Roman governor. Pilate coolly replied that the Jews should judge the man according to their own laws. The Jewish leaders countered that they did not have the right to put anyone to death.[7]

A reconstruction of the Antonia Tower fortress overlooking the Temple Mount once thought to have been the *praetorium* where Jesus was interrogated by Pilate.

WHO WAS PILATE?

Historians know very little about the Roman governor named Pontius Pilatus. He was appointed the fifth prefect of the Roman province of Judaea in AD 26, just one or two years before Jesus began his public activity in Galilee, and served for ten years. According to both Josephus and the Jewish philosopher Philo of Alexandria (ca. 25 BC–AD 50), Pilate was brutal even by Roman standards.[8] A contemporary of Jesus who himself visited Jerusalem around this time, Philo recounts how Jewish leaders wrote to the Emperor Tiberius himself to complain about Pilate's "corruption . . . cruelty, and his continual murders of people untried and uncondemned, and his never ending, and gratuitous, and most grievous inhumanity."[9] While previous Roman governors had made allowances for Jewish objections to graven images in the holy city, one of Pilate's first acts as governor was to march into Jerusalem with the Roman standards raised high, emblazoned with the emperor's image. This triggered protests across the entire region. Thousands of Jews flocked to the seat of Roman government in Judaea, Caesarea Maritima on Israel's central coast, to protest the sacrilege. After a week of demonstrations, Pilate finally agreed to meet with a Jewish delegation. However, the Jews did not know that he also planned to surround them with Roman soldiers, their weapons hidden under their clothes.[10]

Pilate announced to the delegation that they must immediately cease their protests or be executed. His soldiers then drew their swords. To Pilate's surprise, the Jews dropped to their knees, bared their throats, and announced that they would rather die than permit the violation of their ancient laws. No doubt furious, Pilate backed down. He knew that the slaughter of thousands of unarmed men would not win him many points in Rome. As a result, he reluctantly ordered that the Roman standards be withdrawn from Jerusalem.[11]

But that was merely Pilate's letter of introduction. Over the following decade, the stubborn Roman with a notorious temper[12] embarked on a reign of terror that made previous Roman governors look like philosopher kings in contrast. One of his more notorious acts was to fund his aqueduct project in Jerusalem with temple funds. He sent his troops to raid the temple treasury, where Gentiles were forbidden to enter on pain of death, taking hundreds of talents in gold. He then put down the resulting riots by having his troops beat the protestors, killing many.[13] He also placed golden Roman shields along the outside walls of the *praetorium* in Jerusalem; this was supposedly to honor the emperor, but in reality, according to Josephus, it was meant "to annoy the multitude."[14] This last provocation earned him a public rebuke from the emperor himself, and again the Roman governor had to back down, removing the shields.

Eventually, Pilate went too far. When a group of Samaritans gathered in the town of Tirathaba, near their holy mountain of Gerizim, Pilate ordered an assault on the entire group, killing many. He had the leaders summarily executed. As a result, in AD 36, the Syrian legate Lucius Vitellius (ca. 7 BC–AD 51), Pilate's immediate superior, ordered him to report back to Rome to explain his actions.[15] According to the later Christian historian Eusebius, Pilate was banished to Gaul, in what is now modern-day France, and there committed suicide.[16]

JESUS BEFORE PILATE

When Pilate encountered the Jewish delegation and asked them why they had brought Jesus to him, the Jewish leaders leveled charges against Jesus that were sure to make an impression.

"We found this man perverting our nation, forbidding us to pay taxes to the emperor," they said pointedly, "and saying that he himself is the Messiah, a king" (Luke 23:2 NRSV).

That got Pilate's attention. In John's account, Pilate went back into the *praetorium,* Herod's inner courtyard, and brought Jesus with him.

"Are you the king of the Jews?" Pilate asked Jesus directly, according to all four gospels.[17]

The Synoptics report Jesus replied somewhat evasively, "You have said so," and then refused to answer any more questions.[18]

But John reports a much longer and more complex conversation.

"Do you say this of your own accord, or did others say it to you about me?" Jesus inquired in reply when Pilate asked if he were a king.

"Am I a Jew?" Pilate snapped. "Your own nation and the chief priests have delivered you over to me. What have you done?"

"My kingdom is not of this world," Jesus replied, in what must have seemed to the brutal Roman to have been a sign of insanity. "If my kingdom were of this world, my servants would have been fighting, that I might not be delivered over to the Jews. But my kingdom is not from the world."

"So you are a king?"

"*You* say that I am a king," Jesus replied. "For this purpose I was born and for this purpose I have come into the world—to bear witness to the truth. Everyone who is of the truth listens to my voice."

At this, the philosophical Pilate asked, "What is truth?" (John 18:34–38).

It is easy to see why many modern scholars have found this entire exchange to be highly improbable—if only because the text provides no clue how anyone besides Jesus and Pilate could have heard and recorded it.[19] Considering what we know of Pilate's bloodstained career, he was not one to stand around debating philosophy with Jewish rabbis from Galilee. Many writers have claimed that the Jewish leaders were utterly powerless in the first century, that Pilate would not have shown the slightest hesitation in condemning Jesus, and that therefore the entire Gospel account of what happened with Pilate can't be historical.[20] In particular, they see John's version as an attempt to curry favor with the victorious Romans and lay the guilt of Jesus' execution solely on the Jewish leadership.[21] This is possible, but it ignores the fact that many experts believe the author of John's gospel was himself Jewish because of his extensive knowledge of Jerusalem and Jewish customs.[22]

And there is another side to the story. It is precisely because Pilate had such a deep-seated hostility toward the Jews and the temple administration that he may have not wanted to do what they were so obviously demanding—that is, get rid of Jesus. Pilate wasn't one to take orders, least of all from the high priest. He may have hesitated to condemn Jesus more out of spite than anything else. According to Philo of Alexandria, Pilate did not want to do *anything* that was acceptable to his subjects.[23] In any event, Luke and John report that Pilate declared he could find no Roman crime for which Jesus was guilty.[24] The evangelist Luke reports that the Jewish leaders informed Pilate that Jesus "stirs up the people" throughout the country and in Judea, from Galilee all the way to Jerusalem (23:5). Luke adds that when Pilate heard the word *Galilee*, he had the bright idea of pawning off Jesus on the titular ruler of Galilee, Herod Antipas, who was then in Jerusalem for the Passover feast (v. 6). Herod Antipas supposedly wanted to see Jesus in person, hoping to see a "sign" (v. 8), but in the end, according to Luke, Antipas merely mocked Jesus, dressed him in royal garments, and sent him back to Pilate (vv. 11–12).

At this point, all the gospel accounts portray Pilate as being reluctant to condemn Jesus[25]—a claim that, again, many skeptical and Jewish commentators find highly unlikely.[26] From what we know of Pilate, they say, he didn't hesitate to condemn anyone, but that's not wholly accurate.[27] He *did* choose not to kill the protesting Jews of Caesarea. Indeed, Philo of Alexandria reports that Pilate was actually *fearful* that a delegation of Jews would go to Rome and report his conduct as governor.[28] This coincides with what John's gospel says about how Pilate responded when Jewish leaders threatened to inform Caesar that Pilate was showing mercy to a potential rebel.

All four gospels say that Pilate sought a politically expedient way to appease the Jewish leadership while also not condemning Jesus.[29] There was a custom at the time that, during the Passover festival, the Roman governor would release one Jewish prisoner. Pilate knew that one of the prisoners was Barabbas, a political rebel who had supposedly committed murder. The Gospels insist that Pilate proposed releasing either Barabbas or Jesus, the Messiah, King of the Jews; he seems to have assumed the people would choose Jesus over a notorious killer.[30]

"Whom do you want me to release?" Mark, Matthew, and John report Pilate asked the crowd.[31]

In reply and to Pilate's obvious surprise, the crowd shouted the name . . . not of the popular prophet Jesus of Nazareth . . . but of the imprisoned murderer.

"Barabbas!"

"Then what shall I do with the man you call the King of the Jews?"

"Crucify him," the crowds yelled (Mark 15:12–13).

"Why? What evil has he done?" the Synoptics record Pilate asking, his frustration evident.[32] "I have found in him no crime deserving death; I will therefore chastise him and release him" (Luke 23:22 rsv).

Is this plausible? Would a crowd of Jews shout at a Roman governor they hate, asking him to kill, by the most horrible means possible, one of their own? Especially a religious celebrity like Jesus, someone who drew crowds by the thousands all over the country?

For more than a century, scholars have assumed that the portrayal of Jewish mobs calling for Jesus to be killed couldn't be historical and was the invention of the early church already locked in a hostile struggle with Judaism.[33] But in recent years, critical scholars have taken a closer look, and some Jewish experts now concede that there could very well have been sizable crowds in Jerusalem sincerely opposed to Jesus and the new "Way" he proclaimed.[34] Some Jews were actively campaigning not for peaceful coexistence with the Roman barbarians but for armed resistance and freedom. We know from the writings of one Jewish Pharisee, the later evangelist Paul, that opposition to the Way was very strong—strong enough that Paul could lead a small police detachment all the way to Damascus to arrest Jesus' followers (Acts 9:1–2). So it's quite plausible that a vocal crowd of Jews opposed to Jesus could have been calling for his death even while other Jews, including some temple officials, wanted desperately to save Jesus.[35]

JESUS IS BEATEN AND MOCKED

Jesus was then scourged with the Roman *flagrum*—a whip made up of several leather thongs each with pieces of iron on the end, tied to a wooden handle. He was brought out of the *praetorium* and displayed to the crowds. The Torah limits the number of "stripes" a prisoner can receive to thirty-nine ("forty less one," Deut. 25:3), but the Romans had no such scruples. Flogging was often, for them, part of the execution process, designed to weaken the prisoner.

"Ecce homo!" Pilate yelled to the crowd, perhaps in his native Latin. "Behold the man!" (John 19:5). Earlier, to mock his claim to be King of the Jews, the Romans dressed Jesus in a purple cloak and placed a crown of thorns on his head. The soldiers knelt down before him and called out, "Hail, King of the Jews."

In John's telling, Pilate at this point still wanted to release Jesus, but Jesus' enemies had one last card to play. "If you release this man, you are not Caesar's friend," the temple aristocrats pointed out. "Every one who makes himself a king sets himself against Caesar" (19:12 rsv). That fixed Pilate's resolve. It also fits exactly what Philo of Alexandra wrote about Pilate, that he was fearful of what a delegation of Jewish leaders might say to Caesar.[36]

Inspired by this fear, Pilate had Jesus brought before him, then sat down in his ceremonial judgment seat in an area of the *praetorium* called "The Pavement" (John 19:13 rsv). Matthew alone—the most Jewish of the evangelists—reports that when Pilate saw that a riot was about to break out, he took water and washed his hands before the crowd, saying, "I am innocent of this man's blood; see to it yourselves" (27:24).

Pilate then asked those present one last time, "Shall I crucify your King?" And the crowd replied: "We have no king but Caesar" (John 19:15).

Pilate therefore decreed that Barabbas should be released, but that Jesus was to be condemned to death and crucified. It was, John reports, the Day of Preparation for the Passover—that is, the fourteenth day of Nissan—around the "sixth hour" (19:14).

CHAPTER 11

The Crucifixion

Dogs encompass me;
a company of evildoers encircles me;
they have pierced my hands and feet.
—Psalm 22:16

The situation in which Jesus' hundreds of friends and disciples found themselves would have been agonizing. In the gospel accounts, large crowds had gathered outside the *praetorium*. Jesus' followers were shouting in defense of Jesus, even as others in the crowd were loudly demanding his execution.[1] Given the tense atmosphere, fights could well have broken out between the two groups. For a short while, it looked as if Pilate was going to release Jesus, letting him go with only a good Roman beating. But then, suddenly, it became clear that he wasn't. From that point on, events moved very quickly. The Romans knew how to kill people. They were experts.

If Pilate's *praetorium* was indeed the former palace of Herod the Great, then it was located adjacent to Jerusalem's massive First Wall, just south of the three towers of Phasael, Hippicus, and Mariamne. When Jerusalem was destroyed by the Romans in AD 70, the towers were spared; one still exists in an area now called the Citadel, just south of the Jaffa Gate. The practice of crucifixion was not unique to the Romans; they just perfected it. It was designed to be a slow, agonizing form of execution. The victim was tied and sometimes nailed to an upright pole or tree in a wide variety of positions. The Romans weren't particular. Typically the vertical pole, which the Romans called the *staticulum* or scaffold, was fixed and semipermanent. Wood was scarce in Judaea, and the Romans didn't waste it. This upright pole would often have a V-shaped notch at the top or sometimes on one of the sides into which could be placed a crossbeam, the *patibulum*. It's not true that most Roman crucifixions involved a T-shaped or Tau cross, with the crossbeam at the top. The Romans did crucify people that way, but they used other types of crosses as well—including simple stakes in the ground. Many crucifixions had the crossbeam affixed down the side of the upright pole, making a cross in the traditional form depicted in Western art. This is likely the shape of the cross in Jesus' case because the Gospels report that the *titulus*, or summary of the charge against him, was placed *above* his head on the cross, which implies that the crossbeam was not placed on top of the vertical pole but somewhat down the side of the pole.[2]

Typically the condemned man carried only the crossbeam to the place of execution, usually on his shoulders and with his hands tied to the wood. In Jesus' case the Roman scourging had been so brutal and thorough that he did not have the strength to carry even the crossbeam, which, depending upon its thickness, could have weighed as much as one hundred pounds all by itself.[3] The Roman execution detail, seeing that Jesus was too weak to carry the cross himself, conscripted an unfortunate passerby coming in from the countryside to carry it for him.[4] The man's name was Simon of Cyrene, and Mark adds that he was the father of Alexander and Rufus (15:21). If Pilate's condemnation of Jesus occurred around noon, then it's possible that Simon was returning to the city for lunch. Cyrene was a town in Libya, in North Africa, where there was a large Jewish population. In 1941, archaeologists from the Hebrew University in Jerusalem discovered in a cave in the Kidron Valley an ossuary, or bone box, inscribed with the words "Alexander son of Simon" in Greek and Hebrew, leading the experts to wonder if the ossuary was related to the Simon of Cyrene mentioned in the Gospels. The artifacts found in the burial cave all dated to before AD 70, and the names found on other ossuaries in the cave (Sara, Sabatis, and Jacob) were rare in Israel but common outside Israel.[5]

THE WAY TO GOLGOTHA

Simon of Cyrene picked up the *patibulum* and began to walk where the Roman officers pointed. There were four soldiers, one a centurion, all armed with Roman broadswords and the narrow, razor-sharp javelins they called *pila*. They were marching Jesus and two other condemned men. At this point, Jesus was weak from loss of blood but could still speak. According to Luke, a multitude of people, including many women, were following behind the execution detail, loudly wailing in sorrow and defiance. Jesus turned and addressed them directly, giving them a final warning of what was coming to the holy city. *"Banat Orushalem,"* Jesus said in Aramaic. "Daughters of Jerusalem, do not weep for me, but weep for yourselves and for your children. For behold, the days are coming when they will say, 'Blessed are the barren and the wombs that never bore and the breasts that never nursed!'" (Luke 23:28–29). Forty years

The annual reenactment of the Passion of Christ in Cainta, Rizal, in the Philippines, accurately depicts the massive blood loss that Jesus likely suffered from scourging with the Roman *flagrum*.

later, in AD 68, the Roman general Titus and four legions surrounded the holy city, laying siege for two years. At one point, the Romans were crucifying five hundred people a day outside the city walls, eventually running out of wood for the purpose.[6] The Kidron Valley and the Valley of Hinnom were filled with rotting, diseased corpses. In the end, between three hundred thousand and one million people may have been slaughtered, although contemporary historians say it could have been "only" three hundred and fifty thousand.[7] Like the prophet Jeremiah before him, Jesus was warning his people that this was the fate that lay in store for them if they took up the sword against the world's empires. "[People] will begin to say to the mountains, 'Fall on us,'" Jesus added, as he began moving again, "and to the hills, 'Cover us'" (Luke 23:30).

ARCHAEOLOGY ILLUSTRATED

A reconstruction of Golgotha, or Calvary hill, believed by archaeologists to have been outside Jerusalem's Second Wall and north of Herod the Great's old palace. In the AD 40s, a Third Wall was built that incorporated this area into the city of Jerusalem.

The normal place of execution lay outside the city walls. According to all four gospels, it was a place called Gulgulta or Golgotha, the Place of the Skull.[8] Outside the walls of the city, just north of Herod's Palace, a rock quarry and a garden had been present for decades. The quarry was used for tombs; archaeologists have uncovered numerous *kokhim*-style tombs, in which bodies were laid on niches or tables, in this area.[9] In the middle of this quarry, a steep rocky hill ascended to a height of about forty feet. Somewhere on the side of this hill, although probably not at the very top, the Romans had placed fixed poles to use for executions. This hill, called *calvarius* (skull) in Latin, likely still exists. It's located just inside the Church of the Holy Sepulcher in Jerusalem's Old City where a Christian church has stood since AD 335.

Jesus, the two other condemned prisoners, and Simon of Cyrene did not have far to walk. The distance from Herod's palace at the Citadel to the likely location of Calvary is no more than four or five hundred yards. The real *Via Dolorosa*, or "way of sorrows," was far different from the traditional path walked by pilgrims in Jerusalem today—the one that presupposes the execution detail began at the Antonia Fortress and walked west, across the city toward Golgotha. It's more likely that they began at the Gennath or Garden Gate, just north and east of Herod's Palace, which led to the gardens that lay outside the city walls.[10] Outside of the Gennath Gate they continued left, where there was a large pool or reservoir, sometimes called Hezekiah's Pool, that the locals called the Pool of the Towers. (Although now dry, the pool structure still exists in a large open space surrounded by buildings, hidden from the public, in the Christian Quarter.) The first-century Jewish historian Josephus calls this enormous reservoir the Amygdalon Pool in Greek, thought to be a corruption of the Hebrew word *migdal*, or tower.[11] Built by Herod the Great, this large reservoir, which was about 140 feet wide by 240 feet long—or about twice the size of an Olympic swimming pool—was fed by an aqueduct (also still visible) and provided water for the lush gardens just outside the city's walls.[12] Thus, Jesus and his executioners walked out the Garden Gate, past the Pool of the Towers, and continued north on the path that ran along the Second Wall to their right and the gardens on their left. They then descended steps down into the quarry area and over to the mound where the execution poles were upright.

The Romans frequently drove iron spikes through the wrists of the crucified.

ONTO THE CROSS

At this point, the crowds would have been kept back some distance by the soldiers, the tips of their javelins glistening in the hot sun. Many of the onlookers observed what happened from the hill above the quarry. The Roman soldiers did not waste any time. They had this down to a science. The Gospels report that Jesus was crucified along with two robbers (*lestai*), which could mean either brigands or political insurgents, but imply that Jesus was crucified first (Matt. 27:38). The soldiers first offered Jesus the customary drink of wine mixed with "myrrh" (Hebrew *mor*), an aromatic resin thought to be from the Commiphora plant and also known as the Balm of Gilead.[13] It had been used for millennia throughout the Middle East as a potent analgesic and narcotic. Jesus refused the drink. Next, the Roman soldiers stripped Jesus naked. Unlike the more modest Jews, the Romans were accustomed to nudity; the stripping was part of the humiliation. The *patibulum* was laid on the ground and Jesus was forced to lie on his back as they bound his arms to the crossbeam with ropes or leather thongs. As a method of torture more than anything else, the soldiers then pounded iron spikes through both of his wrists or lower forearms. The Romans frequently did this, but not always.[14] The Gospels do not mention nails during the crucifixion scene itself. They say merely that "they crucified him."[15] However, in the accounts of Jesus' resurrection, Luke reports that Jesus told the apostles to "see my hands and my feet," implying that there were marks there (24:39).

After driving the spikes into his wrists, the Romans then used forked sticks to hoist the crossbeam up onto the upright stake, sliding the beam into the notch cut at an angle in the side of the vertical pole. The Romans used stakes of different heights, some so short that the condemned man's feet could almost touch the ground.[16] In Jesus' case the stake was about ten feet high or higher, since, as Jesus was dying, a man had to use a reed to try to reach his mouth with a drink of vinegar (Mark 15:36 RSV). A ladder was placed against the upright pole so a Roman soldier could secure the crossbeam with rope and nail a wooden board with the charge against Jesus above his head. All four gospels report that this board, which the Romans called the *titulus*, held the inscription "The King of the Jews."[17] John's gospel alone reports that Jesus' name was also on the *titulus*, "Jesus of Nazareth, the King of the Jews," and that it was written in Hebrew, Latin, and Greek (19:19–20). In Latin the charge read *Iesus Nazarenus Rex Iudaeorum*, which is why, to this day, the letters *INRI* appear at the top of crucifixes.

John's gospel also alone reports a strange scene in which Pilate argues with the chief priests over the exact wording of the *titulus*. The priests were offended that Pilate had written, "King of the Jews" on the wood plaque, in effect saying that Jesus really was the king of the Jews. According to Josephus, Pilate never missed an opportunity to insult his subjects. "Do not write 'The King of the Jews,'" the priests complained, "but, 'This man *said*, I am King of the Jews.'" Pilate must have laughed at that. He replied with a phrase that has become a kind of proverb, "What I have written I have written" (John 19:21–22 RSV).

The last part of the crucifixion process involved the feet. The Romans could either lash the legs of their victims to the upright pole or just let the legs dangle. However, this latter option could lead to a faster death—the weight of the body hanging made it very difficult to breathe—and the entire point of crucifixion was to prolong the agony. Thus, the Romans frequently put a footrest on the cross, a *suppedaneum*, so the condemned man could push up a little and relieve some of the pressure from gravity. They also would sometimes make a little seat for the same purpose.

As for whether the Romans nailed feet to the cross, experts were once skeptical because there was little evidence for it in Israel, and the New Testament does not describe the Romans doing so. But in 1968, archaeologists uncovered a first-century tomb at Giv'at ha-Mivtar, northeast of Jerusalem. Inside the tomb they found an ossuary containing the skeleton of a crucified man—the first and only relic of a crucified man found in Israel. Inscribed on the ossuary was his name in Hebrew: Yehochanan. On top of the bone of his right heel was a wooden board, and through the board, and his heel, was a 4.5-inch iron nail. The archaeologists concluded that the executioners, when they removed his body from the cross, couldn't get the nail out of the board due to a knot and so just buried the condemned man with the wood board and nail attached. It appears that the Romans nailed the man's feet on each side of the upright pole. This proves that it's quite possible that Jesus' feet *were* nailed to the cross just as the gospel of Luke implies (24:40). At that point, the soldiers were finished. The gospel of Luke says that, after they had finished securing his hands and feet to the cross, Jesus prayed out loud, "Father, forgive them, for they do not know what they are doing" (Luke 23:34 NIV).

BYSTANDERS AT THE CROSS

All four gospels report that the soldiers divided up Jesus' clothes among themselves, casting lots, or dice, to see who got what.[18] What were those clothes like? They were not long robes, as we often see Jesus depicted in.

Long robes were actually a sign of wealth and high status—and Jesus criticized people who wore them. "Beware of the scribes, who like to walk around in long robes [*stolai*] and like greetings in the marketplaces and have the best seats in the synagogues and the places of honor at feasts," he said (Mark 12:38–39). Instead, Jesus probably wore a knee-length, Greek-style tunic, called a *chiton*, with colored bands, perhaps blue, running from top to bottom. Over the shorter Greek tunic or undergarment, Jesus would have also worn a long woolen cloak or blanket, a *himation*, that reached almost to the ground. Jewish men frequently would have also worn the distinctive *tallit*, or fringed Jewish prayer shawl, as a cloak. John reports that they divided up his clothes and other belongings into four piles, one for each soldier—which means there were four soldiers present. He adds that Jesus' tunic, the *chiton*, was "without seam, woven from top to bottom," so they cast dice for it (19:23 RSV).

Some modern skeptics claim that once Jesus was arrested, the Romans took him away, killed him, allowed his body to decompose and be attacked by animals, buried the remains later in a secret location, and no one knew what became of his body.[19] This is a misunderstanding of how the Romans did things, which was very much in public. The Romans *wanted* people to see what they did.[20] Nothing was done in secret. The condemned man's friends were allowed to watch everything, even to talk to him as they all waited for him to die (Matt. 27:39–40). The soldiers stood guard to make sure no one helped the prisoner escape, but everything was done very much out in the open. The entire point of crucifixion was to provide a hideous spectacle as a deterrent for future would-be rebels. In the case of a celebrity like Jesus, hundreds, perhaps thousands of people watched from the high ground above the rock quarry, along Jerusalem's walls. That's what the Romans wanted. That's *why* they crucified people in the first place.

In addition, the Gospels all report that a number of Jesus' followers and relatives were at his side during the ordeal. Luke says "all" of Jesus' acquaintances and the women who had followed him from Galilee stood at a distance and saw these things (Luke 23:49). Mark and Matthew report some of their names: Mary Magdalene, Mary the mother of the younger James and Joseph, Salome, and "many other women who came up with him to Jerusalem" (Mark 15:41). Many more watched from a greater distance, perhaps from Jerusalem's walls.

Jesus' execution was a public spectacle, and the Romans hid nothing from the public. The Gospels' depictions of passersby taunting Jesus on the cross is consistent with what historians know of Roman crucifixion customs.

In addition, the Gospels report that passersby and even one of the men condemned with him mocked Jesus on the cross. They called out to him, "You who would destroy the temple and rebuild it in three days, save yourself. . . . Come down from the cross" (Matt. 27:40). Others mocked, "Let this Messiah, this king of Israel, come down now from the cross, that we may see and believe" (Mark 15:32 NIV). There is no reason to believe these jibes are not historical. These are the sorts of things people believed Jesus was claiming—that he was the Messiah, the king of Israel, the "son of God." Even one of the men crucified along with Jesus got into the act, mocking him along with the crowd. The other condemned man was horrified at this and protested Jesus' innocence, asking Jesus to remember him when he, Jesus, inherited his kingdom.

This incident reveals that Jesus was still lucid and could speak because he promised the criminal: "Today you will be with me in Paradise" (Luke 23:43).

FINAL MOMENTS

From this point on, it was simply a matter of waiting for the condemned men to die. At some point, four of the onlookers gathered up their courage and approached as close as they could. They were Jesus' mother, Mary; "the other Mary" (Matt. 27:61, whom John describes as Jesus' aunt, the wife of Clopas[21]); Mary Magdalene; and a mysterious figure, widely believed to be the evangelist John, known simply as the "disciple whom Jesus loved" (John 21:20).[22] By this time, Jesus was having trouble breathing. His lungs were filling up with fluid and, weak from the loss of blood, he could no longer push his weight up to relieve the pressure on his chest. Recent medical studies, such as one in the *Journal of the American Medical Association*, have hypothesized that the weight of Jesus' body eventually caused his heart to rupture in a sudden catastrophic event. It's more likely that the scourging with the Roman *flagrum* caused severe blood loss that resulted in "hypovolemic shock, exhaustion asphyxia, and perhaps acute heart failure."[23]

Jesus winced—and looked into the horror-stricken eyes of his mother, Mary.

"Woman, behold, your son!" Jesus gasped between agonized breaths, nodding toward the beloved disciple. Then he looked at the young man keeping Mary from collapsing on the hard ground. "Behold, your mother!" (John 19:26–27). The gospel of John says that, from that time forward, the disciple took Jesus' mother into his own home. This scene is why some Christian churches believe Jesus did not have any biological siblings and that the "brothers" and "sisters" mentioned in the Gospels were actually cousins or other relatives.[24]

It took Jesus only three hours to die, from the "sixth hour," or around noon, until the "ninth hour" or three o'clock in the afternoon.[25] A darkness descended over the whole land at this time. Both Mark and Matthew report that Jesus cried out in a loud voice, quoting from Psalm 22.[26] Matthew records the words Jesus used in Hebrew (27:46), but Mark records them in Jesus' mother tongue of Aramaic: *Eloi, Eloi, lama sabachthani*. Both give the translation: "My God, my God, why have you forsaken me" (Mark 15:34). The onlookers mistakenly believed Jesus was calling for the prophet Elijah, taken up alive to heaven by a whirlwind, to rescue him.

Some of the people mocking Jesus eventually felt sorry for him, took a "sponge," probably hyssop, dipped it in *posca*, the vinegar-wine drink popular with the Roman legions, and, taking a reed, lifted it up to Jesus to drink.[27] The Romans permitted such little acts of mercy, if only because they extended the condemned man's agony by keeping him alive longer. In Jesus' case, it didn't work. According to John, as soon as he took a sip of the vinegar—which some interpreters claim is the postponed fourth cup of the Passover meal—he said, "It is finished," bowed his head, and died (v. 30). Luke adds that Jesus issued a final prayer of surrender, saying, "Father, into your hands I commit my spirit!" (Luke 23:46).[28]

Thus, Jesus of Nazareth, the Savior of the world, true God and true man, died around three o'clock on the Friday before Passover and the Sabbath, the Day of Preparation for both that year, the fourteenth day of Nissan, April 7, AD 30. He was about thirty-five years old. [29]

CHAPTER 12

A HASTY BURIAL

He was assigned a grave with the wicked, and
with the rich in his death, though he had done no
violence, nor was any deceit in his mouth.
—ISAIAH 53:9 NIV

Jesus likely died just as the Passover lambs were being ritually slaughtered in the temple, their blood caught in golden and silver goblets—a
chilling coincidence not lost on later Christians. They would come to see
Jesus as the Agnus Dei, the Lamb of God, whose blood was poured out,
as Jesus himself is quoted as saying in Mark's gospel, "as a ransom for
many" (10:45). The eerie timing of Jesus' crucifixion and death—the
way it was bound up with the ancient Passover ritual, combined with
Jesus' strange talk of his own blood as the blood of the new covenant
(Matt. 26:28)—all contributed to how Jesus' followers understood what
happened in the months and years that followed.

A great darkness came upon the earth at the moment of Jesus'
death—a spring thunderstorm, perhaps, or a solar eclipse; it's difficult to
say. One of the Roman soldiers watching Jesus die, a centurion, thought
Jesus innocent of the charges against him. Mark even quotes the centurion as saying, "Truly this man was the Son of God!" (Mark 15:39).[1]
Many of the onlookers fled to their homes. Strange stories began to

circulate. It was said there was an earthquake, that tombs were opened and the dead were raised to life.[2] The curtain or veil in the temple, the *parochet*, which separated the outer hall of the temple from the Holy of Holies, was split down the middle.[3]

These reports are part of the ancient Christian tradition of the "Harrowing of Hell," the belief that Jesus, at the moment of his death, liberated the souls of the righteous dead then trapped in the shadowy netherworld the Jews called *sheol*, the Greeks *hades*, and medieval Christians *purgatory*. There is little explicit scriptural support for this ancient belief, widely held in the early Jesus community. However, there is an odd teaching from the first letter of Peter, traditionally believed to have been authored by Simon Peter (or dictated to a scribe). "Christ was put to death as a human, but made alive by the Spirit," the author of 1 Peter writes. "And it was by the Spirit that he went to preach to the spirits in prison" (3:18–19 CEB). The phrase "spirits in prison" is widely believed to refer to the souls of the righteous in *sheol*.

CONFIRMATION OF DEATH

There was one final coda to the crucifixion. According to John, who frequently gives details that turn out to be eerily accurate, Jewish officials came to Pilate in the early afternoon.[4] It was the Day of Preparation before the Sabbath, John reports, and the officials were concerned that Jesus might linger on the cross or die in the night, his body left on the cross— thus desecrating the holy city on the Sabbath as well as on Passover. As a result, they asked that Jesus' legs be broken—the Romans called this act the *crurifragium*—to hasten his death so his body could be taken down before sundown. Without the ability to push off from the footrest on the cross, a condemned man with broken legs suffocated quickly.

Pilate agreed, so soldiers were dispatched to the execution site and broke the legs of the other men crucified with Jesus. But when they saw that Jesus was already dead, they decided not to break his legs; but they made sure he was dead another way. One of the soldiers took a spear and thrust it into Jesus' side, and blood and "water" (lymph fluid from his pericardial cavity) came flowing out (John 19:34). John insists that this incident was reported by an eyewitness (v. 35). In verse 37, John would remember a line from the prophet Zechariah: "When they look on me, on him whom they have pierced, they shall mourn for him" (12:10).

CUSTODY OF JESUS' BODY

What happened next is remarkable. A man named Joseph of Arimathea—a member of the Sanhedrin but also, perhaps, a secret follower of Jesus—went hurriedly to the *praetorium* and requested an audience with Pilate. That alone took considerable courage. But then he dared to ask Pilate for the body of Jesus, an act that would have instantly made the Romans suspicious. The Romans frequently left the bodies of condemned men to rot on crosses for days, as a deterrent. That is why some skeptics today claim that Jesus was never given a formal burial but his body left on the cross and then disposed of in an anonymous grave that none of his followers knew about.

However, we know from the writings of the Alexandrian Jewish philosopher Philo that the emperor Tiberias insisted that Jewish religious sensibilities be respected, especially by the Roman governors.[5] Tiberias had publicly rebuked Pilate on more than one occasion for his stubborn refusal to respect Jewish customs. It's fairly certain that Pilate knew the Jews considered leaving dead bodies hanging right outside the holy city's walls to be a desecration, especially during the Passover festival. Therefore, as much as he hated to do so, Pilate certainly knew he had to honor Jewish scruples and placate the emperor. But he was surprised Jesus had died so soon. So he summoned the centurion in charge of the execution detail and asked if Jesus was really dead. When the centurion replied that he was, Pilate granted permission to Joseph of Arimathea to retrieve the body.[6]

Joseph thanked the Roman governor and walked out of the main gate of the *praetorium*, into the north-south street that led to the Garden Gate. There he met Nicodemus, the Pharisee with whom Jesus had spoken late one night about being reborn. What they were about to do was risky. They were exposing themselves at the very least as admirers of the condemned man, if not something more. Joseph in particular would certainly face the scorn of his colleagues in the Sanhedrin.

Nevertheless, they were determined to do what was right. Nicodemus had brought servants with him, carrying one hundred pounds of burial spices, myrrh, and aloes. Joseph, Nicodemus, and the servants walked north to the Garden Gate, past the Pool of the Towers, and back down to the Golgotha hill below in the quarry. When they got there, they found that the soldiers had already taken Jesus' body down from the cross. The nail had been pulled out from his feet and the *patibulum* lowered back down to the ground. The soldiers were carefully pulling the iron spikes out of the wood, to be reused later.

The "Tombs of the Prophets" on the Mount of Olives in Jerusalem. The chamber forms two concentric passages containing thirty-eight burial niches.

Joseph had use of a brand-new rock-cut tomb just nearby, one he had likely recently purchased for his own family's use. Like most tombs in the area, it was nothing more than a large room cut out of the rock with a small doorway for an opening. From studying about a thousand similar rock-cut tombs dating to this era around Jerusalem, archaeologists believe Jesus' tomb was very small, roughly six feet square, with a single stone bench against one wall. Sometimes this bench would be cut into the side of the wall with an arched recess, called an *arcosolium*, above it.[7]

The entrance was fairly small, just two or three feet high and requiring visitors to crawl inside on their hands and knees. (The gospel of John says that Mary Magdalene had to stoop to look inside [20:11].) Sometimes, a large circular stone placed in a grooved incline would be rolled into place to block the entrance once a body was placed inside. This "high-tech" solution was generally reserved for the wealthy, although a Jewish aristocrat such as Joseph of Arimathea might have been able to afford it. If not, the entry stone, known as a *golal*, would have been a rectangular block that several men would have had to push into place to cover the entryway.

LOSING TRACK OF THE TOMB

Where was this tomb actually located? The gospel of John reports that the tomb was close to Golgotha and near a garden (19:41–42). This fits very closely with the area near the Pool of the Towers, now an abandoned lot just north of the Petra Hotel in the Christian Quarter of Jerusalem, on Ha-Notzrim Street. A few hundred feet up this modern-day street, and to the east, lies the ancient Church of the Holy Sepulchre. Not all archaeologists agree, but a surprising number of them believe that Jesus' tomb was indeed located in this general vicinity, somewhere inside this ancient church.

A decade after the crucifixion, around AD 41, Herod the Great's grandson Herod Agrippa began building a Third Wall to the northwest of Jerusalem, to incorporate areas then outside the city's walls that had been built up. This wall wasn't finished until the early AD 60s and war with Rome was looming, but it was massive: fifteen feet thick and rising thirty feet in the air. The Third Wall encircled the old quarry, its tombs, and the rising hill of Golgotha within the city's walls. The followers of Jesus in Jerusalem, of course—including James, "the Lord's brother" (Gal. 1:19)—would have watched all this as it was happening, beginning about ten years after Jesus' death. As the Third Wall was being built, the owners of the tombs removed the remains of anyone buried in the tombs to other locations because Jewish law forbade burial within city limits.

What happened over the coming eighty years was the "wars and rumors of wars" that Jesus had warned the people of Israel about—a series of three increasingly desperate revolts against Roman rule that each ended in disaster. Events during these wars made it difficult, but not impossible, for his followers to know the location of Jesus' tomb. After the final Jewish revolt failed in AD 136, the Roman emperor Hadrian, who had briefly considered rebuilding the Jewish temple, instead decided to wipe Jerusalem off the map forever. He leveled the city and rebuilt a new Roman city, Aelia Capitolina, on the ruins of the old Jewish capital. Jews could not enter on pain of death—a ban that lasted for six centuries. As a deliberate insult, the Roman builders erected a temple of Venus on the site of Calvary Hill—although the sharp, pointed top of the hill was still visible rising up into the street. According to Melito of Sardis (ca. AD 190), the spot where Jesus was crucified was located in the middle of a street and well-known.[8]

Everything changed when Rome became a Christian empire. Following the conversion of the emperor Constantine to Christianity, the emperor's mother, Helena, came to the Holy Land in search of relics and the holy places of Christianity. When Empress Helena arrived, she ordered the temple of Venus torn down and the mound of Calvary excavated. The Roman engineers uncovered the rocky limestone hill and, beneath it in the surrounding area, numerous tombs. They built an enormous Christian basilica on top of the rocky mound of Calvary, known as the Martyrion, dedicated by a Bishop Macarius on September 17, 335. Incredibly, that rocky mound is still there: it's located just to the right inside the Church of the Holy Sepulchre, up a steep flight of stairs, in Jerusalem's Old City. The current building, which dates to the Crusader period, was built on the ruins of the old Martyrion. Even many skeptical Israeli archaeologists believe that this is, in fact, the rock of Calvary on which Jesus was crucified, although they believe the area now visible was too steep to have been the precise spot. Many believe Jesus was crucified down the hill on a lower, more level area. They say the pointed top now inside the Church of the Holy Sepulchre functioned as a kind of marker of the general area of Calvary.

The Church of the Holy Sepulchre was first built in AD 335 over the remains of a rocky hill that the Christian community then believed was Calvary, where Jesus was crucified. The hill still exists inside the church to the right of the entrance.

Identifying the precise tomb where Jesus was laid is more difficult. Excavations beneath and within the Church of the Holy Sepulchre have intriguingly revealed numerous rock-cut tombs dating back to the first century. Unfortunately, the site that Empress Helena and Bishop Marcarius identified as the actual tomb of Jesus was housed in a stone structure, called an Edicule, located in front of the church built on the site (the Martyrion). Hardly anything of that original structure still exists. The church and the Edicule were destroyed by invading Arab armies in the eleventh century. Today the Church of the Holy Sepulchre houses an Edicule built in 1801, an elaborate marble shrine about two stories high, that is maintained by the Greek Orthodox Church. Inside, amid hundreds of lamps and icons, is a slab of marble beneath which they claim, Jesus' body was laid inside the tomb.

A TEMPORARY RESTING PLACE

Joseph of Arimathea probably assumed the use of his tomb would be a temporary situation, that they would move Jesus' body later to a more suitable final resting place. But they had to hurry. If John's chronology is correct and Jesus was crucified on the Day of Preparation for the Passover, both the Sabbath and Passover would begin at sundown, around 7:00 p.m. at that time of year in Israel (John 19:42).

Joseph, Nicodemus, and the servants placed Jesus' naked body on a large sheet of linen and carried him about one hundred yards to the entrance of the tomb, near the lush gardens just north of the Pool of the Towers. Some of Jesus' other disciples, Peter, James, and John, were possibly there as well, although they are not mentioned in the gospel accounts. They do mention that Jesus' closest women followers—Mary Magdalene, "the other Mary," and the mother of Jesus—were watching everything from close by. They saw the tomb and how Jesus' body was laid inside.[9]

No doubt with some difficulty, and racing to beat the arrival of the Sabbath at dusk, Joseph and Nicodemus pulled Jesus' body through the low opening of the tomb. Once inside, they quickly bathed the body and then wrapped it, along with the aromatic spices Nicodemus had brought, in a burial shroud of linen, called a *tachrich* in Hebrew.[10] A separate cloth was wrapped around Jesus' head. That would have to do for now. They would come back after the Sabbath, on Sunday, and finish the job properly. The men left the tomb and struggled to move the heavy stone to block the entrance. The women watching understood that more had to be done. They went to their homes to buy and prepare spices and perfumes, determined to return on the day after the Sabbath.[11]

The Stone of Anointing and mosaic icon on the wall at the entrance to the Basilica of the Holy Sepulchre designate the place where tradition claims Jesus' body was prepared for burial.

When Joseph and Nicodemus left the tomb, they were surprised to see members of the temple guard standing outside. The guards explained that the chief priests had complained to Pilate that Jesus' followers might steal his body. Pilate had given permission for the temple authorities to station guards by the tomb to make sure nothing happened. The apocryphal gospel of Peter—an early second-century work that some scholars believe contains some reliable traditions about Jesus—adds that Pilate also sent a Roman soldier, a centurion named Petronius, to join the temple guards and seal the tomb.[12] These guards would become critical witnesses to the shocking events to come.

PART II

ALIVE

Then he said to me, "Prophesy over these bones, and say to them, O dry bones, hear the word of the LORD. Thus says the Lord GOD to these bones: Behold, I will cause breath to enter you, and you shall live. And I will lay sinews upon you, and will cause flesh to come upon you, and cover you with skin, and put breath in you, and you shall live, and you shall know that I am the LORD."

—EZEKIEL 37:4–6

CHAPTER 13

A GLIMMER OF HOPE

After two days he will revive us;
on the third day he will raise us up,
that we may live before him.
—HOSEA 6:2

The day Jesus had foretold had finally arrived. His followers had been warned that he would follow in the footsteps of other prophets, that he would be killed just as John the Baptist had been killed. Throughout the two years and a few months of their training, Jesus had tried to show them that this outcome was inevitable. Their time together had been a suicide mission from the start, the disciples knew. But it was a risk Jesus was willing to take because, he said, that was why he had come: to proclaim the good news of the kingdom of God (Luke 4:43). Walking into the precincts of the temple itself and proclaiming a new Way—one that did not involve paying tithes to the treasury—could not end well. It was like walking into the Roman Senate and announcing the end of Caesar's rule: you couldn't expect anything but the cross.

That was what Jesus had done. Yet it had all happened so fast, and in a way no one had expected. Peter, James, and John had been *sleeping* while Jesus prayed in the garden. They had been woken up, startled, as Jesus was arrested and dragged off to an interrogation at the home of Caiaphas. Instinctively, Peter had lashed out, swinging his sword and cutting off the ear of the high priest's slave. As soon as they could, the disciples had run for their lives, eventually staggering back to the upper room in the Upper City. Peter had mustered the courage to sneak into Caiaphas's inner courtyard but had only succeeded in fulfilling Jesus' prophecy about Peter, that he would deny even knowing Jesus three times before dawn. Now, not even a day later, Jesus was dead. The women who watched the entire spectacle had seen it with their own eyes: the Roman soldier thrusting the razor-sharp javelin, the *pilum*, into Jesus' side (John 19:31–37).

A typical first-century tomb near Nazareth. Only the more affluent could afford a round *golal*, or stone door, used to block the entrance.

By the start of Passover, most of the disciples huddled together all Saturday in the room Jesus had arranged for the Passover meal. All of the Twelve were there, minus Judas. So were the three Marys—Jesus' mother, Mary; Mary, the mother of the younger James; and Mary Magdalene. Salome, the mother of James and John and the wife of the rich fisherman Zebedee, was in this room as well. Joseph of Arimathea and Nicodemus probably returned to their own homes in Jerusalem.

Also present were other friends and associates of the Way, rich and poor, who lived in Jerusalem and in the villages nearby, such as Mary and Martha of Bethany and Joanna, the wife of Herod Antipas's steward, Chuza. They now all met together around the table, weak with grief, terrified of what might befall them, overwhelmed with guilt and sorrow. Simon Peter, in particular, could barely speak as he remembered again and again, in his mind, how he had betrayed the Master.

The community spent the next day, the Sabbath, locked inside this room. Few slept. Fewer still ate anything. Some of the Twelve, Andrew and John, James and Bartholomew, may have sat talking quietly, recalling things Jesus had told them about this day, things they had forgotten but that now came flooding back into their anguished minds. Peter probably remained nearly paralyzed, barely moving. Everyone slept where he or she could find a spot on the floor, curled up on the pillows the Twelve had sat on during their final meal with the rabbi. Every now and then, someone knocked quietly on the door, asking if anyone had any news.

Finally, sometime after sundown and the end of the Sabbath, some of the women went out. They were preparing more ointments and spices. Jesus' body had not been prepared properly. Everything had been done in haste. They owed the rabbi a proper burial. The women would go to the tomb to perform the *mitzvah* of Tahara, the cleansing, ritual washing, and dressing of a deceased person's body.

EASTER MORNING

The next day was Yom Rishon, the first day of the Jewish week, Sunday by the Roman reckoning. The women awoke long before dawn, packed their supplies, and left the upper room. They were about to witness the greatest miracle ever reported in history—a miracle that almost no one believed at the time and many still do not believe to this day. The Gospels disagree slightly about which women went to visit Jesus' tomb this day, but they all agree that one of them was Mary Magdalene. Also present were "the other Mary," the mother of James; Joanna, the wife of Chuza; and Salome, the wife of Zebedee and mother of James and John. The group left the upper room in the southern part of the Upper City, walked north past the *praetorium,* left the city through the Garden Gate, and continued along the city's northern wall to the quarry area.

They were certainly frightened. It was just light. As they walked they asked one another what they were going to do when they reached the tomb. After descending the steps into the quarry and hurrying past Golgotha, the execution site, one of the women asked, "Who will roll away the stone for us from the entrance of the tomb?" (Mark 16:3). But just as the woman said this, they reached the tomb itself.

They couldn't believe what they were seeing. The sun was rising, and it was light enough to see clearly.[1] The large stone blocking the entrance to the tomb had already been rolled back. As Luke reports, the women stooped down and, probably on their hands and knees, went into the tomb. Much to their astonishment and horror there was nothing inside. *The body wasn't there!* Mary Magdalene immediately exited the tomb.

The gospel of John at this point reports that Mary Magdalene actually ran all the way back through the streets of Jerusalem to the upper room (20:2). She woke Simon Peter and John and, panting and out of breath, gasped that someone had taken Jesus' body out of the tomb. She had no idea, she said, where they had put him. Upon hearing this, both Peter and John raced to the tomb, with Mary Magdalene following behind. John, a younger and probably thinner man, easily outran Peter and got to the tomb first. It was now fully light outside. John stooped down, looked inside the tomb, and could see the linen cloths that had been used to wrap Jesus' body but didn't go in. Perhaps he was frightened. When Simon Peter arrived, just seconds later, he immediately crawled inside the tomb. Just as Mary Magdalene had said, the body was not there. Instead, Simon found the linen burial shroud and, rolled up by itself, the cloth that had been used to cover Jesus' face. John went in and saw everything as well. This account is corroborated by the gospel of Luke, which says simply that Peter ran to the tomb, bent down, and saw the burial clothes alone (24:12).

GINO SANTA MARIA

A reconstruction of what the interior of Jesus' temporary tomb may have looked like when Simon Peter crawled inside with the burial cloths left to the side.

Simon Peter and John, their hearts no doubt racing, then decided to go back to tell the other disciples what they had seen. They left. Mary Magdalene stayed with the other women, who were still standing beside the tomb, crying. At this point, the women decided to go back and look into the tomb again—but this time they saw something, or someone, they hadn't seen before.

The reports differ, but they saw either one young man or two, dressed in white robes.[2] The gospels of Matthew and John call them *angeloi*, the Greek word for "messengers." "Do not be amazed," the young man or young men in white told the women in Mark's and Matthew's accounts. "You seek Jesus of Nazareth, who was crucified. He has risen, he is not here" (Mark 16:6 RSV).

The young man or men then told the women that they were to go and tell Jesus' followers that he had risen from the dead and that he was going before them to Galilee. They would see him there. At this point, at least some of the women then returned to where the disciples were all staying—and reported what they had seen.[3] *Yet no one believed them!* Their story was considered "nonsense" (Luke 24:11 NIV).

John includes more details. According to John, the two young men in white first asked Mary Magdalene, while she was outside the tomb, why she was crying. "They have taken away my Lord," she replied, "and I do not know where they have laid him" (20:13).

As she said this, Mary turned and spotted someone whom she thought was a gardener! This man too asked her why she was crying and for whom she was looking. "Sir, if you have carried him away, tell me where you have laid him," Mary replied, "and I will take him away." At this, the "gardener" said simply, "Mary," and, in astonishment, she yelled out, *"Rabboni,"* which is an Aramaic version of rabbi. The "gardener" then replied that Mary was not to touch him but was to go to his "brothers" and tell them that he was "ascending to my Father and your Father" (John 20:15–17).

John's account is mirrored somewhat by Mark. According to the long ending of Mark, not found in the earliest Greek manuscripts, Jesus indeed appeared first to Mary Magdalene—a woman from whom he had exorcised seven demons (16:9). She returned to where the other disciples were staying, as they "mourned and wept," and reported that Jesus was alive and that she had seen him (Mark 16:10). But no one would believe her. In Luke's account, none of the women saw Jesus himself, they saw only the angels; but in Matthew, as the women were running away from the tomb to tell the disciples that they had seen the empty tomb and an angel, Jesus greeted them on their way. They approached him, embraced his feet, and paid him homage. Then Jesus told the women, "Do not be afraid; go and tell my brothers to go to Galilee, and there they will see me" (Matt. 28:10).

BEYOND BELIEF

One common theme that Mark and Luke share is *disbelief*. "These words seemed to them an idle tale," is how Luke puts it (24:11). Skepticism wasn't invented in the modern world. Ancient literature is riddled with attempts on the part of the urbane, highly skeptical Romans and Greeks to debunk religious eccentricities and superstitions. For example, the Roman historian Publius Cornelius Tacitus (AD 56–117), in his *Annals*, referred to the early Jesus movement as "a deadly superstition (*exitiablilis superstitio*)."[4] The Jews also were well-known in the ancient world for their rejection of pagan myths and legends and their insistence on worship of one God.

According to the gospels of Mark, Luke, and John, the skepticism of the apostles ended that first evening of Easter. John portrays the apostles huddled together, the doors "locked . . . for fear of the Jews" (John 20:19).[5] By "the Jews," of course, John must have meant the Jewish temple authorities who had just arrested Jesus only twenty-four hours earlier. At this point, Jesus' closest followers all assumed they were wanted men. John doesn't say where they were, but only that they were together.

But both Luke and John agree that Jesus suddenly came and "stood among them," saying, "Peace be with you"—the standard Jewish greeting (Luke 24:36 NIV, John 20:26). In Luke's account, the disciples "were startled and frightened and thought they saw a spirit" (24:37). But Jesus promptly told them to calm down. Jesus showed them his hands and feet and bluntly pointed out that a spirit does not have flesh and bones. "See my hands and my feet, that it is I myself," Jesus said, no doubt pointing to the marks of crucifixion. "Handle me, and see; for a spirit has not flesh and bones as you see that I have" (Luke 24:39 RSV).

While they marveled at all this, Jesus suddenly asked, "Have you anything here to eat?"—a comment so odd that it rings true even to some skeptical historians, some of whom think Jesus must have survived the crucifixion and was simply hungry.[6] The disciples gave him a piece of broiled fish, and "he took it and ate it in front of them." After he had finished eating, Jesus then explained to the astonished men that everything that had happened had been written about in the law of Moses and in the prophets and psalms. "Thus it is written that the Messiah would suffer and rise from the dead on the third day," Luke quotes Jesus as saying, "and that repentance, for the forgiveness of sins, would be preached in his name to all the nations, beginning from Jerusalem." Jesus then told the disciples, "You are witnesses of these things," and added that he was sending "the promise of my Father upon you" (Luke 24:41–49 NABRE). In Mark's briefer version, Jesus said simply, "Go into all the world and proclaim the gospel to the whole creation" (16:15).

EYEWITNESS ACCOUNTS

This is as close a reconstruction of what happened on Easter as is possible with the sources we have. On this much, there is a certain amount of agreement, although the Gospels do vary in the details. In Matthew's account, there are no appearances to the disciples in Jerusalem but only in Galilee (28:16–20). They all agree Mary Magdalene and perhaps two or three other women (the "other Mary," Salome, and Joanna) found the tomb where Jesus was buried empty.[7] Mark, Luke, and John all agree that Jesus appeared initially to at least Mary Magdalene and perhaps to the other women as well. At first, the followers of Jesus refused to accept these reports, but later that same day, in the evening, Jesus appeared alive to members of his inner circle, the Eleven, while they were having dinner.

And there is something else: We actually possess an *independent eyewitness account* of Jesus appearing alive after death—and few secular historians question its authenticity. This is known as Paul's first letter to the community he founded at Corinth. Likely written by Paul when he was staying in the Greek city of Ephesus, between AD 53 and 57, the document we know as 1 Corinthians contains the very earliest report of the resurrection in existence—a report issued within a couple of years from the events they describe. Speaking of the gospel message that he proclaimed in Corinth, Paul wrote that he "delivered" to the Corinthians what he had himself received:

> That Christ died for our sins in accordance with the Scriptures, that he was buried, that he was raised on the third day in accordance with the Scriptures, and that he appeared to Cephas, then to the twelve. Then he appeared to more than five hundred brothers at one time, most of whom are still alive, though some have fallen asleep. Then he appeared to James, then to all the apostles. Last of all, as to one untimely born, he appeared also to me. (1 Cor. 15:3–8)

Skeptical scholars debate endlessly whether the resurrection reports in the Gospels were inventions of the evangelists or legends that they collected.[8] But in the case of Paul's testimony in 1 Corinthians, there is no doubt that this is Paul's own eyewitness testimony of what he experienced and what he heard from the eyewitnesses themselves, James and Peter, when he visited them around AD 33–34 in Jerusalem.

CHAPTER 14

The First Reports

For you will not abandon my soul to Sheol,
or let your holy one see corruption.
—Psalm 16:10

The day following Easter, there must have been hell to pay for the soldiers who were supposed to be guarding Jesus' tomb. Caiaphas and the other temple priests had wanted to avoid someone stealing Jesus' body, but that was apparently what had happened. The story was bound to get out. With Jerusalem still bursting at the seams with hundreds of thousands of devout Jewish pilgrims, many of whom were ardent supporters of the wild rabbi from Galilee, well, who knew what crazy stories would be told?

Matthew reports that the guards went back to the city and told the chief priests what had occurred. However, rather than having them punished, the priests decided on a different course. After consulting with some of the temple elders, the priests paid the soldiers some money. According to Matthew, the priests told the soldiers, "Tell people, 'His disciples came by night and stole him away while we were asleep'" (28:13). They also promised to cover for the soldiers if word of this exploit came to Pilate's ear. The soldiers took the money and did what they were told. That is why, Matthew claims, the story of Jesus' body being stolen has "spread among the Jews to this day" (v. 15).

If premature burial was an issue at the time, how do we know Jesus didn't just survive the crucifixion and then appear "alive" to the disciples later? One reason: had this happened to Jesus, his followers would have instantly understood what had occurred—as a barely breathing, whipped and scourged Jesus staggered before them. As for Jesus' body being stolen, this is actually *very* plausible but would not explain the resurrection. Over the centuries, various skeptics have proposed that the empty tomb can be explained by someone stealing Jesus' body—and that is certainly the case. A variation on this theory was recently proposed on TV and in books, alleging that Jesus was buried temporarily in Joseph of Arimathea's tomb, due to the Sabbath, but that Joseph had returned on Saturday and relocated the body to a more permanent resting place— namely, in a tomb located beneath a modern apartment building in south Jerusalem, near the modern suburb of Talpiot. The problem is, had this occurred, the followers of Jesus, along with everyone else in Jerusalem, would have simply and very reasonably assumed that someone had moved the body. Moving bodies was a common occurrence at that time. The empty tomb, by itself, wouldn't have made anyone think that Jesus was raised from the dead. In fact, in John's account, the first thought that Mary Magdalene had, when seeing the empty tomb, was that someone had moved Jesus' body (20:2). Not for a moment did she suppose that Jesus was somehow alive.

But Jesus' followers did know that he was somehow alive—and not just "alive," resuscitated from a premature burial, like Lazarus or Jairus's daughter, but utterly transformed. The reports of Jesus' resurrection are odd, and not what you would expect. On one hand, the risen Jesus appears to have had supernatural abilities humans simply do not have, such as the ability to appear in a locked room so suddenly that his closest friends assumed he was a ghost (Luke 24:37). But on the other hand, some of the accounts stress that he was so normal looking that one of his closest friends, Mary Magdalene, mistook him for a gardener (John 20:14–15)! His other friends heard him ask for something to eat, and then he proceeded to eat some broiled fish (Luke 24:42–43). These are strange details—details that are not what you would expect if the stories of Jesus' resurrection were invented. They are too strange to have been simply made up.[1]

REACTION FROM THE AUTHORITIES

From Monday onward, Jerusalem was in chaos. It's almost certain that word got back to Pilate about the fiasco at the tomb. It's equally certain that Pilate and the chief priests weren't about to sit back and do nothing about it. Squads of Roman auxiliaries no doubt fanned out from the *praetorium* barracks and the Antonia Tower, searching for whoever had stolen Jesus' body. It's also likely that they began hunting for Jesus' followers as well—if only to question them about what had happened. One of the reasons historians know that Jesus was not a revolutionary "Zealot," plotting the overthrow of Roman occupation forces, is that we have solid proof that the Romans allowed Jesus' followers to operate unhindered in Jerusalem for decades after the crucifixion. Had they really believed Jesus was a political rebel, there would have been a thousand crosses on Golgotha, not just three. For this reason, the account in the Gospels is actually far more plausible than many skeptical reconstructions: that Jesus was executed on trumped-up charges of sedition that even the Romans themselves didn't really believe. Pilate likely thought Jesus was a politically naïve, somewhat otherworldly prophet like John the Baptist, but not a real threat. It was only when Jesus admitted that he was, in fact, the Messiah, the long-prophesied "king of the Jews," that Pilate felt he had to act. In any event, Jesus was clearly trouble . . . and Pilate didn't like trouble. But for the rest of his rule, until he was sacked in AD 36 for massacring some Samaritans, Pilate allowed the followers of the Nazarene to continue to operate in Jerusalem.

Nevertheless, at this stage there is little doubt both the Romans and the Jewish authorities wanted to question Jesus' followers. His inner circle were now being hunted—and had to lie low. They no doubt stayed indoors. Trying to flee the city immediately would have been too risky. The Roman and Jewish guards would be at every gate, watching for them. By now, the authorities probably had detailed descriptions of the key followers of Jesus—Simon Peter, James and John, the rest of the Twelve, Mary Magdalene, Joanna, and Salome. Now that they had seen Jesus, the Eleven wanted to leave Jerusalem and return to Galilee. They knew they would see Jesus there. He had told them that (Mark 16:7).

JESUS REAPPEARS

Reports of the empty tomb spread like wildfire throughout the city. Everyone was talking about it. And Jesus was about to make another appearance. The gospel of Luke features an unusual and lengthy anecdote, mentioned in a single sentence by Mark, about two of Jesus' disciples encountering him alive just two days later on the road to Emmaus, a small village about seven miles from Jerusalem. According to Luke, as the disciple Cleopas and a companion were walking on the road to Emmaus, Jesus himself came up to them and walked along with them. The two followers did not recognize that it was Jesus. In Mark's brief mention of the same incident, he says simply that Jesus appeared "in another form to two of them, as they were walking into the country" (16:12). Jesus asked the two what they were talking about, and Cleopas, incredulous, asked Jesus (only he didn't know it was Jesus) if he was the only visitor to Jerusalem who didn't know what had happened in recent days. Jesus asked what the events were that Cleopas was speaking about. "Concerning Jesus of Nazareth," Cleopas replied, "who was a prophet mighty in deed and word before God and all the people, and how our chief priests and rulers delivered him up to be condemned to death, and crucified him" (Luke 24:19–20 RSV). He then added that they had hoped he was the one who would redeem Israel, and that it was now the third day since all this had happened. "Moreover, some women of our company amazed us," Cleopas continued. "They were at the tomb early in the morning and did not find his body; and they came back saying that they had even seen a vision of angels, who said that he was alive. Some of those who were with us went to the tomb, and found it just as the women had said; but him they did not see" (vv. 22–24 RSV).

Luke then recounts how Jesus, beginning with Moses and all the prophets, interpreted the Jewish Scriptures for them and showed them how all of these ancient oracles pointed to Jesus himself. As they approached Emmaus, it appeared that the stranger was going to continue walking, but the two men invited him to stay with them. He agreed. But when they sat down to eat, the man took the bread, blessed it, and then broke it, and gave it to them. Their eyes were immediately opened, Luke concludes, and they recognized that it was Jesus; but he then vanished from their sight (vv. 25–31).

They then got up and immediately returned to Jerusalem, where they found the Eleven gathered together and heard that "the Lord has arisen indeed, and has appeared to Simon!" (v. 34 RSV). The two men then reported what they had witnessed, and how Jesus was known to them in the breaking of the bread—a clear reference to the eucharistic rite of the early Jesus community.

By the end of the first week, the disciples were once again all together, gathered in a locked room. Perhaps it was the upper room, but perhaps not. They had to be careful. Temple spies were everywhere, and they were still all wanted men and women. An incident then occurred that is reported only by the gospel of John. The apostle Thomas was missing when Jesus had appeared to the others on Easter night, and, unlike the others, he didn't believe the stories he had heard. "Unless I see in his hands the print of the nails, and place my finger in the mark of the nails, and place my hand in his side, I will not believe," said Thomas—as definitive an expression of skepticism as you are likely to find (John 20:25 RSV). Now, eight days later, the Eleven were again in the house and, once again, Jesus "stood among them" and said, "Peace be with you" (20:26 RSV).

This time Thomas was there, and Jesus spoke directly to him.

"Put your finger here, and see my hands," he said, "and put out your hand, and place it in my side; do not be faithless, but believing." Of course, Thomas did believe. He answered, "My Lord and my God!" But to that Jesus replied, "Have you believed because you have seen me? Blessed are those who have not seen and yet believe" (John 20:27–29 RSV).

CHAPTER 15

"I Am with You Always"

I saw in the night visions,
and behold, with the clouds of heaven
there came one like a son of man.
—Daniel 7:13–14

The appearances of the risen Jesus lasted for forty days after Easter—that is, until roughly mid-May of that year. We have records of only a handful of these appearances, and very little information even on these. But during this period, Jesus continued to appear, "[presenting] himself alive to them after his suffering by many proofs" (Acts 1:3). During this period Jesus began to show his followers everything that had been written about him in the law of Moses, the Prophets, and the Psalms. Jesus "opened their minds" to understand the ancient writings (Luke 24:45).

At some point during the first month after Easter, Jesus' followers must have returned to Galilee and even, briefly, to their professions. The disciples who followed Jesus to Jerusalem would naturally have wanted to share the news that they had seen Jesus alive with the rest of his followers, and their families, who had not journeyed to Jerusalem. They would have returned to their homes, perhaps to collect their spouses and children.

The Gospels portray two incidents of Jesus appearing in Galilee. The first is an appearance on the Sea of Tiberias, reported by John, in which Jesus appeared as a regular living man and the disciples again did not recognize him at first (John 21:1–14). The second was an appearance reported by Matthew alone, in which Jesus appeared on a mountain in Galilee, proclaimed that all authority on heaven and earth had been given to him, and was worshiped there (Matt. 28:16–20).

According to ancient Christian traditions, the appearance of the risen Jesus to his followers while they were out fishing, recounted in the gospel of John, took place at this beach at Tabgha, south of Capernaum.

In addition to these accounts, the apostle Paul presents the catalog of appearances in 1 Corinthians—including some that are *not* recorded in the Gospels. These included appearances to: "Cephas, then to the twelve. Then he appeared to more than five hundred brothers at one time, most of whom are still alive, though some have fallen asleep. Then he appeared to James, then to all the apostles" (15:5–7).

The appearance to Simon Peter (Cephas) is not described in the Gospels at all, but it is referred to obliquely in the gospel of Luke. Upon returning to Jerusalem, the two disciples who saw Jesus on the road to Emmaus found the Eleven and the others gathered with them, and they told them exultantly, "The Lord has risen indeed, and has appeared to Simon!" (24:34). Thus, there must have been an early tradition about an appearance of Jesus to Simon alone—perhaps on his way back from visiting the empty tomb. Similarly, there is no description in the Gospels of an appearance to James (the brother, half brother, or cousin of Jesus) nor to the "five hundred brothers at one time" (1 Cor. 15:6–7). Paul likely received this information directly from James and Simon Peter when he visited Jerusalem three years after his encounter with Jesus on the road to Damascus.

The appearance to the five hundred has long puzzled both ordinary Christians and scholars. There have been attempts to link this appearance either with Pentecost (when, according to Acts 1:15, a large group of 120 followers of Jesus were likely present), or with the appearance on the mountain in Galilee. Pentecost is a dubious candidate because it did not involve an appearance of Jesus at all. But Paul could have been referring to the appearance on the mountain in Galilee (Matt. 28:16–20) when he spoke of the five hundred. However, in both cases, there is very little information; so these ideas are speculative. The appearance on the mountain in Galilee takes up only eighty-five words in Matthew 28, and it is not mentioned explicitly in any other New Testament source. What's more, Matthew only mentions "the eleven disciples" witnessing the event, not five hundred people (v. 16).

THE ASCENSION

In addition to the appearances in Jerusalem and Galilee, and those recorded in 1 Corinthians, we also know that the risen Jesus continued to appear even *after* this initial forty-day period. He would be seen in a vision by the first Christian martyr, Stephen (Acts 7:55). Then he was at least heard by Saul, the Pharisee and persecutor of the early Jesus movement, on the road to Damascus (Acts 9:3–6). However, it is true that after this initial flurry the appearances of the risen Jesus came to an end with a mysterious event called the Ascension.

The long ending of Mark (16:19), Luke (24:51), and Acts (1:9) all mention the Ascension, but Matthew and John do not—at least not directly. Matthew ends with the Great Commission on the mountain in Galilee (28:16–20). John ends with the disclaimer that Jesus did so many wondrous deeds that the whole world could not contain the books that would have to be written in order to record them all (21:25). In John, the only mention of ascension is when the risen Jesus tells Mary Magdalene not to touch him "for I have not yet ascended [*anabainō*] to the Father" (20:17).[1]

The Dome of Ascension of Jesus on the Mount of Olives in Jerusalem, Israel. Inside are footprints in the rock that some Christians believe was where Jesus stood before he was "lifted up" at the event known as the Ascension (Acts 1:9).

As Luke tells the story, the risen Jesus ordered his followers to stay in Jerusalem until they were "clothed with power from on high."[2] He then led them "out as far as Bethany," where Martha, Mary, and their brother, Lazarus, lived and where Jesus stayed the entire week before his arrest (Luke 24:49–50). Today, the site is commemorated inside a large walled courtyard abutting Rub'a el-Adawiya Street, just outside Jerusalem's eastern wall, where there stands an octagonal stone structure topped with a plain stone dome. It was built by the Crusaders on top of a Byzantine chapel constructed as early as AD 392.[3] Inside the small, plain, empty building—controlled by Muslims since 1198—there are some footprints in stone on the floor where, it is said, Jesus stood immediately before he ascended into heaven. These footprints have been venerated for at least fifteen hundred years. Devotional candles burn nearby.

WHAT IS AN ASCENSION?

The Bible clearly tells us that Jesus "passed through the heavens" (Heb. 4:14). But what exactly did this mean? Did Jesus rise bodily into the air like a helium balloon? Stories of such an event would, naturally, inspire skepticism. Why would New Testament writers have made up such an unlikely episode? In the twentieth century, it was common to claim that the New Testament writers adhered to a primitive cosmology in which the (flat) earth lay at the center of the universe, with hell, or hades, located physically below ground and God and his angels dwelling up in the sky. Thus, the description of the Ascension of Jesus, of Jesus being "lifted up" to heaven, merely reflected this primitive cosmology, it was said. But of course, the ancient Jews understood very well that God did not live up in the sky the way the Greeks imagined the gods dwelling above the clouds on Mount Olympus. In fact, in the record of the oracles of the ancient Jerusalem prophet Isaiah, who lived around 750 BC, it's easy to see that the ancient Israelites viewed God as so far above the known universe that even the sun, the moon, and all the stars were his handiwork. The Almighty, Isaiah proclaims,

> has measured the waters in the hollow of his hand
> and marked off the heavens with a span,
> enclosed the dust of the earth in a measure
> and weighed the mountains in scales
> and the hills in a balance. (40:12)

So whatever the ancient Israelites meant when they spoke about other figures ascending to heaven—such as Enoch (Gen. 5:24) and Elijah (2 Kings 2:11–12)—they did not mean people flying up into outer space and entering into orbit around the earth. Rather, they described entering into another dimension beyond (and yet still mysteriously part of) this world. In the story of Enoch, the Torah says merely that "Enoch walked with God, and he was not, for God took him" (Gen. 5:24). Elijah, it's true, "went up by a whirlwind into heaven"—and not, as is sometimes thought, riding in a fiery chariot (2 Kings 2:11). But that doesn't mean that the ancient Hebrews thought of Elijah as living up in the sky. The appearance of the fiery chariot and horses seems to have been more for the benefit of Elijah's apprentice, Elisha, and the fifty "sons of the prophets" watching nearby (vv. 12, 15).

For the early followers of Jesus, ascension meant that Jesus "was taken up into heaven and sat down at the right hand of God" (Mark 16:19). It meant that Jesus now somehow reigned "with" God in a dimension beyond space and time. This is an idea that is clearly repeated throughout the New Testament epistles. Jesus was not merely restored to life in some luminous state as a reward for his trials. Rather, he was exalted above all of creation. In the first letter of Peter, the author writes that Jesus "has gone into heaven and is at the right hand of God, with angels, authorities, and powers having been subjected to him" (1 Pet. 3:22). The author of the book of Hebrews proclaims that Jesus is now "the radiance of the glory of God" and adds that "after making purification for sins, he sat down at the right hand of the Majesty on high" (1:3). Late in life, while he was in prison, probably in Rome around AD 62, Paul wrote to the people who lived in the Macedonian city of Philippi. He referred to an early Christian creed that he received, probably in Aramaic:

> Therefore God also highly exalted him
> and gave him the name
> that is above every name,
> so that at the name of Jesus

> every knee should bend,
>
> in heaven and on earth and under the earth,
>
> and every tongue should confess
>
> that Jesus Christ is Lord,
>
> to the glory of God the Father.
>
> (Phil. 2:9–11 nrsv)

It is of course true that God does not live in outer space—and whatever the event that marked the end of Jesus' bodily presence on the earth, it's doubtful that he flew up into the sky. That's not what the text says in any case. It actually says that Jesus was "lifted up, and a cloud took him out of their sight" (Acts 1:9). It is clear that this was the point when the followers of Jesus understood that their mission—for which Jesus had been preparing them for several years—was about to begin.

Immediately before he was "lifted up," Jesus' followers asked him if he was now going to "restore the kingdom to Israel" (Acts 1:6). Luke reports that Jesus did not directly answer the question and replied that it was not for them to know the "times or seasons" that God had established by his authority. But then he made them a promise: "You will receive power when the Holy Spirit has come upon you, and you will be my witnesses [*martyres*] in Jerusalem and in all Judea and Samaria, and to the end of the earth" (vv. 7–8).

After Jesus left them, Luke reports that two men in white garments, presumably angels, appeared next to them. They asked Jesus' followers, "Men of Galilee, why do you stand looking into heaven? This Jesus, who was taken up from you into heaven, will come in the same way as you saw him go into heaven"—a comment that has led Christians ever since to expect Jesus' return (Acts 1:10–11). But before that would happen, the followers of Jesus knew they had a lot of work to do.

CHAPTER 16

THE RETURN OF THE SPIRIT

"And it shall come to pass afterward,
that I will pour out my Spirit on all flesh;
your sons and your daughters shall prophesy,
your old men shall dream dreams,
and your young men shall see visions."
—JOEL 2:28

In late spring, Jerusalem is one of the most beautiful places on earth. The mornings are cool and sunny, the air fresh and clean. The rocky hills of Judea are covered in pine, cypress, and olive trees, and there are many hilly meadows bedecked with colorful wildflowers, such as red poppies. The houses in the city are made today, as in Jesus' time, with pale, yellow-tinted limestone blocks—known as *even Yerushelaim*, or Jerusalem stone—that seem to radiate a warm glow in the sunshine. In Jesus' day, there were also many open pools and natural fountains throughout the city—enormous glistening reservoirs such as the Pool of Siloam in the south and the enormous Pool of the Towers (Amygdalon) just north of Herod's Palace. These pools were also surrounded by lavish, terraced gardens and fruit trees—one of the reasons why Jerusalem, despite its reputation for violence (then as now), was considered one of the world's most beautiful cities.

The stone walkways, steps, and lush gardens of the Jewish Quarter in Jerusalem convey something of what the ancient city would have looked like in the first century.

Around this time, the city was once again being filled to bursting with pilgrims for *Hag ha-Shavuot*, the Jewish harvest festival of Weeks, or firstfruits. It was one of the important festivals mentioned in the Torah, occurring seven weeks after the first day of the barley harvest (roughly between May 15 and June 15).[1] In Jerusalem, local farmers would bring *bikkurim* (firstfruits) to the temple and present them to the priests. By the first century of the Common Era, it also commemorated the giving of the Torah at Mount Sinai in the desert. It was just fifty days after Passover (the festival was called *Pentecost*— "fiftieth"—in Greek).

Jesus' followers were all gathered together in one place when Shavuot began. Suddenly, there was a noise from the sky like a strong, driving wind, and it filled the entire house where the group was meeting (Acts 2:2). After that, "divided tongues as of fire appeared to them" and came to rest on each of them (v. 3). What this phenomenon actually looked like is difficult to say, despite the detailed imaginings of artists over the centuries. The members of the group were "filled with the Holy Spirit" and began to speak in different tongues (Acts 2:4). According to Acts, there were Jews from all different countries in Jerusalem for the festival and, upon hearing the ruckus in this building, a large group gathered outside to see what was going on. The people were amazed because they could see that Jesus' followers were mostly Galileans, yet they appeared to be speaking in foreign languages, with each person hearing what was being said in the language of his or her own country. The crowd was astounded, although some people dismissed what they heard, saying, "They are filled with new wine" (v. 13).

The harvest festival of Shavuot, or Weeks, is celebrated to this day in Israel. It was during this festival, seven weeks after Jesus' crucifixion, that the early Christian community had the experience of the Spirit known as Pentecost.

PETER ADDRESSES THE CROWD

Simon Peter stood before the crowd of onlookers gaping at Jesus' followers on this crisp, sunny morning in late spring. He proceeded to summarize what the Jesus movement was all about—and what it was planning on doing going forward.

"You who are Israelites, hear these words," he began. "Jesus the

Nazorean was a man commended to you by God with mighty deeds, wonders, and signs, which God worked through him in your midst, as you yourselves know. This man, delivered up by the set plan and foreknowledge of God, you killed, using lawless men to crucify him" (Acts 2:22–23 NABRE).

The crowd began to murmur loudly, with a few shouts of protest. It had been less than two months after all these events had occurred, and he was addressing people who witnessed some of what he was describing. And then Simon Peter spoke about the rumor that had been whispered in Jerusalem for weeks. "But God raised him up, releasing him from the throes of death, because it was impossible for him to be held by it," he said (Acts 2:24 NABRE).

Simon Peter then looked around him at the crowd and, raising his voice, made a solemn declaration that would be repeated for months and years to come: "Therefore let the whole house of Israel know for certain that God has made him both Lord and Messiah, this Jesus whom you crucified" (v. 36 NABRE).

Some archaeologists believe Jesus' followers likely gathered together at Pentecost in an area south of Herod's old palace, near the current Zion Gate and Dormition Abbey.

It was a large crowd. Many people listening were outraged, but a surprising number were, as Luke puts it, "cut to the heart." They asked Simon Peter what they should do. What was he asking of them? "Repent and be baptized, every one of you," he replied simply, with an assurance that took many off guard, "in the name of Jesus Christ for the forgiveness of your sins; and you will receive the gift of the holy Spirit" (vv. 37–38 NABRE).

THE HOLY SPIRIT

What exactly happened in this building fifty days after the crucifixion of Jesus? What was behind the tongues of fire? The Synoptic Gospels refer to a mysterious force or power or indwelling divine presence called, in Greek, the *pneuma hagion* or "Holy Spirit." It is not immediately clear what this term means in the New Testament, and modern readers are often bewildered by it. In the Hebrew Bible, the term "Holy Spirit" is only used twice—once in Isaiah 63:10 and once in Psalm 51:11. However, throughout the Hebrew Bible there are references to a mysterious power called the *ruach*—the "breath" or "wind"—of God.

This mysterious spiritual power or force is, in fact, at the very beginning of the biblical story. It is the Spirit of God (*ruach Elohim*) that, at creation, hovers over the face of the waters (Gen. 1:2). This same divine power also fills human beings and can bestow upon them extraordinary mental powers. Like most ancient peoples, the Hebrews believed that divinity could, and sometimes did, enter into the minds and hearts of human beings. In Exodus, Moses told the people that the Spirit of God had filled Bezalel, the son of Uri, son of Hur, of the tribe of Judah, and given him skill, intelligence, and knowledge (35:30–31). The Spirit of God is associated with the gift of prophecy and with anointed kings. The Spirit of God "rushed upon" Samuel (1 Sam. 10:10) and "clothed Zechariah the son of Jehoiada the priest" (2 Chron. 24:20). The Spirit "lifted . . . up" the prophet Ezekiel between earth and heaven and brought him in visions to Jerusalem (Ezek. 8:3).

But many Jews in Jesus' time believed that the Spirit of God had actually abandoned Israel, had left God's dwelling place (the temple) on Zion. The Spirit of God had long been associated with prophets and kings, but there had not been any of either—at least not in any real sense—for centuries. During the days of the Maccabees (ca. 167–63 BC), there was Jewish self-rule by high priests but no real kings. Herod the Great called himself king of the Jews, but he was actually an *Idumean*, a foreigner who had converted to Judaism; and no one accepted him as a true king. As for prophets, Israel had been bereft since the days of the last prophets—Haggai, Zechariah, and Malachi—four hundred years earlier. Israel was and always would be God's chosen people, but the Jewish people were still living in exile, the Spirit of God still absent from the holy city.

Part of Jesus of Nazareth's message, then, was that the Spirit of God was at last returning to Israel. The coming of the kingdom of God meant that God was actively involved once again in saving Israel, and, through them, the entire human race. The problem was, God was not saving Israel the way many wanted to be saved—through military victory over the Romans. God would save the world, not by means of cosmic destruction, not by military conquests, but by transforming individuals and communities through a mysterious outpouring of his own Spirit—his own intelligence and mercy and empathy. The Spirit of God returned in Jesus' own teaching and example, and then, later, through a direct infusion of divine intelligence and mercy in the hearts and minds of Jesus' followers.

Thus, the Jesus movement would be a Spirit-led community, a mystical society in which God's own mind somehow reshaped the thoughts and motivations of those within it, giving them a power and a courage and otherworldly intelligence they could never have imagined. Just as the Jewish feast of Shavuot was all about "firstfruits" being offered to God, so Pentecost was about the "firstfruits" of God's Spirit being poured out. God was remaking the entire human race, one person at a time, one village and town at a time, through the message and example of Jesus of

Nazareth, into what he had always intended his people to be from the dawn of creation.

From the very beginning, ever since the rabbi Jesus told Simon Peter he would make him a fisher of men, the followers of Jesus set about building a spiritual movement that would one day reach all people. It was an effort to create a new community within the heart of much older communities—at first, the community of Israel, and then, later, the community of the Roman Empire. This was Jesus' intention all along. We know this because Jesus' followers began actively recruiting new members to their community and movement almost immediately.

Following Simon Peter's speech on the morning of Pentecost Sunday, many people flocked to join—not dozens, as you might expect; not even hundreds, but thousands. Acts reports that *no fewer than three thousand people* accepted Simon Peter's message and were baptized that day (2:41). The impact would spread as the Jesus movement fanned out to many of the largest cities in the region, including, as we will soon see, Damascus and Rome.

PART III ————————————————

THE BEGINNING OF PERSECUTION

"If the world hates you, know that it has hated me before it hated you."

—JOHN 15:18

"Neither Gold nor Silver"

O Lord my God, I cried to you for help,
and you have healed me.
—Psalm 30:2

From that day forward, everything changed—and virtually overnight. It is with good reason that Pentecost is widely considered the birth of the Jesus movement. It had been a small group of terrified men and women, wanted for questioning by the temple guard, almost certainly in fear of torture or of losing their very lives. Yet suddenly, Jesus' followers were transformed into stalwart champions of an entirely new way of life—and of a message that would set the world on fire.

A CRIPPLED MAN WALKS AGAIN

Soon after Pentecost, Simon Peter and John went up to the temple to pray in the morning, around the third hour of the day (nine o'clock). Earlier, some friends of a crippled man had placed him in front of the Beautiful Gate. Just a few years before Jesus arrived on the scene, an Alexandrian craftsman named Nicanor had created a spectacular and world-famous door for one of the courtyard gates, seventy-five feet high and made of so-called Corinthian bronze—actually an alloy of copper mixed with gold and silver—as a gift to the temple.[1] Immediately before this gate stood an enormous semicircle of stone steps upon which beggars and the sick could sit and cajole pious Jews about to enter into the inner temple precincts to offer sacrifice. As Luke tells the story in Acts, the crippled man asked Simon Peter and John for alms as they were about to go into the temple. Rather than brushing the man off, Peter and John looked intently at him. "I have neither silver nor gold," Peter said, "but what I do have I give you." Then Peter looked closely at the man and said, "In the name of Jesus Christ the Nazorean, [rise and] walk" (Acts 3:4–6 NABRE).

Peter then took the man by his right hand and pulled him to his feet. According to Luke the physician, "immediately his feet and ankles grew strong" (Acts 3:7 NABRE). The man stood on his feet and began to walk around, eventually running and literally jumping for joy. He went into the temple area with Peter and John and was immediately recognized as the man who always sat begging at the gate. People were astonished.

MIRACULOUS HEALINGS

Part of the fascination with the kingdom movement came from Jesus' widespread reputation as a healer. A major component of Jesus' mission appears to have been free healing, or at least, reaching out to people suffering from diseases of the body and spirit. Twenty-five of the thirty-seven miracles attributed to Jesus in the New Testament, or fully 65 percent, are miracles of healing. One of the first things the gospel of Mark says about Jesus is that he was a healer: "[Jesus] healed many who were sick with various diseases, and cast out many demons" (1:34). In the hypothetical sayings source that scholars call Q, there is the report of the Roman centurion who begged Jesus to heal his paralyzed and dying servant.[2] The same is true of the gospels of Luke and John where there are many incidents in which Jesus heals serious, even potentially fatal diseases.[3]

What's more, Jesus charged his followers to continue with this aspect of his mission. According to Matthew's account, Jesus called to him his twelve disciples and instructed them "to heal every disease and every affliction" (10:1). The hypothetical source material unique to Luke, which scholars call L, contains the unique incident in which Jesus sent out seventy-two of his disciples as emissaries of the kingdom, instructing them specifically to "cure the sick...and say to them, 'The kingdom of God is at hand for you'" (Luke 10:9 NABRE). In other words, free healing is one of the ways in which the kingdom of God is made real for people—at least according to the evangelist Luke who was, according to tradition at least, himself a physician. "Heal the sick, raise the dead, cleanse lepers, cast out demons," Jesus told his disciples in Matthew. "You received without paying; give without pay" (10:8). It is hardly surprising, then, that the leaders of the Jesus community quickly gained reputations of their own as healers—particularly Simon Peter.

Solomon's Portico refers to long covered walkways, built with columns, that topped the outer walls of the Temple Mount and provided shade from the sun. They can be seen in this model of first-century Jerusalem behind the temple and to the right.

An enormous crowd followed Peter and John as they moved from the temple to Solomon's Portico, helping the crippled man to walk. With the man clinging to him, Peter addressed a large crowd of Jews and, in essence, repeated much of what he said on the morning of Pentecost Sunday. "You Israelites, why are you amazed at this, and why do you look so intently at us as if we had made him walk by our own power or piety?" Peter asked (Acts 3:12 NABRE). What is remarkable is what Luke, a Greek-speaking Gentile, writes next. He betrays a thorough knowledge of the Jewish holy books, at least in the Greek translation known as the Septuagint, and easily follows Peter's scriptural references but also his blunt accusation against his fellow Jews.

The crowd had grown to an enormous size. From Solomon's Portico outward toward the temple itself, the crowds of people were jostling one another, trying to hear what Simon Peter was saying. In the distance, Simon and John could see sentries from the temple guard, standing and listening to every word Simon said. "By faith in [Jesus'] name, this man, whom you see and know," Simon Peter continued, his hands still holding up the former crippled man, "his name has made strong, and the faith that comes through it has given him this perfect health" (v. 16 NABRE).

Simon Peter stopped. The sentries from the temple guard were making their way through the crowds along with some priests and Sadducees. Suddenly, the guards rushed forward and, with their lances pointed toward the crowd, laid their hands on Simon and John, arresting them. With great shouts, the crowds pressed forward, screaming at the temple guards and the priests. The guards waved their lances menacingly, forcing the crowd to back off, as they then proceeded in a line back toward the tall buildings on the southern wall known as the Royal Stoa.

BEFORE THE AUTHORITIES

The guards took the two men into custody. The next day they were brought before a meeting of the Sanhedrin. Up until this time, the Great Sanhedrin, made up of seventy-one members, had met daily (except for on the Sabbath and during festivals) in the Hall of Hewn Stones located next door to the temple building itself on the north wall. But in AD 30, for reasons that are not entirely clear, the Sanhedrin began meeting instead in the Royal Stoa, the tall basilica built on the southern wall of the Temple Mount, overlooking the Rabbi Steps and the Hulda Gates. The authorities present included both the high priest Caiaphas and Annas, his father-in-law, as well as the priests John and Alexander and many other "leaders, elders, and scribes" (Acts 4:5 NABRE).

During the proceeding, Peter and John were questioned forcefully about what they were doing in the temple precincts, what had happened with the crippled man begging at the gate, and, most important, by whose authority they were doing what they were doing. According to the account in Acts, Peter spoke out fearlessly, now filled with the Spirit of God and no longer hiding what he believed.

"Leaders of the people and elders," he began. "If we are being examined today about a good deed done to a cripple, namely, by what means he was saved, then all of you and all the people of Israel should know that it was in the name of Jesus Christ the Nazorean whom you crucified, whom God raised from the dead; in his name this man stands before you healed," he said (Acts 4:8–10 NABRE).

Half of the men seated leapt to their feet with shouts of "Blasphemy!" echoing off the stone walls. Eventually the crowd of leaders quieted down. Everyone could see who and what Peter and John were—uneducated, ordinary men. Yet at the same time, the crippled man whom they had healed was standing there as well, waiting to be called to testify. He was middle-aged, over forty, yet standing upright before the entire assembly. The cripple was a living rebuke, proof that what Peter and John said was, at the very least, sincere. So calmer heads prevailed, and they ordered the two men out of the hall for a moment so the council members could confer.

As Luke recounts, the council members were genuinely conflicted over what to do with these strange Galilean fanatics. The entire city had heard about what happened in front of the temple gate the day before, with the crippled man getting up and walking. The Sanhedrin could not deny the event without looking like fools. At the same time, they did not want this bizarre movement to spread any further. In the end, they decided that they would let Peter and John go but with a stern warning.

When the two were brought back into the hall, Caiaphas, the high priest, addressed the pair directly. "We have decided to let you go this once," he announced with as much gravity as he could muster. "However, it's on the condition that you never speak or teach in the name of Jesus the Nazorean again" (vv. 17–18, paraphrased).

At this, Peter must have smiled.

"Whether it is right in the sight of God for us to obey you rather than God, you be the judges," he replied. "It is impossible for us not to speak about what we have seen and heard" (Acts 4:19–20 NABRE).

THE COMMUNITY GROWS

After Peter and John were released, they returned to the community house in the Upper City, to great shouts of acclaim. The entire community had been praying for their release but had feared the worst. They all gave thanks to God and prayed that, despite the threats of the Sanhedrin, they could continue to speak out with boldness and that God would continue to work through them to heal and to do great "signs and wonders" in the name of Jesus (Acts 4:30). Each day, more and more people appeared. Some were just curious. Others were intent on joining the new movement, which the followers of Jesus continued calling the Way.

One of the newcomers was a Greek-speaking Levite, a type of Jewish priest, named Yosef. He was from Cyprus, an island off the coast of Syria. He had sold a piece of property he owned and brought the money from the sale and placed it at the feet of the apostles. From then on, the community called him by the nickname Barnabas, which in Aramaic means "son of encouragement" (Acts 4:36). Although little is known about him, Barnabas was to become one of the most important leaders in the community and would accompany the apostle Paul on some of his missionary journeys throughout the Greek-speaking world of the Roman Empire. It's possible Barnabas was the cousin of the John Mark mentioned in Paul's letters who was held prisoner with Paul in Rome (Col. 4:10). According to an ancient tradition, he would eventually be martyred on his home island of Cyprus, in the city of Salamis, around the year AD 61.

Barnabas's donation of money was warmly accepted. Donations such as these allowed the apostles to dedicate themselves full-time to building up the kingdom movement—and that, in turn, allowed the group to grow very quickly. According to Acts, the apostles bore witness to the resurrection "with great power" and, as a result, "great favor was accorded them all" (4:33 NABRE). There was no needy person in the community because, as with Barnabas, anyone who owned property would sell it and share the proceeds with the entire group. At this stage, the community was of one mind and heart (vv. 34–35). Only later would divisions develop.

CHAPTER 18

THE TRIAL BEFORE
THE SANHEDRIN

For the sake of Christ, then, I am content with
weaknesses, insults, hardships, persecutions, and
calamities. For when I am weak, then I am strong.
—2 CORINTHIANS 12:10

Just a month or two later, a young Jewish man stood next to a pillar in
Solomon's Portico, seeking shade in the hot Judean sun. The young
man was of below average height, likely in his midtwenties, with a dark
beard; short, black hair; and piercing eyes. He went by the Hebrew
name of Sha'ul—Saul in Greek—the same name as the first king of
Israel. We don't know exactly what he looked like, but an apocryphal
second-century document, the *Acts of Thecla*, describes him as balding,
not very tall, with crooked or bowed legs, a long nose, and large eyes.[1]
Obviously an observant Jew, he wore the *tzitzit* on his outer cloak, but
his thinning hair was cut short in the Greek style. His eyes were blazing as he and a small group of friends watched what was taking place
before them.

On the surface, nothing important seemed to be happening. The
temple guard, standing nearby, didn't even glance in their direction. But

what Saul saw filled him with rage. Followers of the crucified so-called Messiah, Jesus of Nazareth, met daily in this place. Every morning, they came to the temple courtyard to pray and to spread what this young Jewish zealot believed to be lies and blasphemies among the people.

Even Jews who didn't believe in the superstition brought their sick relatives in case one of the leaders of the group, the Galilean fisherman named Simon, might walk past, believing that even Simon's shadow, as he walked by, might cure them. Saul had seen it with his own eyes. People would carry out the sick and dying on cots, both here and in the Lower City, with that false hope. Such was the folly of this evil sect in his eyes.

WHO WAS SAUL?

We don't know when the young Jewish zealot, Saul of Tarsus, first arrived in the land of Israel. The New Testament says that Saul was a witness to the lynching of the first martyr of the Jesus movement, Stephen, which probably occurred a year or more after Jesus' execution (Acts 7:58). Over the centuries, many have assumed that this meant Saul first came to Jerusalem as a young man, after Jesus was crucified. But neither his later letters nor the Acts of the Apostles confirm that. Saul could have come to Jerusalem as a teenager, studied Torah in the first-century equivalent of the *yeshivot*, or religious academies, that are still scattered all over Jerusalem today, but been away from the city when Jesus visited for the final time.

Saul had an unusual, multicultural background. A Roman citizen, he was from a Greek-speaking Jewish family in Tarsus, a major center of Greco-Roman culture and a city of 250,000 inhabitants, located just a few miles from the Mediterranean Sea on what is now the southern coast of Turkey. Tarsus was a cosmopolitan center for Hellenistic education, a city of philosophers, famous as the place where the Roman general Mark Antony and the Egyptian Queen Cleopatra first met.

According to a tradition recorded by St. Jerome in the late 300s, both of Paul's parents originally came from Gischala, located in the hills of northern Galilee.[2] It seems likely the family had a small factory in Tarsus where they manufactured the goat-hair textiles famous in the region, known as *cilicium*, made from goats bred on the Cilician plateau.[3] The warm, thick fabric was popular with sailors, but making it was hard work that required strong hands. Saul's family was certainly moderately affluent. It takes extra money to dispatch a son to Jerusalem to study religious law.

Saul was almost certainly fluent in Greek, since he was able later in life to address Greek crowds directly on the Areopagus hill in Athens (Acts 17:19). Yet he was also steeped in the language, traditions, and laws of the Jewish people. Saul was fiercely proud of his Jewish heritage. He would write that he was "a Hebrew of the Hebrews," a member of the tribe of Benjamin, someone who had, as he modestly put it, "advanced in Judaism beyond many of [his] peers" (Phil. 3:5, Gal. 1:14 CEB). At this stage in his life, in fact, Saul could rightly be considered a fanatic, a Jewish extremist who believed that heretics deserved not just ostracism or rebukes but death! When it came to the Torah, Saul would not tolerate compromise. God's laws were inviolate. Any Jew who ignored the Law deserved punishment—and it was said that the followers of Jesus believed they could pick and choose which *mitzvot* of the Torah they would obey.

CONFRONTATION AND TRIAL

Suddenly, there was a commotion in the crowd waiting in the portico out of the hot morning sun. The so-called emissaries of Jesus had arrived. They were led by Simon bar Jonah, the one they called the Rock. Saul scowled. They had been arrested only a short time before, and yet here they were, right back in the temple court. Something had to be done— and sooner rather than later.

Suddenly the captain of the temple guard and various court officers appeared. They were followed by dozens of guards. But, Saul noticed, their swords were not drawn. They actually appeared nervous. With hundreds of people crowded into the area, the guards obviously feared that their actions could spark a riot. Saul must have been stunned to hear the guards ask—*ask*—if Simon and his fellow emissaries would accompany them, and then to hear Simon agree without protest. Dozens of his friends followed, and Saul and his friends did as well. They all walked, in an enormous group, toward the large, marble-covered building on the opposite end of the temple court, where the Sanhedrin met.

According to the Talmud, there were actually two Jewish courts, or *bet-din*, called the Sanhedrin—the Bet Din Ha-Katan or "lesser" Sanhedrin, and the Bet Din Ha-Gadol, or the Great Sanhedrin. The Great Sanhedrin, traditionally made up of seventy-one judges, functioned as a kind of Supreme Court and legislature for the Jewish people, issuing definitive rulings on matters of Jewish law but also functioning as a kind of Jewish parliament under Roman occupation. It was led by a president, called a *nasi* or "prince." In the months after Jesus was executed, the president of the Sanhedrin was none other than Gamaliel himself, the renowned leader of the Hillel School. The author of Acts quotes Paul as saying that he was educated at the feet of this great Torah teacher (22:3).

Saul followed as the temple guard marched Simon and the others toward the meeting place of the Sanhedrin. Once inside the building, they stood in the area reserved for observers and watched as the members of the Sanhedrin filed into the building. Built in a modified Greek style by Herod the Great, the room used for this court was an amphitheater with three levels of seats. The accused stood in the center. Saul watched eagerly as the high priest, Caiaphas, walked into the building with his attendants. He was the same man who handed over the false prophet Jesus to Pilate.

Caiaphas stood on a raised platform, looking down at Simon and the others. The room was totally silent. Saul could even hear the spear of a temple guard scratching on the marble floor as he shifted his weight.

"We gave you strict orders [did we not?] to stop teaching in that name," Caiaphas nearly roared down at Simon. "Yet you have filled Jerusalem with your teaching and want to bring this man's blood upon us" (Acts 5:28 NABRE).

Simon and his friends stood in silence for many minutes. Finally, Simon spoke. "We must obey God rather than men," he said as loudly as he could, his voice echoing in the marble chamber (v. 29 NABRE).

Simon's rustic Galilean accent must have seemed almost comical in this magnificent building.

"The God of our ancestors raised Jesus, though you had him killed by hanging him on a tree," he continued. "God exalted him at his right hand as leader and savior to grant Israel repentance and forgiveness of sins" (vv. 30–31 NABRE).

There was a loud gasp in the room. Saul shook with fury at these words. He could see Caiaphas grow red with rage as well. Only God could forgive sins! To say that a man, any man, can forgive sins was blasphemy.

Simon ignored Caiaphas, who was twitching above him on his raised platform.

"We are witnesses of these things, as is the *ruah ha-kadosh*, the spirit of holiness, that God has given to those who obey him," said Simon (v. 32, paraphrased).

Suddenly, the entire building erupted in pandemonium. The members of the Sanhedrin were all shouting at once.

"Blasphemy! Blasphemy!" the voices roared. "Put them to death!"

Amid the uproar, Saul saw Gamaliel himself rise from his seat. He was likely over fifty at this time, probably with white hair, and commanded enormous respect.

He stood quietly until, once again, there was not a sound in the room.

Saul waited eagerly to hear what his old teacher would say, but part of him dreaded it. He knew Gamaliel too well.

"Fellow Israelites," the learned Torah scholar began. "Be careful what you are about to do to these men."

He paused for a moment, waiting.

"Some time ago, Theudas appeared, claiming to be someone important, and about four hundred men joined him, but he was killed, and all those who were loyal to him were disbanded and came to nothing."

Gamaliel walked slowly to the center of the speaking area. All eyes in the building were on him.

"After him came Judas the Galilean at the time of the census. He also drew people after him, but he too perished and all who were loyal to him were scattered."

Saul shook his head in disgust. He knew what his old teacher was about to say.

"So now I tell you, have nothing to do with these men, and let them go," Gamaliel continued. "For if this endeavor or this activity is of human origin, it will destroy itself." He paused again, looking around the court at each member.

"But if it comes from God, you will not be able to destroy them; you may even find yourselves fighting against God" (Acts 5:35–39 NABRE).

Saul looked up at the judges. He could see immediately that Gamaliel's words had had their effect. The judges, who only moments earlier were calling for Simon's death, now looked unsure of themselves.

Exactly as Saul expected, Caiaphas rose again. He consulted with several senior members of the Sanhedrin, then stepped up to his podium.

"Followers of Jesus, we have decided to give you one last chance," the chief priest bellowed, trying to muster as much authority as he could. "You are hereby ordered, once again, to cease speaking or teaching in the name of Jesus. For your impertinence, you will be flogged and then released" (v. 40, paraphrase).

And that was exactly what happened. Simon and his fellow emissaries broke out into small, tight smiles even though they were about to be beaten. Afterward, they returned to Solomon's Portico, telling everyone that they were celebrating "that they had been found worthy to suffer dishonor" for Jesus (v. 41 NABRE). Nothing appeared to stop them.

In both the temple and in people's homes, the "emissaries" continued to proclaim the dead Jesus as the Messiah. Saul and his friends met outside the Royal Stoa to discuss what had happened. It was clear that something had to be done. Beatings and stern lectures did not appear to dissuade these people. Sterner measures were required. And Saul knew that one day the emissaries would cross the line—and the people themselves would take action. It was only a matter of time.

CHAPTER 19

THE MARTYRDOM OF STEPHEN

"Brother will hand over brother to death, and the father his child; children will rise up against parents and have them put to death. You will be hated by all because of my name, but whoever endures to the end will be saved."
—MATTHEW 10:21–22 NABRE

Despite opposition, the Way grew rapidly. Entire neighborhoods in Jerusalem, primarily Jewish ones, were now made up of followers. Then there were those known as "fearers of the Name," or *yirei ha-Shem* in Hebrew. Known in Greek as *theophobes*, or "God-fearers," these were Gentiles who had converted to Judaism in some fashion, often attending synagogue services. The male God-fearers rarely took the extreme step of adult circumcision, though.

Soon a division developed between the Jews from Galilee who spoke Aramaic—and had known Jesus personally—and the Greek-speaking Hellenists who were later arrivals. The Hellenist members were often educated Jews from outside the land of Israel. The men often wore their hair much shorter than their rustic cousins, sometimes even partially shaving their beards. Third-century frescos found in some synagogues in Dura-Europos, located in eastern Syria, show what they may have looked like.[1] The men in the frescos wore the Greek-style *himation*, a woolen, blanketlike garment that looked almost like a Roman toga, with long stripes running vertically from shoulders to the hem. As for the women, they had a surprisingly modern look, their hair braided behind their heads, and often sporting stylish earrings (samples of which are on display in the Israel Museum in Jerusalem).

Eventually, the division between the Aramaic-speaking Galileans and the Greek-speaking "Hellenists" became more noticeable. The Hellenists complained that their widows were actually being cheated in the daily distribution of food supplies (Acts 6:1). In the earliest days, the community maintained a common purse, buying food supplies as a group and distributing them as needed to different members who lived in different houses around Jerusalem. The Greek-speaking members of the community thought the food distribution unfairly favored the Galileans—those who knew Jesus when he taught around the Sea of Galilee.

The Twelve called a meeting of the entire community to talk it out. "It is not right that we should give up preaching the word of God to serve tables," the apostles declared (Acts 6:2). As a result, they created what was, in effect, a new position within the community, what they called deacons, or *diakonoi* in Greek. This word simply means "waiter" in ordinary Greek, but it had a slightly different meaning in this context. The community would choose seven reputable men for this position, and later women as well.[2] They had to be people who were filled with the Spirit of God. They would tend to the physical needs of the community, acting as household managers, distributing food, paying the rent, and tending to other matters of domestic management, all while the Twelve and the other apostles focused on teaching and healing. The names of the seven men chosen at first are recorded in Acts: Stephen, Philip, Prochorus, Nicanor, Timon, Parmenas, and a Gentile-turned-convert to Judaism named Nicholas (Nicolaus) of Antioch (Acts 6:5). Even at this very early stage the Jesus community drew both Gentile converts to Judaism and pious Jews, including, Acts reports, a large group of priests, or *kohanim* (6:7).

The deacons must have been frustrated with their duties to some extent. Like all of the members of the Way, they were filled with the Spirit of God at baptism and eager to proclaim the kingdom to all who would listen. What's more, some of the deacons were highly educated in both the Torah and Greek philosophy, and more than willing to explain how Jesus was Israel's Messiah and the Savior of the world. One, a Greek-speaking Jew named Stephen, was particularly involved in active debates in Jerusalem.

WHO WAS STEPHEN?

According to Acts, Stephen was no mere manager but someone who was "full of grace and power" and who was able to work "great wonders and signs among the people" (6:8). Stephen became involved in an altercation with members of a specific synagogue, called the Synagogue of the Freedmen. Archaeologists have now confirmed that many synagogues dotted the landscape in first-century Israel, and some were quite wealthy, such as one uncovered in 2009 in Magdala on the Sea of Galilee.[3] The "Freedmen" or "Libertines" (*libertinoi* in Greek) of this particular synagogue were possibly the descendants of former Jewish slaves who had been captured when the Roman general Pompey had conquered Jerusalem in 63 BC. The synagogue was made up of Hellenized Jews, like Stephen, who were nevertheless zealous for Torah and temple. Describing the expulsion of the Jews from Rome under the emperor Claudius, the Roman historian Tacitus speaks of "four thousand of the freed-men or Libertine class."[4] Archaeologists are also confident that Greek-speaking synagogues like the one described in Acts existed; in 1913, a team uncovered a plaque in Jerusalem that identified one Theodotus son of Vettenus—a very Greek-sounding name—as a founder, priest, and the head of a synagogue.[5]

In the first century as today, Jews from all over the world met in synagogues in Jerusalem to study Torah. One of these, the Synagogue of Freedmen, became involved in disputes with the Greek-speaking servant-leader (deacon) Stephen.

It's possible that Stephen was himself actually a former member of the synagogue of the Freedmen. According to Acts, members of this synagogue were engaged in heated debates with Stephen. Within a year or less of the crucifixion, Jesus' followers were already engaged in worship practices that shocked pious Jews to their cores. Part of the evidence for this is the reaction of members of the Synagogue of Freedmen to what Stephen was telling them. Proclaiming Jesus the Messiah was no big deal. It merely meant you were a misguided fool. Proclaiming Jesus the Lord of heaven and earth, sitting at the right hand of God, invoking his name in prayer and supplication—that was something else.

The account in Acts insists that the synagogue members were unable to answer Stephen's arguments or to neutralize the "Spirit" with which he made them. So they "instigated" or perhaps bribed men to claim that they heard Stephen utter blasphemous words against Moses and God (6:10–11). We don't know the specifics of these accusations, only that it was alleged Stephen "never ceases" saying things against the "holy place"—that is, the temple—and against the Torah (v. 13). Stephen's accusers then leveled the same charge against him that others leveled against Jesus, that Jesus the Nazorean would one day destroy the temple and the "customs that Moses delivered to us" (6:14).

According to Acts, Stephen's opponents "stirred up the people" against him, and then the elders and scribes seized him and brought him before the Sanhedrin (6:12). It is not clear from the text if this was primarily a mob riot or an actual judicial action. However it happened, Stephen was brought before the Jewish council. The members of the Sanhedrin were doubtless growing weary of this odious sect.

STEPHEN'S TRIAL

The high priest, Caiaphas, stepped forward once again. He listened to the loud accusations the synagogue members leveled against Stephen. Then he asked Stephen a simple question: "Is this true?" (Acts 7:1 ISV).

Stephen's answer was a long, rambling speech that is recorded in painstaking detail in Acts. According to Acts, Stephen first gave the learned members of the Sanhedrin a lengthy history lesson, outlining in considerable detail the history of the Jewish people from the days of Abraham up through the enslavement in Egypt and exodus to the promised land of Israel. He dwelled at length on a prophecy of Moses, recorded in the book of Deuteronomy, that God would send to Israel a future prophet like Moses. From there, Stephen described how Solomon built a temple for God but added that "the Most High does not live in houses made by human hands," quoting the prophet Isaiah to prove his point (7:48 NIV). At this comment, a gasp of outrage no doubt arose from the assembled priests. Who was this Greek-speaking fool to dare address the holy Sanhedrin in such an impertinent manner?

But Stephen was just warming up.

"Which of the prophets did your ancestors *not* persecute?" he shouted above the din, in what must have seemed like a mad frenzy. "They put to death those who foretold the coming of the righteous one, whose betrayers and murderers you have now become. You received the law as transmitted by angels, but you did not observe it" (vv. 52–53 NABRE).

Saul of Tarsus, watching the proceedings from a side aisle, no doubt smiled. This crazy fanatic had sealed his fate. By now, men young and old were rushing at Stephen, shaking their fists at him. It was only the presence of the temple guards that kept them from beating him to death on the spot. Stephen stood, looking upward, and announced that he could see Jesus at that very moment, standing at the right hand of God (v. 56).

By then, Saul almost felt sorry for this deluded lunatic. He was obviously insane . . . or possessed by a demon. The Sanhedrin had no need for a formal judgment. The judgment of the crowd was sufficient. According to Acts, the assembly "covered their ears" at the blasphemy and rushed at Stephen en masse (Acts 7:57 NABRE).

THE FIRST MARTYR

The traditional punishment for blasphemy, as described in the Torah, is death by stoning. According to Leviticus 24:14, the people are to "bring out of the camp the one who cursed, and let all who heard him lay their hands on his head, and let all the congregation stone him." In the Second Temple period of 530 BC to AD 70, the preferred practice was for the executioners to hurl the guilty party from a high place at least twice the height of a man's body and then, if he or she survived the fall, for the principal accuser to drop one large rock directly on the chest, with the intent of causing instant death. Unlike crucifixion, the purpose of stoning was *not* to torture the prisoner in a prolonged agony but to kill him or her quickly, as an act of mercy. If the single stone dropped was not sufficient, then, and only then, would the onlookers attempt to finish off the accused by throwing additional stones.

The account of Stephen's martyrdom in Acts has given rise to many questions. Where were the Romans when all this was going on? If the

Sanhedrin could order the execution of Stephen for blasphemy, why could they not have done the same thing with Jesus? Why the rigmarole of Jesus' trial before Pilate?

The New Testament does not say where Stephen was taken to be stoned. Many rocky cliffs and hillocks surrounding Jerusalem could be candidates. The Torah insists that the condemned person must be executed "outside the camp." From traditions contained in the Talmud and ancient Christian writings, the Place of Stoning was likely a rocky precipice just north of the city, near the cave known as Jeremiah's Grotto. Photographs taken in 1900 show this location to contain rocky cliffs hundreds of feet high.

The execution squad probably marched Stephen to the rocky cliffs and hills just north of Jerusalem's city walls. Once there, the executioners would have stripped Stephen naked. According to the Mishnah, men were typically stripped naked before execution by stoning, but women were not. Acts reports that the men executing Stephen laid their outer garments at the feet of the young man named Saul (7:58).

PUBLIC DOMAIN

Photographs taken in 1900 north of Jerusalem's Damascus Gate show the high rocky cliffs from which the first martyr of the Way, the Greek-speaking Jew Stephen, may have been thrown.

If Stephen was thrown off a rocky ledge at this spot, he would have endured a near-fatal blow but must have lingered for some minutes. Acts reports that the men were stoning Stephen—a sign that he survived the initial fall and dropping of the large stone. Yet, remarkably, Stephen forgave his executioners. "Lord Jesus, receive my spirit," he said. He then fell to his knees and cried out in a loud voice, "Lord, do not hold this sin against them," and then died (Acts 7:59–60 NABRE).

The act of forgiving his executioners is a direct parallel to what Jesus did on the cross—an incident reported only by the author of Luke. Clearly, the author of Luke and Acts wanted to highlight the similarities between the martyrdoms of Jesus and Stephen. However, it's also plausible that reports of such a shocking and unnatural act of forgiveness would have filled the streets of Jerusalem, and certainly the homes of Jesus' closest followers. We know from reports of how later Christians met their deaths in the arenas of Rome that many strove, in conscious imitation of Jesus on the cross, to offer prayers of forgiveness immediately before their deaths.[6] It is therefore possible that Stephen was the first to do so, deliberately offering a prayer of forgiveness as he breathed his last.

Members of the community, who watched the horror unfold before their very eyes, collected Stephen's body and loudly lamented him. According to ancient but not verified traditions, the great Jewish rabbi Gamaliel and Nicodemus buried Stephen in a hidden location just outside of Jerusalem's walls, perhaps in the same ancient tombs found in this area in the nineteenth century.

A PATTERN OF VIOLENCE

Acts tells us undeniably that the Pharisee Saul witnessed the entire incident, and perhaps even supervised it. The contrast between the horror of the execution and Stephen's benign forgiveness must have haunted him. But he was not to be dissuaded from his mission. According to Acts, the execution of Stephen sparked the beginning of a severe persecution of the Jesus community in Jerusalem (8:1). Probably within a year of the crucifixion, or even just months, Jewish authorities went house to house in Jerusalem and the villages of Judea, hunting for members of the Jesus sect. While the Romans permitted them to operate freely in Jerusalem so long as there were no insurrections and everyone paid their taxes, the members of the temple aristocracy were inflamed.

If identified and caught, the followers of Jesus were almost certainly flogged, receiving the Torah-prescribed punishment of not more than forty lashes (Deut. 25:2–3). It was as Jesus himself predicted: his followers would be handed over to courts and beaten in synagogues because of him (Mark 13:9). Saul organized searches throughout Jerusalem. He would drag out men and women suspected of being followers of Jesus and hand them over to temple authorities for imprisonment (Acts 8:3). The first persecution of the early Jesus community was in full swing just months after Jesus himself had been tortured and killed.

As a result of what came to be called the Great Persecution, many of the members of the Way fled Jerusalem. They packed their belongings, took their children, and scattered throughout the countryside of Judea, Samaria, and beyond, staying with families and friends.

CHAPTER 20

PROTECTING THE GOSPEL

As for every matter of wisdom and understanding about which
the king consulted them, he found them ten times better than
all the magicians and conjurers who were in all his realm.
—DANIEL 1:20 NASB

The Jewish authorities would no longer tolerate the proselytizing
efforts of the Way. As a result, the followers of Jesus fled Jerusalem
and its surrounding villages and entered Samaritan territory. The Jesus
movement had already interacted with the Samaritan community,
which was, in itself, a shocking and subversive development. In the first
century, Jews and Samaritans despised one another even though—or
perhaps because—they were related ethnically and religiously. One of
the apostles, Philip, met great success in this thriving, half-pagan region.
Acts reports that the "crowds with one accord paid attention to what was
being said by Philip, when they heard him and saw the signs that he did"
(8:6). Once again, the principal signs that accompanied Philip's efforts
were the exorcisms of unclean spirits and the cure of "paralyzed or lame"
people (8:7).

By this time, Samaria was a region of vast religious diversity in
which conservative Samaritans lived side by side with Roman and Greek
pagans. Once a thriving religious community of more than one million
people, today they number fewer than a thousand in four large families.[1]

Samaria used to be part of the Northern Kingdom of Israel. After King Solomon died around 931 BC, the ancient Israelites were divided into two kingdoms—the northern ten tribes of Israel and the southern two tribes of Judah. Jerusalem was the capital of the Southern Kingdom, and Samaria of the north.

Samaria was conquered by the Assyrians, who performed a kind of ethnic cleansing on the Jews and settled their own people in the north. In Jewish eyes, the remaining population in Samaria became an abhorrent mixture of Israelite and pagan peoples.[2] Yet the Samaritans believed that they practiced the "original," more ancient Israelite religion, handed down from Moses. That is because the inhabitants of Judah were themselves deported from the land and sent to Babylonia—where, the Samaritans believed, they picked up all sorts of strange, pagan ideas from the Zoroastrian priests before returning to Jerusalem in 539 BC.[3]

SIMON THE MAGICIAN

In Samaria, one of the strangest incidents of the early Jesus movement occurred—an incident that would be reflected in the history of early Christianity for centuries. There was in the area a talented and inquisitive man named Simon who was well-known as a religious figure and even a magician. He was known by his stage name, "the power of God that is called Great" (Acts. 8:10). Simon had operated in the region for years, but when the apostle Philip arrived, proclaiming the kingdom and inviting the Samaritans and others to join the Way, Simon paid attention. In fact, Philip baptized Simon, and the young magician became devoted to Philip. As a professional wonder-worker himself, Simon was astounded by the signs that Philip performed, which, as we've seen, consisted largely of free healing and exorcisms.

Word reached Jerusalem of the success of the Samaritan mission. Both Peter and John decided to risk discovery and possible arrest and traveled north to Samaria to join Philip. While there, they laid their hands on new members so that they would receive the gifts of the Holy Spirit. This intrigued Simon. He asked Peter if he could be given this power as well—and even offered Peter and John money if they would give this power to him. This is the origin of the word and concept of *simony*, which means the sale of holy things.

The apostles were appalled. "May your money perish with you," snapped Peter, with a flash of his old anger, "because you thought that you could buy the gift of God with money" (Acts 8:20 NABRE).

Simon was contrite. He asked Peter to pray for him and that nothing of what he said would come upon him.

The incident with the person who became known as Simon Magus illustrates just how soon Jesus' message of the kingdom was corrupted. Very quickly, within a year or two of the crucifixion, religious seekers and charlatans such as Simon Magus began to modify Jesus of Nazareth's message—to put their own "spin" on what he had taught.[4] We have more substantial evidence of this process in the documents known as the Gnostic Gospels.[5]

There were at least thirty of these gospels written in the first centuries of Christianity besides the four canonical ones in the New Testament. We have the complete texts of only five (the Gospel of Thomas, the Secret Book of James, the Dialogue of the Savior, the Gospel of Mary, and most recently, the Gospel of Judas). We have fragments of seven. Most of these Gnostic Gospels date from centuries after the canonical Gospels and merely put their own theosophical ideas into the mouth of Jesus of Nazareth. Different groups quickly "co-opted" the fame of Jesus to spread their own messages.[6]

This helps explain the tremendous emphasis throughout the New Testament on protecting the authentic teachings of Jesus—what became known as the "deposit" (*paratheke*) of faith (1 Tim. 6:20). The incident with Simon Magus, which happened soon after the crucifixion, illustrated for the early Jesus movement why it was so important to pass on the teaching of the apostles—those who had had *direct* personal contact with Jesus while he was preaching in Galilee.

PHILIP AND THE ETHIOPIAN

Philip did not stay only in Samaria. After the incident with Simon Magus, Philip was inspired to travel south to Gaza, on the Mediterranean coast. Acts says that an angel spoke to Philip and told him to take the desert route, the road from Jerusalem to Gaza that still exists today (8:26). The text doesn't actually say where Philip was heading. Gaza was an ancient port city in southwestern Israel on the road from Israel to Egypt. Originally settled by Canaanites, it was later controlled by the Egyptians and Philistines and was where the judge Samson met his death.

As the Acts of the Apostles show, the people of Ethiopia have had a connection to Israel and Judaism for millennia. Thousands of Ethiopian Jews, known as *falashim*, immigrated to Israel under the Law of Return.

While Philip was traveling south on the road to the ancient seaport, he met an Ethiopian eunuch from the court of Candace, the queen of the Ethiopians, who was returning home from Jerusalem (Acts 8:27). The text of Acts is ambiguous. It implies that Candace is the queen's name, but it's more likely that what was meant was *kandake*, the word for queen in the ancient (now dead) Meroitic language of the Sudan. One theory is that the queen referred to was Amanitore, a Nubian *kandake* of the ancient Kushite kingdom of Meroë south of Egypt, who reigned from 1 BC to AD 50.[7] According to Acts, the eunuch was a high court official, in charge of the queen's entire treasury, and had been in Jerusalem to worship in the temple (8:27). This meant he was a *theophobes*, a "God-fearer" who practiced the tenets of Judaism without formally converting. There had long been ties between Israel and the peoples of northeastern Africa, and they continue to this day—so much that the modern State of Israel accepted the application of the *falashim* of Ethiopia, black Africans who claimed to be Jewish, to immigrate to Israel under the Law of Return.

Philip saw the eunuch sitting in his chariot as it moved slowly along. He was reading the scroll of the prophet Isaiah. "Do you understand what you are reading?" Philip asked, coming up beside the vehicle. The eunuch smiled. "How can I, unless someone guides me?" he replied (Acts 8:30–31). The chariot stopped. Philip took the scroll from the man and read it. Despite what some modern scholars claim, some Jews in this period, although perhaps not a very large number, could read the ancient Hebrew holy books.[8] According to Acts, the passage the eunuch was reading was providential:

> Like a lamb that is led to the slaughter,
> and like a sheep that before its shearers is silent,
> so he opened not his mouth.
> By oppression and judgment he was taken away;
> and as for his generation, who considered
> that he was cut off out of the land of the living? (Isaiah 53:7–8)

"I beg you, about whom is the prophet saying this?" [the eunuch asked]. "About himself, or about someone else?" (Acts 8:34 NABRE).

It was a heaven-sent opening. As they traveled along together, Philip told the eunuch all about Jesus of Nazareth and the events that had just transpired in Jerusalem. He explained that Jesus was the Jewish Messiah, the world's Savior long foretold by Israel's prophets. He revealed that a person could become one of his followers and join the kingdom movement by being baptized with water in his name and receiving the Spirit of God in his heart.

Even in the dry Negev Desert, where Philip likely encountered the Ethiopian eunuch, it's possible to find streams of water—as this stream at the bottom of the Wadi Qelt shows.

As Acts tells the story, the two men came upon some water as they traveled. No one knows precisely where this water source was located. However, in the blazing hot Negev there are, down in the deep valleys called wadis, or *nahalim* in Hebrew, many streams of cool, clear water.[9]

"See, here is water!" the eunuch called out, no doubt spying a small stream down in a valley below them. "What prevents me from being baptized?" (Acts 8:36). According to Acts, the eunuch ordered the chariot to stop and then both he and Philip "went down" into the water and Philip baptized the Ethiopian official right there (v. 38). The eunuch went away rejoicing and Philip headed for Azotus, the Greek name for Ashdod, a thriving seaside village north of Gaza. He proclaimed the gospel in all the villages along the Mediterranean as he traveled along the coast north to Caesarea Maritima, the seat of the Roman government in Israel and where Pontius Pilate still spent most of his time. Philip's journey from the God-fearing Ethiopian to the center of Roman power prefigured, in a dramatic way, what would happen to the Jesus community as a whole in the months and years to come.

CHAPTER 21

THE ROAD TO DAMASCUS

Then the LORD spoke to you from the midst of the fire; you
heard the sound of words, but you saw no form—only a voice.
—DEUTERONOMY 4:12 NASB

Why would Saul, a Greek-speaking Jew from the diaspora, make
it his mission to hunt down the adherents of a new group of fellow Jews like the Jesus movement? There were all sorts of strange and
unusual groups in Jerusalem in those days. Some, like the Essenes, were
practically treasonous, insisting that the temple itself had been corrupted
and that true Jews should have nothing to do with it. Why would the
followers of an executed prophet deserve such fanatical investigation?

Yet that is precisely what Saul of Tarsus was doing in the first two
years after Jesus of Nazareth was crucified. We know this from both
the account in Acts and from the letters that Saul himself wrote later.
According to Acts, Saul breathed "murderous threats" against the
disciples (9:1 NABRE). He went from house to house, dragged off both
men and women, and put them in prison. In his letters to the Jesus community in Galatia in central Turkey, perhaps written around the year
AD 50, Saul of Tarsus says he "persecuted the church of God violently
and tried to destroy it" (Gal. 1:13). The question is: why?[1]

It was not because the followers of Jesus were denying the Torah. They weren't. The disciples continued to meet and pray in the temple and to observe the Jewish feasts, such as Shavuot. Nor can it be said that Saul's rage was ignited because Jesus' followers claimed he was the Messiah. There were many messianic claimants in that era, both before and after Jesus, and there is no evidence that any of their followers or supporters were persecuted.

No, it was *something else* . . . some other aspect of the Jesus movement that sparked official opposition among Jewish authorities and from Saul of Tarsus. There is a clue buried in Acts that cuts to the heart of the matter.[2] Saul of Tarsus persecuted the Jesus community because the members of the Way invoked "the name" of Jesus of Nazareth (3:6) in a way that struck Saul, and many other Jews, as blasphemous (26:11). Saul hunted down the members of this odd sect not because they believed that the crucified Jesus was the Messiah, but because they invoked his name the same way that Jews invoke *ha-Shem*, the Name, the word Orthodox Jews use to this day to refer to God.

BOUND FOR DAMASCUS

Saul of Tarsus had connections with the temple leadership, even though he was probably only in his late twenties. Acts says that Saul went to the high priest himself, still Joseph Caiaphas, and asked him to write letters to the synagogue in Damascus; if Saul found any members of the Way in Damascus, he wanted permission to bring them back to Jerusalem in chains (9:1–2). If this is accurate, and there is no reason to suspect it isn't, Saul was asking for political and legal power the high priest did not have the authority to give.

Damascus at this time was a semiautonomous city-state. One of the world's oldest cities, it was and is located in southwestern Syria near the Lebanese border. Saul was attempting to assert legal jurisdiction over Jewish residents of Damascus with the understanding that he could arrest them, with or without the knowledge of local officials, and effect a kind of legal kidnapping.

Unlike other cities in the region, Damascus was a strongly Middle Eastern city with an Aramaic-speaking population largely indifferent to Greek culture and ways. After Pompey swept through the city in 63 BC, the Romans allowed the residents to maintain semiautonomous control. At the time Saul of Tarsus was journeying to the city, it was ruled by a governor appointed by the Nabatean king.[3] It was a key transit station on the caravan routes to the East; exotic characters from all over the region flocked there to do business.

Friends and supporters of Jesus took up residence in the city, perhaps even before Jesus was arrested. Later, following the initial burst of persecution that began with the stoning of Stephen, more followers made their way to Damascus. By the time Saul reached the city, late in the year AD 33 or early 34, there was already a thriving colony of Jesus' disciples living there.

Paul traveled to Damascus along a well-maintained Roman road similar to this one on the border of Jordan and Syria.

The journey from Jerusalem to Damascus was about one hundred and fifty miles of relatively difficult travel. Saul could have taken any number of routes, but the most likely was the direct route north across Samaria to Galilee. He would have traveled on good roads past Mount Gerizim to the Samaritan capital city of Sebaste, all the way to Caesarea Philippi. From Caesarea Philippi, it was a straight shot northeast across what is now called the Golan Heights, directly to Damascus. It was a complicated journey that could have taken as much as two weeks to complete on foot or horseback.

THE APPEARANCE OF THE RISEN JESUS

Along this road, Saul would have a shocking experience that would change his life forever. Acts says that Saul's experience of the risen Jesus occurred near Damascus, so it was on the final leg of the journey from Caesarea Philippi (22:6).[4] This event is described in three different passages in Acts (9:3–9, 22:6–11, and 26:13–18) as well as in Saul's own letters. The initial text in Acts says that a light from the sky suddenly "flashed around him" and Saul fell to the ground. He then heard a voice saying to him, "Saul, Saul, why do you persecute me?" (9:3–4 NIV).

Staggered, lying on the ground, the fierce Pharisee blurted out, "Who are you, Lord?"

"I am Jesus, whom you are persecuting," the voice said in reply. "Now get up and go into the city, and you will be told what you must do" (vv. 5–6 NIV).

The men with Saul stood speechless because, the first passage in Acts says, they had heard the voice as well but saw no one. Later in Acts, the author reports Paul's own testimony about his conversion to the Jews in Jerusalem. He quotes Paul as saying that the men with him saw the light but did *not* hear the voice (22:9).[5]

The bright light left Saul blind. He had to be led by the hand the rest of the way into Damascus where, for the following three days, he neither ate nor drank anything, still unable to see a thing.

During this time, Saul was not the only one to have an experience of the risen Jesus. A man named Ananias also heard Jesus speaking to him. In a vision, Jesus told Ananias that he was to go to the house of a man named Judas, located in "the street called Straight," and inquire about a man from Tarsus named Saul (Acts 9:11). The voice told Ananias that this man Saul was in the house praying, and that he, Saul, had seen in a vision a man named Ananias coming to him and laying his hands on him, so he could regain his sight.

WIKIPEDIA

The mile-long street called Straight, designed by the Greek city planner Hippodamus, still exists in Damascus where it is known, in Arabic, as Al-Shari al-Mustaqim. At one end is a Roman-era triumphal arch restored in 1947.

But Saul's reputation had already preceded him because Ananias was afraid. He replied to the voice that Saul was a dangerous fellow, that he,

Ananias, had heard of the evil things Saul had done to Jesus' followers in Jerusalem, and that Saul was in Damascus to arrest all those who called upon Jesus' name. The voice of Jesus told Ananias that Saul was chosen to carry his name "before the Gentiles and kings and the children of Israel," and that he, Jesus, would show him what he would have to suffer in the future for his name (9:15–16).

Ananias left his own house and walked to the home of Judas, on the street called Straight. He entered the house and found things just as he had heard in his vision. He laid his hands on Saul. "Saul, my brother," Ananias said, "the Lord has sent me, Jesus who appeared to you on the way by which you came, that you may regain your sight and be filled with the holy Spirit." The texts adds that immediately "things like scales" fell from Saul's eyes and he regained his sight. He stood up and was immediately baptized (Acts 9:17–19 NABRE).

The street called Straight still exists. The actual level of the Roman roadway is about twenty feet below the level of the current street. After the Greeks conquered the city, a Greek architect named Hippodamus of Miletus created a new grid layout for the city's streets.[6] One of these streets, called in Latin the *Via Recta*, extended sixteen hundred yards in a straight line and became a main shopping street during and after the Roman period (and still is to this day). A Roman triumphal arch, dating to the time of Saul, has been raised and reconstructed at one end of the street. There is also an underground stone structure nearby, a few blocks north, which is alleged to be the remains of Ananias's house and which has been revered as such since at least the sixth century.

PAUL JOINS THE DISCIPLES

Saul, who was eventually renamed Paul, recounted his own version of his conversion in his letters. In his first letter to the Corinthians, Paul recounts the detailed report of Jesus' resurrection appearances mentioned earlier: first to Peter/Cephas and the Twelve, then to five hundred brothers at once, then to James and all the apostles. Paul ends by saying that last of all Jesus "appeared" to him also, "as to one untimely born" (1 Cor. 15:3–8). However, he doesn't describe in any more detail what this "appearance" was.

In another letter, written to the residents of Galatia, he says that the gospel that he preached he received "by revelation from Jesus Christ" (Gal. 1:12 NIV) and that God "was pleased to reveal his Son in me" (1:15–16 NIV). Some people make much of the word *in* (Greek *en*), but it can also be translated "to." Thus, unlike the detailed accounts of Jesus' resurrection appearances to others, such as Mary Magdalene and the Twelve, the appearance of Jesus to Paul is often understood by many New Testament scholars more as a vision than as a physical manifestation.[7]

Yet however modern readers view the appearance of the risen Jesus to Saul of Tarsus, his was the most famous and dramatic conversion in history. He went from being a merciless persecutor of the kingdom movement to its greatest and most influential champion. The author of Acts makes clear that this transformation was virtually instantaneous. Within days of his baptism, Saul began to proclaim the risen Jesus in the synagogues of Damascus, insisting that Jesus was the Son of God and using his considerable rabbinic training to show that he was the Jewish Messiah. Naturally enough, the author of Acts reports great skepticism and astonishment among the members of the Way in the city. "Is not this the man who in Jerusalem ravaged those who call upon this name," they asked, "and came here expressly to take them back in chains to the chief priests?" (9:21 NABRE).

But then Saul of Tarsus, the fierce Jewish zealot, simply vanished. The encounter with the risen Jesus on the road to Damascus transformed him. By his own account in his letter to the Galatians, he did not consult with any leaders in the Jesus movement but simply slipped off on his own "into Arabia," which could have been anywhere from eastern Syria south to the Arabian peninsula (1:17). When he returned after about three years, he was no longer Saul the Zealot but Paul the apostle.

Paul then made the long journey back to Jerusalem—the first time he had been there in three years since he left to arrest Jesus' followers in Damascus. It was now AD 36. When Paul arrived in the holy city, he tried to make contact with the apostles—but to his dismay, no one would see him. Everyone assumed, quite naturally, that his conversion was a trick and Saul the persecutor was back to his old habits. However, after days of fruitless searching, Paul eventually made contact with none other than Barnabas, the Greek-speaking Levite who had joined the community in the weeks immediately after Pentecost and who had become one of the most prominent leaders. Barnabas took Paul under his wing and brought him to the apostles in Jerusalem. He recounted to them how Paul had personally seen the risen Jesus and spoken to him, and how he had boldly proclaimed the gospel message in Damascus (Acts 9:27). By Paul's own account, in his letter to the Galatians, he spent two weeks with both Simon Peter and James, the brother or stepbrother of Jesus, who had become one of the main leaders in the community, and did not see any other apostles (1:18–19). This apparent discrepancy with Luke's account in Acts can perhaps be explained by different definitions of *apostles*. If an apostle was someone who had been with Jesus during his mission and seen him alive after the crucifixion, then Barnabas was not an apostle. In any event, Paul spent two intense weeks with Simon Peter and James, no doubt questioning them intently about Jesus' life and teachings.

According to Acts, Paul soon began proclaiming Jesus in Jerusalem. He even debated with Hellenists—the Greek-speaking Jews who were not members of the Jesus community—and quickly aroused their ire. Apparently Paul had a singular talent for stirring up trouble, because Acts reports that very quickly members of the Hellenistic Jewish community sought to kill him (9:29). As a result, and no doubt in an effort to prevent another flare-up of persecution against the community, the disciples escorted Paul down to the port at Caesarea Maritima and put him quietly on a ship back to his hometown of Tarsus.

While the text does not say this, there is little doubt that the

Jesus community in Jerusalem was glad to see Paul—convert or no convert—on his way. He had been nothing but trouble for them since the very beginning. What they didn't know was that this fierce and argumentative Pharisee would one day become one of the greatest defenders and promoters of Jesus' message in history. In many cases, he would single-handedly create entire communities of believers throughout the Mediterranean world.

CHAPTER 22

THE HEALING
MINISTRY OF PETER

Is anyone among you sick? Let them call the elders of the church to
pray over them and anoint them with oil in the name of the Lord.
—JAMES 5:14 NIV

After Saul of Tarsus left Jerusalem the first time, things quieted
down considerably. Active persecution of Jesus' disciples initially
eased off, at least for a time. Then, in the year AD 36, around the time
when Paul returned for a brief visit, an uprising occurred in Samaria
that would eventually result in the Roman governor, Pontius Pilate,
being recalled from his post. Early in that year, a Samaritan appeared
who claimed to be the long-awaited prophet that Moses promised God
would send to rescue his people (Deut. 18:14–18). One of the cherished
beliefs of both the Samaritans and the nationalistic Essenes was that
the Messiah would be identified by the finding of certain sacred vessels,
which were buried somewhere on the Samaritans' holy Mount Gerizim.
This is what the Samaritan prophet said he would do: he would take the
people up the mountain and show them the lost treasures!

According to the first-century Jewish historian Josephus, the
Samaritan prophet gathered together a huge mass of followers—a group
large enough to excite the worry of the Romans in Caesarea. As a result,

Pilate himself led a force of one thousand Roman troops made up of both mounted cavalry and heavy infantry. Before the Samaritan prophet could even begin his pilgrimage up the holy mountain, the Roman force, their spears and short swords gleaming in the sun, descended on the masses of people, killing many and putting the rest to flight. Pilate ordered the wounded and many of the leaders arrested—and then, with the severity for which he was famous, ordered the prisoners executed without trial.[1]

The Samaritan community was understandably outraged. Why did Pilate feel it necessary to slaughter so many people when all they were doing was going on a religious pilgrimage? The Samaritan leaders appealed to the Roman legate in Syria, Lucius Vitellius, a consul and father of a future emperor. This was the final straw for Pilate, who had been the subject of numerous complaints during his ten-year reign as governor. Vitellius ordered Pilate to return to Rome and give the emperor himself an account of his actions. Pilate obeyed orders and traveled to Rome, but he arrived just after Emperor Tiberius died, which occurred on March 16, AD 37. Vitellius appointed his friend Marcellus to take Pilate's place as a temporary caretaker. Then later in AD 37, a new governor, Marullus, arrived to take charge as the seventh prefect to rule Judea.

The next few years brought a time of growth and consolidation in Judea—between AD 37, after Paul was put on a boat back home to Tarsus, and the persecution that broke out in AD 43 under King Herod Agrippa. Acts says simply that the community in Judea, Galilee, and Samaria "had peace" (9:31). The community had spread throughout the land of Israel due to the first persecution in Jerusalem, and so now there were Jesus communities established in many different villages and towns in the region. And as usual, the community was continuing to grow at a rapid pace.

At first the community focused entirely on recruiting fellow Jews to the kingdom movement—but then, very quickly, they attracted Greek-speaking Hellenists who resided in and around the holy city. As we saw earlier, Jesus saw the kingdom of God as a tiny mustard seed—a leaven for the entire world that would start first with the people of Israel and then gradually spread to "all nations" (Matt. 28:19). Jesus insisted that his followers concentrate at first on the "lost sheep of the house of Israel" (Matt. 10:6), because, he said, "salvation is from the Jews" (John 4:22). But Jesus' outreach was far more inclusive than what his followers could have imagined. He showed it, for example, in his visits to Samaritan villages and pagan cities such as Tyre and Caesarea Philippi, and in his willingness to praise the faith of non-Jews, such as that of the Roman centurion at Capernaum (Luke 7:9). Later, the Jesus community followed this same pattern. Having first witnessed to the Jews, the small Jesus community was driven outward, expanding their reach to include the "heretics" or "half-Jews" in Samaria.[2] Eventually, the community reached out to the "God-fearers," those Gentiles who worshipped the Jewish God and did their best to follow a Jewish way of life. Finally, it would embrace all-out pagans, those Gentiles who knew little if anything about Judaism and learned about the one God solely through the teachings of Jesus of Nazareth.

PETER'S OUTREACH GROWS

At first, Simon Peter appears to have concentrated on his fellow Jews. This lasted roughly for a dozen years, from about AD 31 until AD 43. During this period, Simon Peter was the leader of the Jesus community in Jerusalem and throughout Israel. His work centered mostly in Israel, but that would soon change. Eventually, he, like Paul, would travel far from Israel and would bring the message of the kingdom into the very heart of the Roman Empire—the city of Rome itself.

Many readers of the New Testament assume that Simon Peter was a simpleton. But that is a big assumption. First, it's possible that he could speak Greek fluently and was considerably more sophisticated than he is given credit for. Simon Peter's hometown of Bethsaida, mentioned in all four gospels, was located in the heavily Hellenized district of Gaulanitis where Greek was the common language.[3] What's more, Simon Peter headed up a fairly prosperous fishing enterprise—prosperous enough that he could afford to hire employees. To do business on this scale, selling his catch to the international fishing exporters operating in nearby Magdala, certainly required both business savvy and a conversational knowledge of Greek. He had his own home, just steps from the lakeshore (Matt 8:14).[4] In addition, the teaching attributed to him in both his eponymous letters and in the Acts of the Apostles—even if "polished" later by professional writers, such as Luke, or by his followers—is not something associated with simpleminded fishermen. Finally, his willingness to go off with Jesus of Nazareth on his brazen, seemingly quixotic crusade for the kingdom speaks of an inner depth and intelligence.

Jesus repeatedly predicted that he would be killed in fulfillment of his mission, and he needed someone he could trust to carry on his work—someone who could lead the community during a potentially dangerous period. That's why Jesus chose the impetuous, not always reliable but big-hearted entrepreneur Simon bar Jonah, and named him "the Rock" upon which he would build his kingdom community (Matt. 16:18).

Under his leadership, the apostles traveled around the country to visit the various communities to teach, to baptize, to heal, and to bring the gift of the Spirit through

A statue of the apostle Peter at Capernaum, on the Sea of Galilee. Just steps away lies the foundation of a first-century *insula*, or stone town house, where archaeologists believe Peter likely lived due to the presence of early Christian symbols carved into the walls.

the laying on of hands—a practice that later generations of Christian leaders, by then known as "guardians" or *episkopoi*, would continue. During this period, around the year AD 39, Peter visited the community established at Lydda, known in the Old Testament and today as Lod, about ten miles inland from the coastal town of Joppa. While he was there, Peter visited a man named Aeneas who was paralyzed and had been confined to his bed for eight years. As was his custom, Peter healed Aeneas by invoking the name of Jesus. "Aeneas, Jesus Christ heals you," Peter told him. "Rise and make your bed." According to the account in Acts, this is precisely what Aeneas did (9:34). When the inhabitants of the area saw him up walking around, many joined the community.

Peter then visited the nearby town of Joppa, on Israel's central coast. Known in Hebrew as Yafo and currently a posh northern suburb of Tel Aviv, this hilly seaside village has been used as a major port for three thousand years. It was from here that the biblical Jonah fled to Tarshish and here that the Lebanese cedar planks used to build Solomon's first temple were unloaded. Josephus reports that after the outbreak of the Jewish War against the Romans in AD 66, more than forty-two hundred inhabitants of the town were massacred.[5]

According to Acts, Joppa too had a small community of Jesus' disciples (9:36). They spent their time doing what Jesus' followers did in every town—building up a small, welcoming community of friends, teaching about Jesus and the kingdom, and offering free food and healing when they could. One of their number, a woman called Tabitha in Aramaic but who also went by the Greek name of Dorcus, was renowned for bringing food and money to the destitute in her area. But while Peter was visiting Lydda, Tabitha became very sick and, Acts reports, died (Acts 9:37). Her friends and associates washed her body and placed it in an upstairs room. When the disciples of Jesus heard that Peter was nearby in Lydda, they sent two men to bring him to Joppa without delay. It is not clear if Peter was sent for when Tabitha was sick or after she had been declared dead.

When Peter arrived, the followers of Jesus immediately took him upstairs to the room where they had laid Tabitha. Peter asked everyone to leave, knelt down, and prayed. Then he turned to the woman and said, "Tabitha, rise up." According to Acts, the woman opened her eyes, saw Peter, and quickly sat up (9:40 NABRE). Naturally, word of this amazing occurrence quickly spread through the town of Joppa and beyond. People flocked to the area to see Simon Peter. He stayed in the town, Acts says, for a long time, residing in the home of another Simon, a tanner by trade (v. 43). Throughout this time, the kingdom community continued to grow as the apostles both taught and demonstrated the power of God primarily through free healing.

CHAPTER 23

THE BAPTISM OF CORNELIUS

All nations whom You have made shall come and worship
before You, O Lord,
And they shall glorify Your name.
—PSALM 86:9 NASB

When Pontius Pilate was recalled to Rome to answer for his massacre of the Samaritans, he arrived shortly after the death of the
Roman emperor Tiberius Caesar, who died on March 16 in the year AD
37. Roman history is hazy in many places but is very accurate about the
births and deaths of its emperors. Tiberius's replacement as the most powerful man on earth ended up being a sadistic madman known to history
as Caligula—a nickname he had received as a boy when he accompanied
his father, the famous Roman general Germanicus, on long marches in
the army. The word *caligula* means "little boot" in Latin. His real name
was Gaius Julius Caesar Augustus Germanicus.

At first, the young Caligula was welcomed by the Roman people.
Only twenty-nine years old, he was handsome, and, at least at first, generous as a ruler—handing out bonuses to the army, enacting tax reform,
undertaking other improvements. Yet he also spent a staggering amount
of money on himself. In just his first year in office, Caligula managed to

spend his predecessor's entire fortune of 2.7 billion *sestertii* (the equivalent today of at least $270 million and perhaps as much as $3.4 billion).[1]

A marble statue of the Roman emperor Caligula is remarkably lifelike. Toward the end of his rule, in AD 39, Caligula tried to have a statue like this erected in the temple in Jerusalem, which may be the "abomination of desolation" referred to by Jesus in the gospel of Mark.

In Judea, the political situation was becoming unstable. After Caligula became emperor in AD 37, he appointed his longtime friend Herod Agrippa I (11 BC–44 AD), the grandson of Herod the Great, as the ruler of the northern Israel territories of Gaulanitis, Auranitis, Batanaea, and Trachonitis. These territories had once been ruled by his uncle, the tetrarch Philip, who died in AD 34. Agrippa had been raised in Rome and educated alongside the emperor Tiberius's own son, and he was great friends with Caligula before he became emperor. After just two years as ruler of his uncle's territories, he sailed to Rome and informed Caligula that his uncle Herod Antipas had been plotting a rebellion against Rome with the Parthians. (This was the same Antipas who had executed John the Baptist and whom Jesus had called a "fox" in Luke 13:32.) Antipas confessed that the charge was true, and he was summarily banished. Herod Agrippa was given his territories of Galilee and Peraea.

Around this time Caligula was struck down by a near-fatal illness. Historians suspect, and Caligula himself suspected, that he had been poisoned. As a result, he became paranoid and began executing suspected rivals and traitors without trial. He also began to see himself in divine terms, appearing for meetings dressed as a god and having shrines and statues erected for the worship of himself. The Jews in Judea objected to the creation of a Roman altar in Jamnia (modern Yavne), a village south of Joppa. So around AD 39–40, Caligula decided to teach them a lesson and ordered that an enormous statue of himself be erected in the temple in Jerusalem. This came to be known as the "Caligula crisis," and some modern scholars believe that the statue of the mad emperor may be the "abomination of desolation" that would be set up in Jerusalem, which Jesus spoke of in Mark 13:14 and Matthew 24:15–16.[2]

The Hebrew words translated as "abomination of desolation" (*sikutz misomem*) often refer to idols, and a statue of Caligula would certainly qualify. However, the statue was never actually erected.[3] Rightly fearing that such a desecration would trigger civil war on the part of the Jews, the Roman legate in Syria, Publius Petronius, did his best to delay the implementation of the imperial order for an entire year until it was eventually rescinded.

PETER AND THE GENTILE MISSION

All this was going on when Simon Peter was spending time on Israel's central coast, slowly making his way up to the luxurious seat of Roman government in Judea, Caesarea Maritima. Originally built by Herod the Great, Caesarea was one of the most beautiful cities in the ancient world. It was a planned Greco-Roman town with paved seaside promenades, public pools, enormous statues, and a vast deepwater harbor extending eight hundred feet out into the Mediterranean, welcoming ships from all across the Roman Empire. In the center of town, running parallel to the beach, was an enormous oblong hippodrome or horse-racing arena that could hold ten thousand spectators and is still visible today. The city was full of lavish seaside villas. At the southern edge of the town, near the city's amphitheater, stood an enormous palace that served as the official residence of the Roman governor, now Marullus.

According to the record in Acts, there was a Roman centurion there (roughly equivalent to a captain in a modern army) named Cornelius, a leader of a unit of the Roman army known as the Cohort Italica (10:1).[4] He was a "God-fearer," which meant that he followed the beliefs and teachings of Judaism without formally converting and undergoing circumcision. He and his entire household adhered to this life—including his wife, children, and slaves. They gave alms generously and almost certainly attended worship services at the synagogue in Caesarea—which, twenty-six years later, according to Josephus, would be the occasion of a massacre that would trigger the war against Rome.

Cornelius was something of a mystic, an unusual vocation in a Roman legionary. He prayed constantly to God. One afternoon—Acts even specifies the time, around three o'clock—Cornelius had a vision of an angel of God (10:3). This vision struck terror into the heart of the battle-hardened Roman soldier. "What is it, Lord?" Cornelius blurted out (v. 4). The angel replied that his prayers and acts of sacrifice had been answered. "Send men to Joppa and bring one Simon who is called Peter," the angelic visitor told him (v. 5). He added that the fellow he was to send for was staying with another Simon, a tanner, who had a house.

When the vision ended, Cornelius immediately dispatched two of his servants and a solider under his command and ordered them to proceed to Joppa and bring back this Simon Peter fellow to him. Unbeknownst to Cornelius, Peter would see a vision of his own—one that would forever change the direction of the fledgling Jesus movement. Around noon the following day, Peter went up on the roof terrace of Simon the tanner's house to pray. He was hungry and wanted something to eat. While he was waiting for lunch to be prepared, he too, as Cornelius had done the day before, fell into a kind of trance. Christian theologians have been discussing what Peter saw ever since. According to Acts, Peter saw something like a giant sheet being lowered to the ground from heaven (10:11). Inside the sheet was a kind of Noah's ark in miniature, all the creatures of the earth—four-legged animals, reptiles, even birds.

Peter heard a voice cry out, "Get up, Peter. Slaughter and eat." Peter, a Jew, was taken aback. Jews don't eat reptiles, for example. He protested: "Certainly not, sir. For never have I eaten anything profane and unclean." The voice then replied, "What God has made clean, you are not to call profane" (vv. 13–15 NABRE). Acts reports that this same dialogue was repeated three times, and then the giant sheet of animals was taken back up into the sky.

The vast ruins of the Roman seaside city of Caesarea Maritima, on Israel's central coast, are one of the greatest archaeological sites in the world. It was here that Simon Peter baptized the God-fearing Roman centurion Cornelius.

The vision must have left Peter dazed and more than a little confused because, Acts says, he sat quietly "pondering" what he had just witnessed (v. 19). He then felt an interior voice speak to him, telling him that some men were looking for him and that when they arrived, he should go with them without hesitation.

Just as Simon Peter was experiencing all this, Cornelius's three men arrived at the door of Simon the tanner. They no doubt knocked on the door and inquired whether Simon called Peter was staying in the house. Peter descended the ladder from the rooftop and replied to the men, "I'm the one you are looking for. Why have you come?" (Acts 10:21 NIV). The three men explained that they had been sent by Cornelius, a centurion and a God-fearer, well loved by the Jewish people, who had been visited by an angel and was told to summon Peter. Upon hearing this, Peter invited the men into the house, offered them something to eat and drink, and suggested they spend the night.

The next day, Peter went with the three men from Joppa to Caesarea, bringing with him six members of the Jesus community, all Jews. It took them a whole day and a half to walk to Caesarea, a distance of about forty miles that normally takes about twelve hours on foot. They must have camped a few hours away from the city, near the modern Israeli city of Hadera, and then walked the last ten miles or so into Caesarea. Cornelius was waiting for them in his house. He had gathered together all his friends and relatives for the occasion. When Peter walked into Cornelius's villa, the Roman centurion fell at his feet. Taken aback, Peter quickly protested, pulling Cornelius to his feet and, no doubt chuckling, insisted that he was just an ordinary man like everyone else.

Seeing himself surrounded by Romans, Greeks, and other pagans, Peter smiled. "You know that it is unlawful for a Jewish man to associate with, or visit, a Gentile," he said, aware that this might strike some of his listeners as insulting. "But God has shown me that I should not call any person profane or unclean" (Acts 10:28 NABRE).

Cornelius then recounted to Peter his vision of the angel. He told him that four days earlier, at precisely three o'clock in the afternoon, he had seen a vision of a man in dazzling robes. The man in the vision had told him to send for Peter in Joppa and had even told him precisely where he, Peter, had been staying. "So I sent for you immediately, and you were kind enough to come," Cornelius concluded. "Now therefore we are all here in the presence of God to listen to all that you have been commanded by the Lord" (Acts 10:33 NABRE).

It was silent in the room. Everyone was waiting to hear what Peter would say. He was about to give a speech that would forever change the course of Christian history.

"I see that God shows no partiality," Peter began. "Rather, in every nation whoever fears him and acts uprightly is acceptable to him" (vv. 34–35 NABRE).

The people in the room likely smiled at this—both the pagan "God-fearers," most of them Romans and Greeks, and the Jews from the local synagogue who welcomed them.

Peter then told them all about Jesus of Nazareth. He said that God had proclaimed peace through Jesus the Messiah, who is Lord of all, and whom God had anointed with the Holy Spirit and with power. He added that he and his fellow apostles were witnesses to all that had happened in Israel and in Jerusalem (vv. 36–39 NABRE).

Peter paused briefly. The entire room was hanging on every word he said.

Looking directly at Cornelius, the Roman soldier, Peter continued. "They put him to death by hanging him on a tree," he said. But, he added, God had raised Jesus on the third day and "granted that he be visible, not to all the people, but to us, the witnesses chosen by God in advance, who ate and drank with him after he rose from the dead."

Peter explained that it was the mission of the apostles to testify that Jesus had been raised by God and that everyone who believes in him will receive forgiveness of sins through his name (Acts 10:39–43 NABRE).

What happened next is not entirely clear. Acts merely reports that while Peter was speaking, the Holy Spirit "fell upon all who were listening" to him (10:44 NABRE). Whatever this manifestation of the indwelling Spirit was—whether it was some sort of ecstatic trance, the phenomenon known as *glossolalia* or "speaking in tongues," or just ordinary prayer and worship of God—it was immediately visible and obvious to all who saw it. Acts says only that the six Jewish believers in Jesus who came with Peter were astonished (v. 45). They couldn't believe that the gifts of the Spirit, which they had up until that point believed were *exclusively* for Jewish believers in Jesus, were being manifested among Gentiles, even among Roman officers!

Finally, Peter spoke again. "Can anyone withhold the water for baptizing these people," he asked his Jewish fellow believers, "who have received the holy Spirit even as we have?" (Acts 10:47 NABRE). As a result, Peter made the fateful decision that Cornelius and the members of his household should be baptized in the name of Jesus Christ on the spot. Thus, while people today think of Saul/Paul as the "apostle to the Gentiles," in fact it was Peter who first authorized the baptism of large groups of Gentiles into the Jesus fellowship. It was an enormous step, one that would divide the Jesus movement for years—and not be resolved for at least another decade.

REACTION AGAINST THE GENTILES

When Peter returned to Jerusalem, he was immediately confronted about what had happened in Caesarea. Word had already reached the community of Jewish believers that Peter and his friends had baptized a Roman centurion. "You entered the house of uncircumcised people and *ate with them*," objected the members of the Jesus community in Jerusalem (Acts 11:3 NABRE). Because of the laws of *kashrut*, or kosher dietary laws, observant Jews generally avoid eating with Gentiles. Peter retold the entire story of his vision, how he had seen a sheet descend from heaven with all sorts of creatures and had heard a voice sing out that he should "slaughter and eat" (v. 7 NABRE). He made a point of saying that he had had the same vision *three* times, and had known in advance that people were coming to see him, and that he was told that he should go with them. Peter even related how Cornelius had had a vision as well, seeing an angel. "I remembered the word of the Lord," Peter concluded, "how he had said, 'John baptized with water but you will be baptized with the holy Spirit.' If then God gave them the same gift he gave to us when we came to believe in the Lord Jesus Christ, who was I to be able to hinder God?" (vv. 16–17 NABRE).

As a result of all this, the Jesus community in Judea gradually and reluctantly began to accept all sorts of people into their fellowship—pagans, even Romans. This had begun earlier with the spread of the community into Samaria, which, as we saw, the Jews regarded as half-pagan. It continued with the willingness of the apostle Philip to baptize the Ethiopian eunuch. But now it included even Roman soldiers. Of course, there was a caveat: at this point, all the Gentiles who joined the Jesus movement were "God-fearers," nominal converts to Judaism, who kept all or nearly all of the *mitzvot* of the Torah. The next controversy would be over whether "pure Gentiles," those who had *not* first converted to Judaism, could also be welcomed into the Jesus community and be baptized. Yet it was already happening.

THE GENTILES IN ANTIOCH

After the martyrdom of Stephen, the members of the original Jerusalem community had scattered throughout Judea and into Samaria—even as far as Antioch in northern Syria. Antioch, a bustling metropolis on the Orontes River, was one of the largest cities of the Roman Empire, with a population well over a half million inhabitants. It was also where the main Roman army in the Middle East was stationed. In AD 44, people from all over the Roman Empire flocked to Antioch to attend the first formal Olympic Games in four hundred years (the last Olympiad having been held in 393 BC). The ancient sporting contests of the pentathlon (which included the discus and javelin) were revived, as was the ultimate "mixed martial art" of *pankration*, a combination of wrestling and bare-knuckle boxing. It's possible that Saul, then living in nearby Tarsus, witnessed these events as a spectator.

"Do you not know that in a race all the runners run, but only one gets the prize?" Paul would one day write to his friends in Corinth. "Run in such a way as to get the prize. Everyone who competes in the games goes into strict training . . . I do not fight like a boxer beating the air. No, I strike a blow to my body and make it my slave so that after I have preached to others, I myself will not be disqualified for the prize" (1 Cor. 9:24–27 NIV).

In Antioch, members of the Jesus community had already begun to evangelize Greeks, speaking to them of Jesus of Nazareth. These were presumably not "God-fearers" but ordinary Greco-Roman citizens. According to Acts, a group of Cypriot and Cyrenian believers had first taken this step (11:20). Once again, word had reached Jerusalem of this development—and so the leaders in Judea had sent the trusted Barnabas, himself a Cypriot, to Antioch to investigate. Far from being scandalized, Barnabas was thrilled with what he saw. Hundreds, even thousands of pagans were joining the Jesus community in this multicultural city. Barnabas encouraged them all, urging them to remain strong in the faith and loyal to Jesus of Nazareth (11:19–24).

In Antioch, Barnabas realized that he was not far from Tarsus, the hometown of the former persecutor of the community turned convert, Paul. It was only about 150 miles around the Karatas peninsula to Tarsus. He must have felt that Paul, the Greek-speaking Pharisee, would be of great use in Antioch. So Barnabas decided to track down Paul in Tarsus. He was able to find him and brought him back to Antioch. The two of them spent a year there, teaching large numbers of people. In fact, it was in the cosmopolitan city of Antioch that the followers of Jesus were first called *christianoi* or Christians.[5]

In addition to Saul and Barnabas, the community had its own teachers and even prophets—a colorful and ethnically diverse lot. We know some of their names: Symeon, also known as Niger, a black-skinned Syrian or perhaps African; Lucius from Cyrene; and Manaen, a wealthy and well-connected Jew and a foster brother of Herod Antipas, the banished former tetrarch of Galilee (Acts 13:1 NASB).

CHAPTER 24

PERSECUTION RESUMES

When reviled, we bless; when persecuted, we endure.
—1 CORINTHIANS 4:12

While Saul and Barnabas were busy in Antioch, the grandson of Herod the Great, Herod Agrippa I, was away in Rome. He was visiting his childhood friend Caligula when, in January of AD 41, Caligula was assassinated by members of the Praetorian Guard. According to the first-century Jewish historian Josephus, Agrippa was in the thick of things: he found Caligula's body, covered with stab wounds, and laid it on a bed; he counseled Caligula's uncle, Claudius, about what to do; he even advised the Roman Senate.[1] Having spent much of his childhood in Rome, speaking Latin and growing up so close to Caligula, Agrippa understood the complexities of Roman government better than most.

Caligula's uncle Claudius was a quiet, learned man who was content with his fortune and just wanted to be left in peace to study Greek philosophy. At first, he assumed the army would murder him as the last surviving member of the family. The Praetorian Guard—who, at this point, made and unmade emperors—had already killed Caligula's wife and young daughter in cold blood as they bent weeping over the emperor's body. So when the soldiers approached him, Claudius begged for his life. But rather than killing him, the soldiers took him away by force and declared him emperor instead. Yet the Roman Senate was unsure whether to accept Claudius or to wage a civil war to prevent another emperor from taking power.

At this point, according to Josephus, Agrippa intervened. The Jewish ruler, who controlled most of what is now the kingdom of Jordan and the Galilee region, convinced Claudius to stand up manfully to the Senate. Then he advised the Senate to spare the nation civil war and to allow such a moderate, philosophically inclined man as Claudius to return sanity to the empire.[2] Whether Josephus's account is accurate or whether Agrippa was involved to this degree is unclear, but Claudius was finally accepted as emperor. To repay whatever services Agrippa had done for him, Claudius agreed to make Agrippa ruler not merely of Galilee and the other territories, but also of Judea and Samaria. In other words, Agrippa took over rule of Judea from the Roman procurator— and he briefly became, for the first time since Herod the Great, the king of the Jews, ruler of the entire land of Israel on both sides of the Jordan River. Yet Agrippa's reign as king of the Jews would only last three years.

In Josephus's eyes and the eyes of the sages of the Mishnah, Herod Agrippa was a good and kind king, one who took his religious responsibilities seriously.[3] He even agreed to undertake the ritual reading of the Torah to all the people, as commanded by the book of Deuteronomy. He borrowed and spent vast sums (Josephus mentions twelve million *drachmae*) on public works and on the people. Yet his sincere dedication to the Jewish religion may have influenced his attitude toward Simon Peter and the Jesus movement. According to Acts, one of Herod Agrippa's very first actions after he had returned to Jerusalem as ruler of the Jews was to arrest the apostle James—the brother of John and son of Zebedee—and have him beheaded by the sword.

We have no idea why James was singled out in this way. Along with Peter and James's brother, John, he was part of an elite inner circle as Jesus' intimate confidants. They were the ones who witnessed the event Christian tradition calls the transfiguration (Mark 9:2) when Jesus' true nature was revealed to them. James appears to have come from a more affluent family in Galilee because his father, the famous Zebedee, could afford servants, and his brother, John, if he was indeed the "beloved disciple" in the gospel of John, was known personally by the high priest Joseph Caiaphas (John 18:15). James was not meek and mild: Jesus nicknamed him and his brother the "Sons of Thunder," implying they were a bit hotheaded and loud (Mark 3:17). On one occasion, when Jesus and his followers were refused lodging in a Samaritan village, the two brothers proposed that they call down fire from heaven upon the village (Luke 9:52–54)! Despite or perhaps because of this, Jesus asked James to stand guard with his brother and Peter in the garden of Gethsemane, as he, Jesus, prayed to God for his life to be spared.

THE DEATH OF JAMES

According to ninth-century Christian traditions, James traveled in the fourteen years after the crucifixion, eventually visiting a Jewish colony in Spain.[4] He supposedly returned to Jerusalem by the time Herod Agrippa was declared King of the Jews. One of the most famous medieval pilgrimages in Europe—the *Camino de Santiago de Compestela*, across the width of northern Spain to the Atlantic Ocean—is still made in James's honor.

James was given no trial. Herod Agrippa, now undisputed king of the Jews, did not have to ask permission of a Roman governor to execute someone. Like John the Baptist, James would probably have been brought out into the courtyard of the stone building where he was being held. There would have been no ceremony, no final words. His hands would have been shackled to a stone pillar, and he would have been flogged. After he could barely stand from the loss of blood, a very large, very strong man would have raised the razor-sharp steel blade then used for executions—either a Roman ax or possibly a Celtic *spatha* sword—and cut off James's head in one flashing stroke. James was thus the first of the twelve apostles to be a "witness" (*martyr*) to Jesus . . . but he would not be the last. According to reports in the second and third centuries, all of the apostles except for one, John, were executed for their faith in Jesus.[5]

AGRIPPA CONTINUES PERSECUTING

The following spring, during Passover in the year 44, King Herod Agrippa decided to take further action against the rapidly expanding Jesus community. He ordered that Simon Peter be arrested and held in prison, with four squads of four soldiers each to guard him. Archaeologists can only guess where this particular prison was located. It's doubtful that Peter was held in any dungeon at the high priest's house, as Jesus probably was. The government of Herod Agrippa had its own prison system, taken over from the Romans and the temple administration, and there were many fortress-like structures in Jerusalem in the mid-AD 40s that would have served as excellent prisons. On the Via Dolorosa in Jerusalem, there is a famous tourist site that claims to be the prison where Peter was held after his arrest, but it is a relatively recent building with little claim to historical remains.

According to Acts, Peter was not long in the prison. Since Peter was known far and wide as the leader of the Jesus community, Herod Agrippa planned on a very public trial. But on the night before the trial was to begin, the author of Acts reports, Peter was the subject of a strange supernatural visitation. He was sleeping in a cell of some kind, secured to the wall by two double chains, with a guard on each side of him. Two additional guards were on duty outside the cell door. Suddenly, a light shone in the dank cell and an "angel of the Lord" tapped Peter on his side, awakening him and saying, "Get up quickly" (Acts 12:7). The chains miraculously fell from Peter's arms and the angel told Peter to put on his belt, sandals, and cloak and follow him.

Acts relates how even Peter didn't believe what was happening to him. He assumed that he was dreaming or seeing a vision (12:9). Yet Peter and his angelic visitor somehow managed to pass the first guard outside, then the second, and then they came to the iron gate that led out to the city, which somehow opened on its own. From the context, it sounds as if Peter was being held outside of Jerusalem in some sort of military complex and he was actually trying to sneak back into the city. The two then walked down an alley—a very believable detail in Jerusalem—but then suddenly Peter found himself alone, no angel in sight. The text says simply that "Peter recovered his senses" and realized he had been rescued by God (v. 11 NABRE).

Peter headed quickly to the house of Mary, the mother of the New Testament figure called John Mark. There, a large group of disciples was gathered, praying for Peter's safe return. Peter knocked on the outside gate and a young woman named Rhoda answered it. She instantly recognized Peter's voice and, overjoyed, ran to tell everyone in the household that Peter had arrived—without realizing that she had, in fact, left him outside on the street and hadn't even opened the door! The crowd in the house scoffed and told Rhoda flat out that she was out of her mind. Meanwhile, Peter was still at the gate, knocking plaintively, until finally some members of the group went outside to the courtyard. They opened the gate and were astonished to find that it was Peter in the flesh!

They no doubt yelled out his name in excitement, because Acts reports that Peter quickly made a sign with his hand for them to be quiet, explained what had happened to him, and asked someone to "report this to James and the brothers" (Acts 12:17 NABRE).[6]

Peter then left the house and went into hiding at some other, unnamed location. The next day, Peter's escape was discovered—and there was certainly pandemonium among Herod Agrippa's officers. Soldiers quickly began a house-to-house search for the escaped leader. When he wasn't found, Herod ordered that the guards who were watching Peter be summarily executed—hardly the act of a benign and enlightened ruler.

Herod Agrippa would soon meet his own destiny, however. Shortly after Peter escaped, Herod Agrippa left Jerusalem for Caesarea Maritima. He had spent an enormous amount of money in the city organizing a festival of athletic games and contests in honor of Emperor Claudius. Of course, observant Jews would not attend these games or even set foot in the pagan city without grave reason. But the land of Israel had a large pagan community at this time, and plenty of people would flock to Caesarea's enormous beachside hippodrome to watch the colorful events.

The Greek-style amphitheater at Caesarea Maritima, facing the Mediterranean Sea, has been completely reconstructed by Israeli archaeologists and was probably where the Jewish king Herod Agrippa addressed the groups as recounted in Acts.

According to Acts, Herod Agrippa, then fifty-five but in excellent health, attended the games partly to hear the suit of the people of Tyre and Sidon in the north, with whom he had had a long political disagreement (12:20). Despite Herod's anger toward these northern peoples, he had allowed food supplies to be sent to them during a recent famine. For this, the people of Tyre and Sidon were very grateful, and they attended the games at Caesarea in large numbers to sue for peace.

Dressed in royal robes, Herod Agrippa addressed the crowds with much fanfare. The people present called out that Agrippa's voice was that of a god, not a man. According to Acts, at once an angel of God struck him down because he did not give the honor to God (12:23). A fuller account of what happened, which varies in the details but confirms the main points, is found in Josephus's *Antiquities of the Jews*.[7] This is one of the many incidents in the New Testament that have eerie confirmation from outside, non-Christian sources—confirmation that shows the degree to which the New Testament accounts were based on real events.

In Josephus's version, Agrippa came out to the amphitheater on the second day of the games and addressed the people, just as Acts says, but his "royal robe" was made entirely of silver threads. The robe sparkled in the bright Mediterranean sunlight, and flatterers called out that Agrippa was a god and begged him for mercy. Agrippa was immensely pleased by the flattery, but soon afterward he spotted an owl, a traditional ill omen, perched on a rope nearby. He recalled that a German prisoner had once told him that an owl would be an omen of his death. Suddenly, Agrippa felt a sharp pain in his abdomen and realized that his time had indeed come. He was carried back to his grandfather's lavish villa just steps from the Mediterranean and spent the following five days in agony. Physicians were summoned, but no one could stop the pain. On the fifth day, he died. Agrippa was survived by his wife, Cypros; their three daughters, Bernice, Mariamme, and Drusilla; and their seventeen-year-old son, also called Agrippa.

Herod Agrippa I's sudden, unexpected death caused a small political crisis, but eventually the emperor Claudius decided that the experiment in having a new king of the Jews, one person ruling the land of Israel, was ill considered. Plus, he wasn't about to give that much power to young Agrippa, a teenage boy about whom he knew very little. As a result, the Romans went back to their old system.

PERSECUTION UNDER NEW RULE

To keep a watchful eye on Herod Agrippa II, the emperor Claudius brought the young man to Rome to be educated. After three or four years in Rome, young Herod Agrippa II got his chance: Claudius appointed him "king" over the tiny principality of Qinnasrin in northern Syria, which the Romans called *Chalcis ad Belum*, Chalcis on the river Belus. He would report directly to the Roman legate in Antioch but he was given the special privilege of exercising control over the temple in Jerusalem, including the right to appoint the high priest.

Over the years, the Romans added to the young man's territories, eventually giving him control over the important cities of Tiberias and Magdala (Taricheae) on the Sea of Galilee. According to Josephus, the young Herod Agrippa II lived in an incestuous relationship with his own sister, Bernice[8]—and it was before Agrippa and Bernice that the apostle Paul would eventually appear at Caesarea Maritima, probably in AD 59. When the Jewish War against Rome broke out in AD 66, Agrippa II, although at least partially a Jew, naturally sided with the Romans. He sent troops to aid the Roman attacks upon the holy city and the Jewish rebels. When he died childless around AD 93, at the age of sixty-five, he was the last surviving king of the house of Herod.

PART IV

The Expansion of the Jesus Movement

Go therefore and make disciples of all nations, baptizing them in the name of the Father and of the Son and of the Holy Spirit.

—Matthew 28:19

CHAPTER 25

SPREADING THE WORD

For the Lord has commanded us, saying,
"'I have made you a light for the Gentiles,
That you may bring salvation to the ends of the earth.'"
—ACTS 13:47

After Peter miraculously escaped from Herod Agrippa's prison, we know that he fled Jerusalem and traveled north with John Mark, possibly Barnabas's cousin (Col. 4:10), to Antioch. We know this because Paul would write a letter to the Jesus-following community in Galatia that tells us all about it. This was in the year AD 44. By this time there was a flourishing community in Antioch. The apostles sent leaders and teachers from Jerusalem to Antioch to continue to build up the community there. With this group was a Jewish prophet named Agabus.

Prophets were common in the early Jesus community and were one of its distinguishing characteristics; the return of God's Spirit meant the return of prophecy. Agabus foresaw a period of severe famine in the near future. As a result, the word went forth and one of the first Christian missionary relief efforts was launched. All across Syria and probably into what is now the eastern part of modern-day Turkey, the various Jesus communities took up collections for famine relief. They raised a significant amount of money. The various communities eventually entrusted all the money to Paul and Barnabas who, two years later, brought it to the community in Jerusalem (Acts 11:28–30).

Yet, despite such obvious signs of the Spirit working in the community, the old divisions had reappeared. Most of the members of the Jesus community in Antioch were Gentiles, both "God-fearers" (those who had first converted to Judaism) and many pagans who only discovered the Jewish Scriptures *after* they joined the Jesus fellowship. There was also a group of observant Jews who believed that Jesus was the Messiah. The two communities interacted, but there was some tension over table fellowship.

Table fellowship was a tricky subject between Gentiles and Jews. The dietary rules of *kashrut*, described in the Torah and elaborated later in the Talmud, do not actually forbid Jews to eat with Gentiles.[1] But, as a practical matter, it was difficult for Jews to avoid eating forbidden non-kosher foods at a Gentile table. According to the Torah, meats must be prepared and animals slaughtered in a special way (Lev. 17:1–10); milk and meat products cannot be eaten together (Ex. 23:19); and breads made from new grain are forbidden (Lev. 23:14), among other restrictions. Then there was the problem that, in the ancient world, the "restaurants" available were usually pagan temples where both the foods and the wines were dedicated to idols.

So, for simplicity's sake, many observant Jews would avoid eating with Gentiles to ensure that they did not violate any of the commandments of the Torah. This is still an issue with Jews and Gentiles today. "Keep yourself separate from the nations, and do not eat with them," proclaimed the book of Jubilees, an extracanonical Jewish work written before 100 BC. "Do not imitate their rites, nor associate with them; for their rites are unclean and their practices polluted, an abomination and unclean. They offer sacrifices to the dead and worship demons and they eat among the graves."[2] Eventually, this attitude was distilled into a rule in the Mishnah, *bishul Yisrael*, that asserts that Jews should avoid foods cooked by a non-Jew (Avodah Zarah 2:6).

In Antioch, the Jesus community was aware of this sensitive issue. So, to make things easier, they appear to have organized themselves in such a way that the "Greeks" celebrated the Eucharistic meal in Greek homes and the Jewish believers in Jewish homes. It was just simpler that way. They would then come together in occasional joint meetings of the entire fellowship when food was not an issue.

Little remains of the Roman city of Antioch where a thriving Christian community developed in the first decade after Jesus' crucifixion. The Orontes River, however, still runs through the city (now called Antakya in south-central Turkey) as it did when Peter, Paul, Barnabas, and other Christian leaders first visited.

When Peter arrived in Syrian Antioch with John Mark, he was, of course, welcomed and celebrated by all, and he happily joined in with *both* communities, delighting that the fellowship of believers was growing so rapidly. In imitation of his Master, Jesus, he ate and drank with everyone. There is no record of Jesus eating with Gentiles; although, given his openness to the Samaritan community, it is possible that he did. The gospels of Matthew and Luke record that Jesus had a reputation for being a "glutton and a drunkard" (Matt. 11:19, Luke 7:34). But we do know that Peter *did* eat with Gentiles. Acts reports that after the conversion of the centurion Cornelius but before his arrest by Herod Antipas, Peter was criticized by some in Jerusalem who said, "You went into the house of uncircumcised men and ate with them" (11:3 NIV).

Yet according to Paul, all that changed when some representatives from James arrived in Antioch. Peter was embarrassed to be found eating with Gentile believers in front of "James's people," very devout and observant Jews, so he began to separate himself from the Gentile households, staying and eating only in Jewish homes. According to Paul, even his old friend and coworker Barnabas drew back when James's party showed up—and Barnabas normally advocated a policy of inclusion and outreach to all peoples (Gal. 2:12–13). This enraged the easily aroused Pharisee Paul because he claims to have confronted Peter to his face, referring to what Peter and Barnabas were doing as hypocrisy. During a gathering of the entire Jesus community, both Jews and Gentiles, Paul challenged Peter out loud. "If you, though a Jew, live like a Gentile and not like a Jew," Paul proclaimed, "how can you force the Gentiles to live like Jews?" (Gal. 2:14). We only have Paul's version of this debate. Acts is silent on the matter. The two letters attributed to Peter also do not mention any conflict with Paul. Yet Peter backed down and eventually agreed with Paul's criticism (Acts 15:7–11).

After he heard that Herod Agrippa I had suddenly collapsed and died in Caesarea, Peter returned to Jerusalem. The community in Antioch decided that the debate between Peter and Paul was a revelation from God—a sign of what God wanted the community to do. While worshipping and fasting, the members of the community felt the Spirit was commissioning them to continue the outreach to the Gentiles that had flourished so obviously in Antioch. This applied to Paul and Barnabas in particular. As a result, the leaders laid their hands on Paul and Barnabas—to this day a sign of ordination in many Christian communities—and sent them on what became the first direct and sustained mission to the pagan Gentiles.

THE MISSION TO THE GENTILES

Paul and Barnabas took with them the mysterious John Mark, the man who had accompanied Peter to Antioch and whose mother's house Peter had gone to after his arrest by Herod Agrippa (Acts 12:12). It's possible that this man was the author of the gospel of Mark because the gospel is written in relatively poor Greek, contains many Aramaic words, and shows many signs of being based on the eyewitness testimony of Peter—all things you would expect from a native Galilean who followed Jesus. In addition, the early Christian writer Papias (ca. AD 70–163) claims that the gospel of Mark was written by Mark, a companion and interpreter of Peter's in Rome, who "wrote with great accuracy but not however in the order in which it was spoken or done by our Lord."[3] If true, then the earliest gospel was written by someone who had an intimate familiarity with both Peter *and* Paul, the two most influential apostles and teachers of the early Jesus movement. The gospel of Mark is a remarkable document that almost certainly provides direct access to the eyewitness testimony of Jesus' close disciples.

The trio set off from the nearby port of Seleucia Pieria, or Seleucia by the Sea, a small Mediterranean city in the estuary of the Orontes River about twenty miles from Antioch. Then as now, traveling across the Mediterranean by sailboat was an expensive proposition; it cost the men about sixty *denarii*, or two months' wages, each. Paul, Barnabas, and John Mark booked passage on a squat, round-bottomed Roman merchant ship, called a *ponto* or *corbita*, that transported both goods and passengers short distances around the eastern Mediterranean. Like most Roman ships, this vessel was powered by both sails and oarsmen.[4]

They had already decided to go first to Barnabas's home island of Cyprus and so sailed directly to Salamis, a large town on the southeastern coast of the island. According to Acts, the three men began proclaiming the Way of God's kingdom as soon as they arrived (13:5). Salamis was a large and thriving city at the time, and even today the ruins from this period are extensive. There is an impressive amphitheater, discovered in

1959 and built in honor of the emperor Augustus, that could easily sit fifteen thousand spectators.

As would become their custom, Paul and Barnabas went first to a Jewish synagogue in that city. Then they walked across the island until they got to Paphos, on the western coast, which the Romans had made the island's capital. There they encountered a Jewish false prophet named Bar-Jesus, and, through him, met someone who influenced the outcome of their journey, a Roman proconsul named Sergius Paulus.

Ruins of the ancient city of Paphos, on the western end of the island of Cyprus, where Acts reports that Paul and Barnabas met the Roman proconsul Sergius Paulus and a sorcerer called Elymas.

Sergius Paulus is one of the figures mentioned in the New Testament that has had extensive archaeological confirmation of his existence—confounding those who insist the New Testament is entirely fiction. In fact, there are no fewer than *four* stone inscriptions mentioning this Roman official—an inscription on Cyprus, just north of Paphos and dating to around AD 54, which mentions "the proconsul Paulus"; another inscription on the north side of the island that refers to a "Quintus Sergius"; a stone slab with the name L. Sergius Paulus found in 1912 in Pisidian Antioch in central Turkey; and, most famous of all, a boundary stone in Rome itself, erected under Emperor Claudius, that bears the inscription: "L. Sergius Paullus . . . curators of the river Tiberis . . . Claudius Caesar." In other words, not only was Sergius Paulus a real person but also he appears to have been a fairly important Roman official who performed his duties over a wide area.[5]

HOLYLAND PHOTOS / WIKIPEDIA

Four separate carved inscriptions bearing the name of the Roman proconsul Sergius Paulus, whom Acts reports was converted to the Way by Paul and Barnabas on Cyprus, have been found on Cyprus, in Rome itself, and in Pisidian Antioch in central Turkey.

Sergius Paulus had heard of Paul and Barnabas and wanted to hear for himself what they had to say. According to Acts, Bar-Jesus—who also was called Elymas, a Greek transliteration of the Aramaic word for "magician"—tried to interfere and prevent them from evangelizing the Romans. Never one to mince words, Paul snapped at him. "You son of the devil," the author of Acts records him shouting at the no-doubt startled Bar-Jesus. "Enemy of all that is right . . . Will you not stop twisting the straight paths of [the] Lord?" (13:10 NABRE). Paul still had his old temper, it turns out. He told the Jewish magician that, because of his meddling, God would temporarily blind him—much as Paul had been temporarily blinded on his way to Damascus. As a result, a "dark mist" fell upon the Jewish prophet and he couldn't see (v. 11 NABRE).

The Roman proconsul was astonished. After listening to what Paul and Barnabas had to say, he joined the kingdom movement on the spot. Knowing what we know about Sergius, it appears that the Roman convert told Paul and Barnabas about his home city of Antioch in Pisidia, another Antioch, in what is today west-central Turkey, about four hundred miles overland from the Antioch in northwestern Syria. Sergius must have convinced the two apostles to visit there because, according to Acts, that was their next major destination (13:13–14).

OUTREACH IN ANTIOCH

This part of the world, the enormous peninsula of what became Turkey, was a vast region that was home to successive empires—the Assyrians in the twenty-first century BC, then the Hittites (seventeenth to twelfth centuries), then the Phygians and Galatians, finally the Greeks and then the Romans. To call it "multicultural" would be an understatement. A dizzying array of people and languages—descendants of Hittites, Greeks, Cimmerians and Scythians, Jews and Cypriots—could be found spread out across this region's wild but luxurious steppes and Greek-style city-states. Nominally under the control of Rome, this area, known in ancient times as Anatolia, was in fact a series of semiautonomous regions governed by local magistrates and officials.

So Paul, Barnabas, and John Mark sailed from the island of Cyprus due north to a region called Pamphylia, located in what is now south-central Turkey. They traveled first to the city of Perga, slightly up the river Cestrus from the coast. But then there was some dispute about where they should go next because John Mark left the group and returned to Jerusalem—a minor act of betrayal that Paul was not to forget or forgive (Acts 13:13). In the future, when Paul asked Barnabas to accompany him on another trip, Barnabas again wanted to bring his friend, possibly cousin, along with him; but Paul refused because John Mark had not stuck with them before, so Paul and Barnabas ended up not traveling together (Acts 15:38–39). From Perga, Paul and Barnabas marched due north, across what is now central Turkey to Antioch in Pisidia, a decent-sized city of some fifty thousand inhabitants located about eight miles from the mouth of the Cestrus River.

The remains of the Hellenistic city of Perga, located in what is now central Turkey and visited by Paul and Barnabas, are extensive.

There was a Jewish synagogue in the city. Paul and Barnabas were invited to address the congregation, but eventually some of the leaders of this community came to despise Paul—a reaction he got quite a lot—and hounded him throughout his stay in the region. The author of Acts records a lengthy sermon that Paul delivered to the Jews of Antioch in Pisidia in their synagogue (13:16–41).

The sermon that Paul delivered to the Jews in Antioch in Pisidia was much longer than the one recorded in Acts—which should be seen as a summary of key points, recounted from memory, more than a direct transcription. Paul began, as the first martyr Stephen began, with a lengthy and somewhat tedious recounting of Israel's history. He addressed his sermon to his "fellow Israelites and you others who are God-fearing," meaning pagans who worshipped in the synagogue alongside the Jewish believers (Acts 13:16 NABRE). Paul recounted how God brought the people of Israel out of bondage in Egypt, established their nation, and brought out of the line of David a Savior—Jesus. Then he became much more direct.

"The inhabitants of Jerusalem and their leaders failed to recognize him, and by condemning him they fulfilled the oracles of the prophets that are read sabbath after sabbath," he declared. "We ourselves are proclaiming this good news to you that what God promised our ancestors he has brought to fulfillment for us, [their] children, by raising up Jesus" (Acts 13:27–33 NABRE).

Paul added that the Torah could *not* provide forgiveness of sins and living in a right relationship with God, but every believer in Jesus is offered this freely. This astonishing speech shook up the synagogue congregation. Acts reports that many Jews and Jewish converts followed Paul and Barnabas, and the two were invited to speak again on the following Sabbath (vv. 42–43). But when that day arrived, huge crowds flocked to the synagogue—"almost the whole city," in fact (v. 44 NABRE). This made the leaders of the community uneasy and even jealous, and according to Acts they began to violently refute what Paul said. However, Paul was up to the challenge. "It was necessary that the word of God be spoken to you first," he snapped at one point. "But since you reject it and condemn yourselves as unworthy of eternal life, we now turn to the Gentiles" (v. 46 NABRE).

This was the beginning of a dispute with Jewish communities that would endure for centuries—and for which Paul was flogged five times and even stoned. Eventually, the animosity between the Jewish community and Paul and Barnabas reached such an extreme that the two were expelled from Antioch altogether, no doubt for stirring up trouble (Acts 13:50).

CHAPTER 26

WELCOMING PAGANS

When Jesus heard these things, he marveled at him,
and turning to the crowd that followed him, said, "I tell
you, not even in Israel have I found such faith."
—LUKE 7:9

After leaving Antioch in Pisidia, Paul and Barnabas traveled first to the nearby town of Iconium, the modern-day Turkish city of Konya, just a few miles away. At first they met with great success in Iconium. There was a synagogue in this city as well, and the two missionaries were welcomed there. A great number of both Jews and Gentiles joined the Jesus movement in Iconium, and so Paul and Barnabas decided to remain in the town for longer than was normal for them. They began to perform what Acts calls "signs and wonders," but that was soon short-lived (14:3). The city became bitterly divided between "pro-" and "anti-" Jesus forces. And as before, their very success appeared to stir up trouble.

Unlike in Antioch in Pisidia, where the opposition to Paul was primarily Jewish, in Iconium some of those aligned against Paul and Barnabas were Gentiles. Gentiles were sometimes motivated by financial concerns to persecute the Jesus movement because it was seen as a threat to polytheism in general and to the very real business side of idolatry in particular.[1] Acts reports that both Jews and Gentiles attempted to attack and stone the two men (14:5). For that reason, they quickly fled once again—this time to the two Lycaonian cities of Lystra and Derbe.

The animosity that Paul and Barnabas stirred up continued for years. It's clear from Paul's later writing that other representatives of the Jesus movement visited the same area after Paul and Barnabas, urging the Gentiles in the area to be circumcised and to observe the Torah before or as they were joining the Jesus community. Paul's response was to write one of the most influential pieces of early Christian reflection on what the Jesus movement was actually all about, what we now know as his letter to the Galatians. Scholars disagree about when this letter was written and how to reconcile its factual claims with Acts.[2] Many favor a date in the late AD 50s but some argue it could be among the earliest parts of the New Testament, written just after Paul and Barnabas visited the area around AD 48.

Paul's main point in his letter to the Galatians is that the basis for a relationship with God is faith, not the Torah. The patriarch Abraham's faith in God brought salvation to himself and his descendants, Paul wrote, not Abraham's obedience to a Torah that *hadn't even been revealed yet.* That would only come four hundred years later. Paul argued that while the Torah is truly a gift for the Jews, it was only meant to be a preparation for the salvation that comes through faith. The idea that Gentiles had to obey all the commandments of the Torah—including the laws of purity, the feasts, and other ritual requirements—in order to be full and complete followers of Jesus was to miss the point of what Jesus was all about.

Paul stressed to the Galatians that they should avoid another form of idolatry—an attempt to rely on ritual and religious custom rather than faith in God. Jesus of Nazareth had revealed that everyone was welcome in God's kingdom through faith. "Through faith you are all children of God," Paul told the Galatians. "There is neither Jew nor Greek, there is neither slave nor free person, there is not male and female; for you are all one in Christ Jesus" (3:26, 28 NABRE).

The Greeks have dominated shipping in the Mediterranean for three thousand years. Paul and Barnabas likely took passage in a Greek merchant ship similar to this re-creation.

Later, Paul's writing would be misunderstood to mean that followers of Jesus were free from all moral constraints, not merely the *mitzvot* of the Torah; but that was not what Paul was saying. Even later still, some Christians would claim that faith in Jesus was a kind of "get out of jail free" card and that salvation was guaranteed no matter what someone did. Paul explicitly rejected that misinterpretation in his later letter to the people of Corinth. They were being saved through the message of the gospel, Paul told them, but only if they *held fast* to the message that he had proclaimed to them (1 Cor. 15:2). Writing to followers of Jesus in Rome, Paul would also warn the Gentile believers not to get so full of themselves that they became contemptuous of Jews who did not follow the Way. "For if God did not spare the natural branches," he wrote darkly, referring to Jews, "[perhaps] he will not spare you either" (Rom. 11:21 NABRE).

Still, spreading the message of the kingdom to the pagan Gentiles was quite a bit different from speaking to synagogues of Jews. For example, in Lystra, located just twenty miles north of Iconium, Paul and Barnabas were virtually worshipped as appearances of the Greek gods Zeus and Hermes (Acts 14:11–12). The two apostles had encountered a crippled man, lame from birth, who had been listening to them speak about Jesus and the kingdom. According to Acts, Paul could see that the man "had the faith to be healed," so he, Paul, commanded him, "Stand up straight on your feet" (vv. 9–10 NABRE). The man did so and began to walk about. This greatly impressed the population of Lystra, mostly pagans. The people decided that Barnabas, perceived to be the leader, was Zeus and Paul was Hermes—perhaps because he did most of the talking.

They were serious: a priest of Zeus came from a temple at the main gate of the city with garlands and oxen. They intended to offer a sacrifice to Paul and Barnabas since they were obviously gods in human form. The two apostles were horrified and tore their own clothes in the ancient Jewish sign of protest against blasphemy. The two men rushed into the crowd and told everyone to stop. "We proclaim to you good news that you should turn from these idols to the living God, 'who made heaven and earth and sea and all that is in them,'" they told the people (Acts 14:15 NABRE).

But no good deed goes unpunished. Soon afterward, Jews from Antioch arrived in Lystra and told the people that Paul and Barnabas were frauds and deceivers. Eventually, the Jewish leaders turned the crowds against the two. According to Acts, Paul was "stoned"—probably meaning the people threw rocks at him rather than attempting to formally execute him—dragged out of the city, and left for dead (Acts 14:19). When attended to by disciples in Lystra, Paul revived and stayed that night in the city. He must not have been too seriously hurt, however. The very next day Paul and Barnabas left the town for nearby Derbe, located in the Tarsus Mountains above Paul's hometown.

RETURN TO ANTIOCH AND DERBE

Incredibly, given everything the two men had been through, Paul and Barnabas decided to retrace their steps and, on their way back home to Syrian Antioch, make a final good-bye tour of all the cities they had visited. They wanted to make sure that the Jesus movement was solidly established in each of the towns. To that end, they appointed "elders" (*presbyteroi* in Greek) in each community to function as "overseers" (*episkopoi*)—a practice that the letter to Titus encourages in all of the local communities (Titus 1:5). At this stage, the elders and overseers were the same people, the same office. Later, as the Jesus movement grew and expanded throughout the Mediterranean, local groups of elders or presbyters would answer to a senior "overseer" or *episkopos* in a given region. The *episkopoi* came to be seen as guardians of the authentic teaching passed on from the apostles. By the time of the first post–New Testament leaders, such as the martyr Ignatius of Antioch (ca. 50–98), it was said that it is not permissible to baptize or even celebrate the Lord's Supper without the consent of the local *episkopos*.[3]

Once they reached Antioch in Pisidia, Paul and Barnabas continued retracing their journey, traveling south to Pamphylia and then to the city of Perga a few miles up the River Cestrus. They stayed briefly in Perga but then walked down to Attalia, a seaport, to take a ship east through the channel between Anatolia (Turkey) and Cyprus to the port of Selucia near Antioch. Altogether, Paul and Barnabas had traveled about twenty-five hundred miles together round-trip, a journey that took them about two months.

It wasn't a cheap trip, either. A computer program developed at Stanford University, called Orbis, calculates that Paul and Barnabas's journey cost about 237 *denarii* per person.[4] The program estimates the cost of wheat per day of donkey travel as well as the cost of booking passage on sailing ships at that time. Since a *denarius* was generally thought to be the equivalent of one day's ordinary wage, the total cost of the journey in today's currency would be around $18,960 each—or $37,920 for the two.[5]

When the two missionaries arrived back in Antioch, the entire community welcomed them warmly. According to Acts, they called everyone in the Jesus movement together and gave the whole group a thorough report on everything they had seen and done during their two months away. They particularly emphasized, Acts reports, how God had "opened the door of faith to the Gentiles" (14:27 NABRE).

Despite their success, the old dispute between Jews and Gentiles was about to explode into open conflict and divide the young Jesus movement as nothing else had. The issue was circumcision. As far as Paul and Barnabas were concerned, God had proven to them on their journey that Gentiles could become full participants in the kingdom without first becoming Jews—or being circumcised. But by the time Paul and Barnabas arrived back in Antioch, perhaps in the fall of 48, leaders from Jerusalem were telling everyone that "unless you are circumcised according to the Mosaic practice, you cannot be saved" (15:1 NABRE). Paul and Barnabas opposed these leaders to their faces. As a result, the community decided that this question needed to be settled once and for all. They resolved to send Paul, Barnabas, and some leaders from Antioch to Jerusalem. They were to meet with the apostles and presbyters there and discuss the issue. It was to be a decisive meeting, known as the Council of Jerusalem—the first such council in Jesus' kingdom movement.

CHAPTER 27

THE COUNCIL OF JERUSALEM

As they went on their way through the cities, they delivered
to them for observance the decisions that had been reached
by the apostles and elders who were in Jerusalem.
—ACTS 16:4

Jerusalem in the late AD 40s was becoming an increasingly dangerous place. The Roman procurators Tiberius Alexander (ruled 46–48)
and Ventidius Cumanus (ruled 48–52) faced a restless Jewish population. Two rebel leaders arose, James and Simon, who were either sons
or grandsons of the earlier rebel chieftan named Judas of Galilee, who
led a revolt in AD 6. The Jewish apostate Tiberius Alexander crucified
them for fomenting rebellion. During this period Jewish nationalists
began planning to publicly assassinate Jewish collaborators with hidden daggers—inspiring the term *sicarii* or dagger-men. These murders
occurred a few years later during the procuratorship of Felix (52–60).

These extremists were the forerunners of the Zealots, the men
who eventually ignited a full-blown war against the Roman occupation forces. It would result in Jerusalem and its ancient temple being
utterly destroyed and up to a million Jews slaughtered. The *sicarii* took
advantage of Jerusalem's narrow, densely crowded streets and alleys to
accomplish their purposes. They would slip up behind a victim, stab

him in the back or slit his throat, and then disappear into the crowded alleys before anyone knew what had happened. Eventually, they even dared to strike against a former high priest, Jonathan ben Ananus, in AD 52.

Amid this turmoil, the Jesus community planned its very first council. Paul traveled from Antioch to Jerusalem along with Barnabas and a sizable delegation. Historians know from Paul's later writings that they also brought with them a man named Titus, a Gentile who had joined the Jesus movement in Antioch but who was not, at this point, circumcised (Gal. 2:3). He was still unsure whether that was required of him. The group traveled overland down the coast from Antioch, passing through what is now Lebanon, crossing through Galilee and entering the territory of the Samaritans. Everywhere they went they spoke about the conversion of large numbers of Gentiles to the kingdom movement, which brought "great joy," according to Acts, to all of the brothers and sisters in the community (15:3).

The apostles gathered in Jerusalem in the late 40s to settle the question of whether pagans who wished to join the Jesus movement had to first convert to Judaism and the men undergo circumcision.

WHO WAS JAMES THE JUST?

By the late 40s, the leader of the Jesus community in Jerusalem appears to have been James the Just, the brother, stepbrother, or cousin of Jesus. The gospels of Mark and Matthew report that Jesus had four "brothers" (*adelphoi*)—James, Joses (Joseph), Simon, and Judas—and at least two sisters (Matt. 13:55–56).[1] As noted before, many Christian denominations believe Jesus' mother, Mary, remained a virgin her entire life and that these "brothers" and "sisters" were either cousins or step-siblings, the children of Joseph from a previous marriage. Other denominations say that these relatives were half brothers and half sisters, the children Mary had with Joseph after Jesus was born.

In the decades after Jesus' crucifixion, groups of people called *desposyni*, or "relatives of the Lord," lived in the region around Nazareth. According to one account, two grandsons of Judas, a "brother" of Jesus, were brought before the Roman emperor Domitian and quizzed about their financial assets: they claimed to have had only nine thousand *denarii* between them and then only in the value of their land, consisting of only thirty-nine *plethora* (about nine acres). When the emperor heard how poor they were, relatively speaking, he let them go.[2]

Some scholars believe that James the Just was the same as the apostle the "younger James," son of Alphaeus, mentioned in a few places in the Gospels (Mark 3:18, Matt. 10:3, and Luke 6:15) and once in Acts (1:13). If this is true, then he could have been a cousin of Jesus.[3] However James was related to Jesus, he has remained a little-known figure to modern readers of the New Testament. Most of what we know about him comes from sources outside of the New Testament, such as the writings of Josephus[4] and Hegesippus (ca. AD 110–180), an early Christian chronicler quoted at length by the later Christian historian Eusebius of Caesarea (AD 260–340).

According to Hegesippus, James the Just was famous throughout Jerusalem as an austere and pious Jew, a Nazarite who vowed to abstain from wine, meat, oil, and bathing. In fact, his reputation for holiness was so great that, Hegesippus claimed, he was even allowed to enter the Holy of Holies in the temple, which was off-limits to all but the high priest, and then only on one day a year (Yom Kippur).[5] James appears to have had some connection with the purity-minded Essenes because he went about dressed solely in white linen garments as they did. James was also known to spend most of his time on his knees in the temple, asking for the forgiveness of the people. His knees were said to be as rough as those of a camel.[6]

WIKIPEDIA

Experts disagree sharply over the authenticity of the James Ossuary, which bears the inscription, in Aramaic, Ya'akov bar Yosef achui d'Yeshu'a—which means, "James son of Joseph brother of Jesus." If authentic, it is the first archaeological confirmation of Jesus of Nazareth ever discovered.

Eventually, as the Jesus movement continued to grow at a rapid pace, the leaders of the Pharisees and other sects in Jerusalem came to James and asked him to use his considerable influence to nip this noxious movement in the bud. "We're asking you to restrain the people," the Pharisees said to him, "for they have gone astray in their opinions about

Jesus, as if he were the messiah."[7] Instead of denouncing Jesus, however, James addressed all the people of Jerusalem and proclaimed that Jesus "sits in heaven at the right hand of the Great Power, and shall come on the clouds of heaven."[8]

As a result, the leaders of the Pharisees and Sadducees decided to stone James. Josephus says only that James was "delivered to be stoned," but Hegesippus claims he was actually thrown from the parapet or roof of the temple.[9] Hegesippus adds that James was not killed by the fall and, before he died from stoning, he prayed the same prayer of forgiveness offered by Jesus and by Stephen: "Lord God our Father, forgive them; for they know not what they do."[10] Hegesippus's account strikes some historians as highly implausible because Jewish priests went to enormous extremes to ensure the temple was free of any kind of ritual impurity—and the death of a man would be just such an impurity.

Wherever and however it occurred, the stoning of James happened around AD 62, in the years before war with the Romans would break out. We know the year because, according to Josephus, "the brother of Jesus, who was called Christ, whose name was James" was executed by stoning after the death of the procurator Porcius Festus but before Lucceius Albinus had assumed office.[11] Josephus claims that the high priest Ananus son of Ananus wanted to get rid of James and his companions, so he took advantage of the absence of a Roman governor to convene the Sanhedrin and have them convicted.[12] The stoning of James outraged many in Jerusalem; he was well respected by both ordinary Jews and the followers of Jesus. A delegation wrote to the new Roman procurator, Albinus, informing him of what the high priest Ananus had done. Ananus was, Josephus claims, immediately dismissed from his office.[13]

Strangely, the stoning of James the Just, the "brother of the Lord," is not mentioned at all in the New Testament. However, in 2002, archaeologists announced the discovery of a limestone ossuary, or Jewish burial box, with an inscription that read in Aramaic, "Ya'akov bar Yosef achui d'Yeshu'a"—which means, "James son of Joseph brother of Jesus." This is now one of the most hotly debated archaeological discoveries in history.

Some experts believe that the ossuary itself is genuine, dating to the first century AD, but that the inscription is a forgery. Still others think that the part of the inscription that reads "James son of Joseph" is genuine but that the additional phrase "brother of Jesus" is a forgery, created by a master craftsman. After lengthy court battles and numerous scientific tests, the issue is still not resolved.[14] But if the James Ossuary is eventually declared authentic, it will be the first archaeological confirmation of the existence of Jesus of Nazareth.

THE COUNCIL CONVENES

Paul, Barnabas, Titus, and the other leaders from Antioch were warmly welcomed in Jerusalem. They reported on everything they had done and seen in Syria as well as what Paul and Barnabas had encountered in their travels through Anatolia, or modern Turkey. It's not clear where the group met, but it's possible they met in what became the first "messianic synagogue," the remains of which may lie beneath the structure that today holds the tomb of David and what is claimed to be the upper room.[15]

Acts reports that the apostles and presbyters met with the delegation from Antioch to discuss the community's future and the issues that were causing division. It's also clear that there was significant resistance to the way the community in Antioch was reaching out to pagan Gentiles. The so-called Christian Pharisees, members of the Pharisees who had joined the Jesus movement, insisted that both circumcision and the *mitzvot* of the Torah were essential. They saw the Jesus movement as belonging solely to Israel. Gentiles could participate in the movement only if they first converted to Judaism and, if male, endured circumcision.

A large number of people opposed the Pharisees. They argued for a more tolerant policy, similar to what the Gentile "God-fearers" enjoyed in the synagogues. Gentiles could join the movement and follow the teachings of Judaism in spirit without following the letter of the Torah. Paul's position, of course, was far more radical. It's unclear if he had thoroughly thought through his understanding of the relationship between the Torah and Jesus at this point. Paul took a subordinate role at the council and kept as quiet as possible, if only because many of those present probably still bore the scars from when Paul had ordered many of them flogged. The meetings must have lasted several days, and the debates were loud and occasionally heated.

Finally, after much debate, Simon Peter intervened. He had lived with this issue personally for nearly two decades. He was a pious Jew and understood the sincere convictions of the Pharisess in the movement. Yet he had also witnessed with his own eyes what had happened when the Roman centurion Cornelius had been baptized and received the gifts of the Spirit. It's clear he felt he had to speak out. "My brothers, you are well aware that from early days God made his choice among you that through my mouth the Gentiles would hear the word of the gospel and believe," Simon said to all those present. "And God, who knows the heart, bore witness by granting them the holy Spirit just as he did us. He made no distinction between us and them, for by faith he purified their hearts" (Acts 15:7–9 NABRE).

Peter could see the effect his words were having on the community. Many were nodding their heads in agreement. He walked in the midst of his friends and coworkers.

"Why, then, are you now putting God to the test by placing on the shoulders of the disciples a yoke that neither our ancestors nor we have been able to bear? On the contrary, we believe that we are saved through the grace of the Lord Jesus, in the same way as they" (vv. 10–11 NABRE).

At this, according to Acts, the whole assembly fell silent (v. 13). Then Paul and Barnabas stepped forward and humbly recounted the signs and wonders they had seen God work among the pagans.

All eyes then turned to James. He likely resembled Jesus somewhat, an austere figure who commanded respect among the residents of Jerusalem whether they believed in Jesus or not. According to Hegesippus, after he was killed the people of Jerusalem erected a pillar, or memorial stone, in his memory close by the temple.[16]

The assembled followers of Jesus probably expected James to balance what Simon Peter had just said. He was well-known for his views on the Torah, and how a redeemed Israel was a light to the Gentiles. So what he said must have shocked everyone present.

"My brothers . . . Symeon has described how God first concerned himself with acquiring from among the Gentiles a people for his name," James began, using a variant of Simon's name. He then quoted a passage from the prophet Amos.

> "'After this I shall return
>> and rebuild the fallen hut of David;
> from its ruins I shall rebuild it
>> and raise it up again,
> so that the rest of humanity may seek out the Lord,
>> even all the Gentiles on whom my name is invoked.'"
> (Acts 15:13–17 nabre)

James then paused. There would be no further discussion. He issued what was, in effect, a ruling.

> "It is my judgment, therefore, that we ought to stop troubling the Gentiles who turn to God, but tell them by letter to avoid pollution from idols, unlawful marriage, the meat of strangled animals, and blood." (vv. 19–20 nabre)

SPREADING THE WORD

The decision had been made. So the assembled apostles and presbyters chose representatives to accompany Paul and Barnabas and communicate the decision of this first council. Among those they chose were Judas called Barsabbas and Silas. The men were to carry a letter to the community in Antioch that spelled out what the decision meant. The letter began:

Since we have heard that some of our number [who went out] without any mandate from us have upset you with their teachings and disturbed your peace of mind, we have with one accord decided to choose representatives and to send them to you along with our beloved Barnabas and Paul, who have dedicated their lives to the name of our Lord Jesus Christ. (vv. 24–26).

The letter went on to mention Judas and Silas and insisted that it was "the decision of the holy Spirit" that the Jesus community not place any burden on people beyond the minimal requirements—namely, that those who join the community should abstain from meat sacrificed to idols, blood, meats from strangled animals, and unlawful marriage.

These four prohibitions have been the occasion of many questions and comments over the centuries. The Greek word translated as "unlawful marriage" is *porneia*, the same word Jesus used when talking about the "exception" to his blanket ban on divorce in Matthew 19. The word can mean "adultery," but usually refers to extramarital sexual activity or promiscuity generally, what we might call cohabitation or "living together."

WIKIPEDIA

One of the oldest manuscripts of a letter of the apostle Paul, known as P[46], gives historians some idea of what the letter from the Council of Jerusalem may have looked like. This papyrus, a portion of Paul's second letter to the Christian community in Corinth, was likely copied around AD 175–220.

We can deduce from Paul's letters to the Corinthians that pagans had a very freewheeling attitude toward sexual relationships (1 Cor. 6:12–20), while the Jews were famous for their sexual restraint and modesty. In their letter, James and the Jerusalem community were assuming that the Greeks shared with them the basics of morality, and thus did not forbid such actions as lying, stealing, and murder. Instead they emphasized the unique moral prohibitions of the Jews, specifically their bans on idolatry, casual sexual relationships, and eating blood or strangled animals.

Why these specific rules? Some scholars believe these minimal requirements are similar to the ones derived from Noah in Genesis. The Talmud considers these so-called Noachide laws the seven minimal standards of morality: the prohibition of idolatry, incest/unchastity, shedding blood, the profanation of God's name, robbery, injustice, and eating the flesh of a living animal.[17] However, these aren't an exact match to James the Just's declaration. The rabbinic list mentions neither drinking blood nor eating the meat of strangled animals. More probably, the Jews at the council had been discussing a kind of "secular morality," the bare minimum rules of ethical conduct that could be expected from Gentiles. The four prohibitions could reflect these discussions rather than the rabbinic list.

There is no doubt that the council of Jerusalem was the most significant meeting in the history of what became the early church. After more than two decades of uncertainty and bitter disputes, the Jesus movement had resolved one of the most contentious issues it faced: whether it would actively seek out Gentile members and, if so, whether those members had to first become Jews. The council answered definitely: Gentiles were welcome, and they need not convert to Judaism.

All the apostles' activities were finally vindicated: the initial outreach to the "semi-pagans" of Samaria, the willingness of Peter to eat with and baptize Gentiles and even Roman officers in Caesarea Maritima, the work of the community in Antioch, and the missionary journeys of Paul and Barnabas in pagan Anatolia. Their work was celebrated and accepted as the template for the future. The leaders of the community now all accepted that the kingdom movement would expand outward beyond Israel. Simon Peter, James, Barnabas, Paul, and other leaders could see now what Jesus meant when he proclaimed, in his final exhortation, that his followers were to "make disciples of all nations" (Matt. 28:19).

As Jesus' followers reflected on his actions over the course of his brief time with them, they recalled the many ways he had reached out beyond Israel. They remembered that Jesus had seen more faith in a Roman officer than he had ever encountered among his fellow Jews (Matt. 8:5–10). The apostles, presbyters, and prophets now fully understood that Jesus truly did want them to become "fishers of men"—and by that he meant, as Paul would later put it in his letter to the people of Colossae, *all* men and women, both Jews and Gentiles, slaves and freeborn, barbarians and Scythians (Col. 3:11). This recognition would lead to the remarkable expansion of the Jesus movement: God was calling all people into the unique fellowship of his kingdom.

Other religious and social movements in that period enjoyed brief success and then died out—including Stoicism, Mithraism, and Gnosticism. But the kingdom movement that Jesus began in AD 27/28 continued to grow and expand until it reached nearly all nations on earth. What the brave Jewish freedom fighters were unable to accomplish with the sword in AD 66–70—the overthrow of the brutal Roman Empire—the followers of Jesus would eventually accomplish with alms, free healing, and the gifts of the Spirit. They would carry out Jesus' command to redeem the entire world—a work that is, even now, continuing.

APPENDIX I

TIME LINE

DATE	EVENT	NEW TESTAMENT SOURCE
6–5 BC	Jesus of Nazareth born in Bethlehem of Judea	Matt. 2:1
4 BC	Herod the Great dies	
	Revolt breaks out following death of Herod	
AD 6	Herod the Great's son Archelaus deposed for incompetence; Judea becomes a Roman province	Matt. 2:22
	Judas the Galilean leads new revolt against the census and new taxes	Acts 5:37
AD 8	Jesus, age twelve, visits Jerusalem with his parents	Luke 2:41–50
AD 14–37	Rule of Tiberius Caesar as Emperor of Rome	Luke 3:1
AD 26	Pontius Pilate appointed fifth prefect of Roman province of Judea	Luke 3:1

AD 27	The prophet John the Baptist appears in the wilderness of Judea	John 1:19-23
	Jesus begins announcing the kingdom of God	Mark 1
Late March AD 30	Jesus travels to Bethany, a short distance from Jerusalem, and restores his friend Lazarus to life	John 11:1-44
Early April	As reports about the raising of Lazarus circulate, Jesus' fame grows. The chief priests plot to kill him.	Matt. 26:1-5, John 11:45-53
	Jesus travels to Ephraim, in central Judea, to "lie low" and avoid arrest before the Passover festival.	John 11:54-57
Yom Rishon (Sunday) 9 Nissan, April 2	Jesus is welcomed by large crowds as he arrives in Jerusalem on a donkey in a deliberate allusion to messianic prophecies in Zechariah	John 12:12-16
Monday, 10 Nissan, April 3	Jesus and his followers engage in symbolic protest on the Temple Mount	Mark 11:11, Matt. 21:10-17, Luke 19:45-46
Tuesday, 11 Nissan, April 4	Jesus addresses large groups of Jewish pilgrims on the Rabbi Steps near the southern wall and in the open places around the Pool of Siloam	Mark 11:27-33, Matt. 21:23-27, Luke 20:1-8, John 2:18-22
Wednesday, 12 Nissan, April 5	Jesus continues debating Pharisees and scribes on the Rabbi Steps, dines with Simon the Pharisee in Bethany. Conflict with Judas Iscariot erupts over cost of perfume poured on Jesus' head.	Luke 7:36-50
Thursday, 13-14 Nissan, April 6	Jesus remains in Bethany and then eats a Passover seder meal with his followers a day early in Jerusalem due to his looming arrest, after sundown as 13 Nissan becomes 14 Nissan	Mark 14:12-31

Friday, 14 Nissan, April 7	Jesus crucified on the Day of Preparation before the Passover. Passover officially begins at sundown.	John 19:31-34
Saturday, 15 Nissan, April 8	The first day of Passover	
Sunday, 16 Nissan, April 9	Jesus is seen alive again	John 20:14-18
	Appearances of the risen Jesus cease at Ascension	Acts 1:1-11
	Matthias chosen by lot to replace Judas	Acts 1:26
May 28, AD 30	During the Jewish festival of Weeks, or Pentecost, the followers of Jesus experience the descent of the Holy Spirit	Acts 2
	Peter leads the community and heals the sick	Acts 3
	Peter and John arrested and then released	Acts 4:1-23
	Members of the Jesus community in Jerusalem share their food	Acts 4:32
	Deaths of Ananias and Sapphira	Acts 5:1-11
AD 31	The Greek-speaking deacon Stephen is seized and stoned to death	Acts 6-7
	The Pharisee Saul of Tarsus persecutes the Jesus community	Acts 8:1-3
	The apostle Philip evangelizes the Samaritans	Acts 8:5
	Simon Magus tries to buy the gifts of the Spirit	Acts 8:9-25
	Philip encounters the Ethiopian eunuch	Acts 8:26-40

AD 33-34	Saul encounters the risen Jesus on the road to Damascus	Acts 9:1-9
AD 34-37	Paul leaves Damascus and remains in "Arabia"	Acts 9:19-25, 26:20; Gal. 1:16-17
AD 36	Pilate attacks Samaritan gathering and is ordered back to Rome	
	Marcellus named Roman prefect	
AD 37	Paul returns to Jerusalem and meets with Peter	Acts 9:26-30; Gal. 1:18
	Paul travels to his hometown of Tarsus and remains there for eight years	
AD 37-41	Marullus named Roman prefect	
AD 37	Peter reaches out to pagan Gentiles	Acts 10, 11
	Jewish historian Josephus born in Jerusalem	
	Caligula becomes Roman emperor	
AD 39	Caligula crisis occurs when Roman emperor tries to have a statue of himself erected in temple in Jerusalem	
AD 41	Roman emperor Caligula assassinated by Praetorian Guard	
AD 42	The Cypriot Levite Barnabas is sent to Antioch	Acts 11:22
	Paul suffers from physical ailment ("thorn in the flesh")	2 Cor. 12:7
AD 41-44	Marcus Julius Agrippa named king of the Jews	
AD 41-54	Claudius becomes Roman emperor	
AD 44	The apostle James the son of Zebedee beheaded on order of King Herod Agrippa	Acts 12:2
	Peter freed from Roman prison by angelic visitor	Acts 12:6-17

	Herod Agrippa dies mysteriously in Caesarea	Acts 12:20-23
AD 44-46	Cuspius Fadus appointed procurator of Judea	
AD 45-46	Famine in Judea	
AD 45	Barnabas travels to Tarsus and brings Paul back to Antioch	Acts 11:25-26
AD 46-48	Tiberius Julius Alexander appointed Roman procurator	
AD 47	Paul and Barnabas sail to Cyprus and then to southern coast of what is now Turkey	Acts 13:4-14
	Paul preaches in Pisidian Antioch	Acts 13:13-41
	Paul and Barnabas in Iconium	Acts 14:1-7
	Paul and Barnabas travel to Lystra and Derbe	Acts 14:5-20
	Paul and Barnabas return to Syrian Antioch	Acts 14:21-28
AD 48-52	Ventidius Cumanus appointed Roman procurator	
AD 49	The Council of Jerusalem	Acts 15:1-35
	Paul and Barnabas return to Antioch but part company over dispute about Barnabas's friend/cousin John Mark	Acts 15:36-41
AD 50	Apostle Peter visits Rome	
AD 52-60	Marcus Antonius Felix appointed Roman procurator	
AD 54-68	Nero rules as Roman emperor	
AD 60-62	Porcius Festus appointed Roman procurator	
AD 60	Paul arrested and imprisoned in Caesarea Maritima	Acts 24:1-22
AD 62	Paul appears before Roman procurator Festus	Acts 25:1-12
	Paul appears before Agrippa II	Acts 25:23-27, Acts 26

APPENDIX I

	Paul is sent by ship to Rome	Acts 27:1
	Paul is shipwrecked on his way to Rome	Acts 27:6-44
	Paul comes ashore at Malta	Acts 28:1
	Paul preaches in Rome	Acts 28:17-30
AD 64	Apostle Paul beheaded in Rome, perhaps in June	
	Apostle Peter crucified in Rome after the Great Fire, buried in roadside cemetery just outside an arena near the Vatican hill	

Who's Who in the Early Jesus Movement

THE HERALD

Yochanan (John) the Baptizer (ca. 5/6 BC–AD 29): A Jewish prophet and religious leader who heralded the arrival of the long-promised Messiah, or Savior. After denouncing the marriage of the tetrarch Herod Antipas to his half brother's wife, Herodias, John was arrested and beheaded around AD 29 in Herod the Great's mountain fortress of Machaerus near the Dead Sea.

THE FOUNDER

Yeshu'a bar Yosef (Jesus of Nazareth) (ca. 5 BC–AD 30): Born shortly before Herod the Great's death in 4 BC, Jesus was a charismatic Jewish rabbi who announced and inaugurated a religious and social movement in the late 20s of the common era, which he called the kingdom of God. It spread rapidly throughout the eastern Mediterranean until it became the largest religious society on earth. He was executed as a potential troublemaker by the Romans in AD 30 but then raised from the dead three days later.

THE FAMILY

Miriam (Mary) and stepfather **Yosef (Joseph)**: Devout Jews who may have hailed originally from southern Judea but settled in the Nazareth region in the last years of Herod the Great's reign.

James, Joses (Joseph), Simon, and Judas:[1] Brothers, stepbrothers, or cousins[2] of Jesus.

Unknown sisters: Or female relatives[3] of Jesus.

Elizabeth: Mary of Nazareth's cousin, and her husband, **Zechariah**, a priest, who lived in Judea.

THE INNER CIRCLE

Shimon (Simon) and **Andrew:** Sons of Jonah, from the village of Bethsaida.

Philip: A friend of Simon and Andrew.

Ya'akov (James) and **Yochanan (John):** Sons of a wealthy Galilean man named Zebedee[4] and his wife, **Salome**.[5]

The **"Younger James"**[6] and his brother **Yehuda**[7] (Joses or Jude, short for Thaddeus[8]): Sons of Mary[9] and Alphaeus.[10]

Mattityahu (Matthew), or Levi: The son of Alpheus and possibly the brother of the younger James and Jude.

Shimon (Simon): The Zealot.

Tau'ma (Thomas): The Twin.

Bar-Talmai (Bartholomew): Son of Ptolemy from the village of Kfar Cana.

Yehuda (Judas): Probably from the southern village of Keriot.

EARLY SUPPORTERS

Joanna: The wife of Chuza, house steward for the Jewish king Herod Antipas (Luke 8:3).

Susanna: A wealthy woman and financial patron of the Jesus movement (Luke 8:3).

Mary of Migdal (Magdalene): The first witness to the resurrection (Luke 8:2).

Mary, the wife of Clopas (or Cleopas): The mother of the Younger James and Jude (Mark 15:40, Matt. 27:56). According to the gospel of John, she was one of the women present at the crucifixion of Jesus (19:25).

Eleazar (Lazarus), Marta, and Mary: Of Bethany, in Judea.

Nicodemus: A Pharisee and leader of the Sanhedrin, who visits Jesus at night to discuss various aspects of Jesus' teaching (John 3:1–2). According to the gospel of John, he brought more than a hundred pounds of aloes and spices to anoint Jesus' body after the crucifixion (19:39).

Joseph of Arimathea: A member of the Jewish Sanhedrin who was a secret follower of Jesus, donated his own rock-cut tomb to serve as Jesus' burial place following the crucifixion (Matt. 27:57–60).

THE POLITICAL LEADERSHIP

Jewish

Herod the Great (74/73–4 BC): Son of Antipater and Cypros. A half-Jewish aristocrat from Idumea, south of Jerusalem, he ruled most of Israel as a client king of the Romans and was deeply involved in the intrigues between the Roman leader Mark Antony and Octavian. He is renowned for massive building projects throughout Jerusalem and much of Israel.

Herod Archelaus (23 BC–AD 18): Son of Herod the Great and his Samaritan wife, Malthace, ruled as ethnarch of Samaria, Judea, and Idumea for a decade after his father's death (Matt. 2:13–23), from 4 BC to AD 6.

Herod Antipater or Antipas (20 BC–39 AD): Son of Herod the Great and Malthrace, ruled as tetrarch ("ruler of a quarter") of Galilee and Perea beyond the Jordan. When the prophet John the Baptist criticized his marriage to his half brother's former wife, Herodias, Antipas ordered that John be beheaded. He was deposed by the emperor Caligula in AD 39.

Philip the Tetrarch (22 BC–AD 34): Son of Herod the Great and Cleopatra of Jerusalem (not Cleopatra of Egypt), ruled as tetrarch of the regions of Iturea and Trachonitis in what is now southern Syria and Jordan and rebuilt the pagan resort town of Paneas as his capital, Caesarea Philippi. Philip married his niece Salome, who, according to the gospels of Mark and Matthew, requested that Herod Antipas give her the head of John the Baptist at the urging of her mother, Herodias (Matt. 14:8).

Joseph Caiaphas (dates unknown): Ruled as the high priest (the highest ranked Jewish official) from AD 18 until he was deposed along with Pontius Pilate by the proconsul Lucius Vitellius Veteris in AD 36. According to the Gospels, Caiaphas believed Jesus and his movement were a threat to Jewish society and urged his execution.

Gamaliel the Elder (dates unknown): Grandson of Rabbi Hillel. He was a leading Jewish expert in Torah in the first century and president of the Jewish council, or Sanhedrin, when the followers of Jesus began to evangelize the people of Jerusalem after the crucifixion of Jesus. According to Acts, he urged moderation when dealing with the Jesus movement (Acts 5:34–38). Saul of Tarsus is said to have studied "at the feet of Gamaliel" but that may mean he was a student in Gamaliel's Torah academy in Jerusalem (Acts 22:3).

Herod Agrippa I (11 BC–AD 44): Grandson of Herod the Great and son of Herod's son Aristobulus IV and Berenice, ruled as king of the

Jews for three years, from AD 41–44. Agrippa was raised in Rome and was childhood friends of the future emperors Claudius and Caligula. Appointed by Caligula, he was a king of the regions once held by his uncle Philip the Tetrarch. One of Agrippa's first acts was to behead James, the son of Zebedee.

Roman

Tiberius Caesar (42 BC–AD 37): The all-powerful emperor of Rome from AD 14 until his death in AD 37. According to the gospel of Luke, John the Baptist began his peaching in the fifteenth year of Tiberius's reign—which historians date to around the year AD 28 or 29.

Caligula (AD 12–41): The nickname of the Roman emperor Gaius Julius Caesar Augustus Germanicus. He ruled from AD 37 to 41. Around AD 39, Caligula tried to have an enormous statue of himself erected in the temple in Jerusalem—an event that some scholars propose may be the "abomination of desolation" prophesied by Jesus in Mark 13:14. He arranged the appointment of his childhood friend Herod Agrippa as governor of Philip the Tetrarch's territories.

Claudius (AD 10–54): Was made Roman emperor by the Praetorian Guard following its assassination of Caligula in AD 41. He ruled until AD 54. According to Josephus, the Jewish king Herod Agrippa, who was visiting Rome at the time and found Caligula's body, played an important role in advising Claudius about how he could remain in power.

Pontius Pilate (dates unknown): A Roman military officer, fifth prefect of the Roman province of Judaea from AD 26–36. According to the first-century Jewish writers Josephus and Philo of Alexandria, Pilate was widely considered a brutal governor who despised his subjects. At the urging of some Jewish officials, Pilate ordered the torture and execution by crucifixion of Jesus, probably around April 7, AD 30. Following a massacre of Samaritan pilgrims in AD 36, Pilate was ordered to return to Rome by the Syrian legate Lucius Vitellius.

Marcellus and Marullus: Roman prefects of Judaea from AD 36–41.

Cuspius Fadus: Appointed procurator of Judea by the emperor

Claudius from AD 44–46. According to Josephus, it was Fadus who took action against the false prophet Theudas mentioned in the Acts of the Apostles (5:36).

Tiberius Julius Alexander: A Jewish-born general in the Roman army, originally from Alexandria, Egypt, who ruled as procurator of Judea from AD 46–48. After serving as governor in Egypt, he participated in the final Roman assault against Jerusalem in AD 70, arguing that the famous temple should be spared.

Marcus Antonius Felix: Roman procurator of Judea from AD 52–58, he oversaw the trial of the apostle Paul and spoke with him many times (Acts 24). He is mentioned by the historians Josephus, Suetonius, and Tacitus.

Lucius Sergius Paulus (dates unknown): Proconsul of Cyprus under Emperor Claudius, he suggested to Paul and Barnabas that they visit Antioch in Pisidia, in central Turkey. According to Acts, he was an early Roman convert to the Way of Jesus (Acts 13:6–12). Inscriptions bearing his name have been found in Rome and elsewhere.

Claudius Lysias: A high-ranking Roman military officer, a tribune or commander of a thousand men, who rescued the apostle Paul from a Jewish mob on the Temple Mount at the end of Acts (21:27–32). His brief letter to the procurator Felix in Caesarea, describing the incident, is reprinted there (Acts 23:26–30).

EARLY LEADERS OF THE WAY

Ananias of Damascus (dates unknown): An early follower of Jesus who lived in Damascus and who healed Saul of Tarsus's blindness (Acts 9:10–18).

Saul of Tarsus (5 BC?–AD 62): A Greek-speaking Jew from the large coastal city of Tarsus in what is now southeastern Turkey, and a Roman citizen. He studied Jewish law in the school of Gamaliel in Jerusalem (Acts 22:3), was a member of the Pharisee sect (Phil. 3:5), and was an early and violent opponent of the Jesus movement (Acts 8:3). After seeing a vision of the risen Jesus on the road to Damascus to arrest Jesus' followers (Acts 9:4–6), Saul was renamed Paul and became the greatest early evangelist of the movement among the Gentiles, and Christianity's first theologian. Fourteen of the twenty-seven writings in the New Testament, all public letters, are presented as written by him.

Joseph called Barnabas: A Greek-speaking Jew and Levite from the island of Cyprus, he donated property to the Jesus movement and became an early, popular, and persuasive proponent of Jesus' teachings. He may have been a relative of the New Testament figure of John Mark. He sought out the apostle Paul after he returned to Tarsus and convinced him to return to Antioch. Some apostolic fathers name him as the author of the book of Hebrews in the New Testament.

Stephen (dates unknown): A Greek-speaking Jew and early leader of the Jesus movement who was chosen by Jesus' closest followers to be one of the seven deacons, or financial administrators, of the movement (Acts 6). After getting into a violent dispute with members of a Jerusalem synagogue known as the Synagogue of the Freedmen, he was arrested and tried before the Jewish Council (Sanhedrin) and became the first martyr of the Way just two years or so after Jesus' crucifixion (Acts 7). According to Acts, he was stoned to death and his death was witnessed by Saul of Tarsus (8:1).

John Mark (dates unknown): The son of a wealthy Jerusalem matron named Mary, he was a companion of the apostle Paul and Barnabas on their first journey from Antioch to Cyprus and south-central Turkey (Acts 12:25). The gospel of Mark mentions a young man named John Mark who witnessed Jesus' arrest in the garden of Gethsemane (14:51–52). John Mark may have been a relative of Barnabas, and a dispute arose between Paul and Barnabas over whether John Mark could accompany them, as Barnabas wanted, on a second missionary journey. As a result of this disagreement, Paul and Barnabas parted company.

Andronicus and Junia (dates unknown): Relatives of Saul of Tarsus and early Jewish believers in Jesus who joined the Jesus movement before

Saul's conversion. They were likely husband and wife but could have been siblings. According to Saul/Paul, they were prisoners with him in Rome (Rom. 16:7), arrested as part of the fierce persecution that arose under the emperor Nero.

Cornelius the Centurion: A Roman officer stationed in Caesarea Maritima, the capital of Roman administration in Israel, who became one of the first Gentile converts to the Way of Jesus. He is portrayed in Acts as a "God-fearer," which meant he was a Gentile who informally converted to Jewish beliefs and customs without having undergone circumcision. It was Peter's experience with Cornelius and the pagan believers in his household that convinced Jesus' inner circle, including staunch supporters of the Jewish law, that pagan followers of Jesus did not have to convert to Judaism in order to join the Way.

Joseph Barsabbas: Also known as Justus, he was one of Jesus' earliest followers and a candidate to fill the office of apostle, one of the Twelve, following the suicide of Judas Iscariot. After the remaining members of the Twelve drew lots, he lost out to another early follower, Matthias.

Matthias: An early follower of Jesus who was numbered as one of the Twelve following the suicide of Judas Iscariot.

Lucius of Cyrene: One of the founders of the Jesus movement in Antioch on the Orontes, a Greco-Roman city located on the Mediterranean coast of what is now southeastern Turkey (Acts 13:1).

Simeon Niger: One of the prophets of the Jesus movement in Antioch when Paul and Barnabas first visited (Acts 13:1). The name "niger," or black, might mean he was an African.

Manaen (or Menachem): One of the leaders of the Jesus community in Antioch who laid hands on Barnabas and Paul and sent them on their first missionary journey to Cyprus and central Turkey (Acts 13:1). Early traditions mention him as a household friend of Herod Antipas, the ruler of Galilee, and speculate that he was among the Jewish followers of Jesus who fled Jerusalem following the martyrdom of Stephen.

Acknowledgments

As usual, the writing of any book is a group enterprise in which only the author gets the credit. In my case especially I have depended upon the vast erudition and expertise of innumerable biblical scholars and archaeologists—some of whom have taken the trouble to answer my questions directly and guide me through mountains of scholarly material. To paraphrase the old Willie Nelson song, my heroes have always been biblical scholars—and I know enough to know that I'm not in their guild. I won't embarrass them by naming them now but I am eternally grateful.

I would also like to thank the editors at Thomas Nelson, particularly Jenny Baumgartner, Heather Skelton, and Brigitta Nortker, who kept this project moving forward and (more or less) on deadline. I am also grateful to Greg Jenks, PhD, who took the trouble to read the entire manuscript, looking for egregious errors, and to the meticulous copy editor Jennifer McNeil, who made me dot every *i* and cross every *t*. I would also like to thank my family. My long-suffering wife, Glenn Ellen, has put up with my odd obsessions (and astronomical Amazon bill) for decades. My children, too, have gotten used to seeing mountains of strange books piled up in our family room. I am very grateful for the stimulating, often challenging questions raised by our children, Robert, James, Kelly, Mary, and Jane. It has been their myriad questions about the New Testament over the years that have driven me to write this book. Finally, I would like to thank my father, A'lan, and his wife, Soon, and my many brothers and sisters, for their love and support over the years.

NOTES

INTRODUCTION

1. Robert J. Hutchinson, "The Jesus Seminar Unmasked," *Christianity Today*, April 29, 1996.

2. Robert J. Hutchinson, "What the Rabbi Taught Me About Jesus," *Christianity Today*, September 13, 1993, 28.

3. Without wishing to name-drop excessively, the scholars who have influenced me the most are people such as N. T. Wright, James D. G. Dunn, Larry Hurtado, Richard Bauckham, Luke Timothy Johnson, and Craig Evans. These are top-tier scholars who use all the tools of contemporary biblical scholarship but who also remain faithful Christians.

4. Ehrman says, "The story of Jesus's triumphal entry into Jerusalem has long been recognized by scholars as historically problematic." Bart D. Ehrman, *Did Jesus Exist?* (New York: HarperOne, 2012), 201. See also Bart D. Ehrman, *How Jesus Became God: The Exaltation of a Jewish Preacher from Galilee* (New York: HarperOne, 2014), 157.

5. For those interested in why many Christian New Testament scholars are not bothered in the least by the "discrepancies" and alleged "contradictions" in the Gospels, see Robert J. Hutchinson, *Searching for Jesus* (Nashville: Thomas Nelson, 2015), 46.

6. "Should we, therefore, accept the opposite opinion . . . that all the contents of the Gospels must be assumed fictitious until they are proven genuine? No, that also is too extreme a viewpoint and would not be applied in other fields. When, for example, one tries to build up facts from the accounts of pagan historians, judgment often has to be given not

in the light of any external confirmation—which is sometimes, but by no means always, available—but on the basis of historical deductions and arguments which attain nothing better than probability. The same applies to the Gospels. Their contents need not be assumed fictitious until they are proved authentic. But they have to be subjected to the usual standards of historical persuasiveness." Michael Grant, *Jesus: An Historian's Review of the Gospels* (New York: Charles Scribner's Sons, 1977), 201.

7. There is independent corroboration of some facts reported in the Gospels: both the Jewish Talmud and the Roman historian Tacitus (ca. AD 56–117) report that Jesus was executed. Tacitus adds that he was condemned by Pontius Pilate: "Christus, from whom the name had its origin, suffered the extreme penalty during the reign of Tiberius at the hands of one of our procurators, Pontius Pilatus, and a most mischievous superstition, thus checked for the moment, again broke out not only in Judæa, the first source of the evil, but even in Rome, where all things hideous and shameful from every part of the world find their centre and become popular." Tacitus, *Annals* 15.44, retrieved November 2, 2016, http://classics.mit.edu/Tacitus /annals.11.xv.html. Most historians concede that the passage in Tacitus's ~~False~~ *Annals* does provide independent corroboration of the Gospels' account of Jesus' crucifixion. However, a handful of so-called mythicists, those who believe Jesus never existed at all and that the Gospels are works of fiction, deny this. They claim that Tacitus's account is based on stories in the New Testament that he heard indirectly.

8. The only other record historians have to support or contradict Herodotus's version of what happened comes from the writing of the Sicilian historian Diodorus Siculus, who wrote in the first century BC, more than four hundred years after Herodotus.

9. For example, the Greek author Papias (ca. AD 70–163), quoted at length by the Christian historian Eusebius (ca. AD 260–340), relates how he heard the gospel of Mark came to be written. He says that Mark was a companion and translator of the apostle Peter and wrote down meticulously the anecdotes about and sayings of Jesus as Peter told them, but not in chronological order. This has led many scholars to conclude that the Gospels are indeed based on eyewitness testimony but that the order of events in the Gospels, particularly in the beginning, likely varies from gospel to gospel.

10. "Simon Peter said to him, 'Let Mary leave us, for females don't deserve life.' Jesus said, 'Look, I will guide her to make her male, so that she too may become a living spirit resembling you males. For every female who makes herself male will enter the domain of Heaven.'" Gospel of Thomas, 114, in Robert J. Miller, *The Complete Gospels: Annotated Scholars Version* (San Francisco: Harper San Francisco, 1992), 322.

11. For those interested in Egeria's diary, one contemporary edition is *Egeria: Diary of a Pilgrimage*, trans. George E. Gingras (New York: Newman Press, 1970).

12. Andrew Griffin, "Jesus Trial Site 'Found': Herod's Palace Remains Discovered Near Tower of David in Jerusalem," *Independent*, January 5, 2015.

13. Scholars are divided on whether the James Ossuary, the alleged burial box of James the brother of Jesus, is genuine. Some evangelical scholars, such as Ben Witherington III, believe it is likely authentic. Others, however, including the Israel Antiquities Authority (IAA), believe it to be a well-crafted forgery. See Hershel Shanks and Ben Witherington III, *The Brother of Jesus: The Dramatic Story and Meaning of the First Archaeological Link to Jesus and His Family* (San Francisco: HarperSanFrancisco, 2003). See also Thomas H. Maugh II, "Archaeology Journal Says Burial Box of Jesus' Brother Is Genuine," *Los Angeles Times*, June 13, 2012, http:// articles.latimes.com/2012/jun/13/science/la-sci-sn-jesus-brother-ossuary -20120613; and Hershel Shanks, "Hershel Shanks Explores the Evidence Before the James Ossuary Trial," *Bible History Daily*, video, 54:01, March 13, 2012, http://www.biblicalarchaeology.org/daily/biblical-artifacts /artifacts-and-the-bible/video-hershel-shanks-explores-the-evidence -before-the-james-ossuary-trial/.

14. Jonathan L. Reed, *Archaeology and the Galilean Jesus* (Harrisburg, PA: Trinity Press International, 2000), 80.

15. Bart D. Ehrman, *Jesus Before the Gospels: How the Earliest Christians Remembered, Changed, and Invented Their Stories of the Savior* (New York: HarperOne, 2016).

16. James G. Crossley, *The Date of Mark's Gospel* (London: T&T Clark International, 2004), 22–24.

17. John A. T. Robinson, *Redating the New Testament* (London: SCM Press, 1976), 13.

18. Isabel Kershner, "New Evidence on When Bible Was Written: Ancient Shopping Lists," *New York Times*, April 11, 2016, http://www.nytimes .com/2016/04/12/world/middleeast/new-evidence-onwhen-bible-was -written-ancient-shopping-lists.html; Alan Millard, *Reading and Writing in the Time of Jesus* (London: Sheffield Academic Press, 2001), 223, quoted in James M. Arlandson, "Did Some Disciples Take Notes During Jesus' Ministry?" Bible.org, April 15, 2008, https://bible.org/seriespage /8-did-some-disciples-take-notes-during-jesus-ministry.

19. "Then Jeremiah called Baruch the son of Neriah, and Baruch wrote on a scroll at the dictation of Jeremiah all the words of the LORD that he had spoken to him" (Jer. 36:4).

20. In addition, it appears that Matthew and Luke "correct" Mark's Greek grammar and vocabulary—another indication for scholars that Mark likely wrote first. This is often lost on readers of English Bibles because translators also "correct" Mark. For example, in Greek Mark frequently switches back and forth between the present and past tense in a single sentence—as a writer might do without a good editor! In Matthew's and Luke's versions of the same events, however, the evangelists appear to correct Mark and use the past tense consistently. This is difficult to see without showing the Greek text. However, here is an example: One literal rendering of the Greek of Mark 1:20–21 is "And immediately he called them, and, having left their father Zebedee in the boat with the hired servants, they went away after him. *And they go on to Capernaum,* and immediately, on the sabbaths, having gone into the synagogue, he was teaching" (YLT). The parallel passage in Luke 4:31–32 changes the present tense of "and they go on to Capernaum" (Καὶ εἰσπορεύονται εἰς Καφαρναούμ) to the past tense of "and he came down to Capernaum" (Καὶ κατῆλθεν εἰς Καφαρναούμ; YLT). English translators do the same thing: The English Standard Version, for example, translates Mark 1:21 using a consistent past tense: "And they *went* into Capernaum, and immediately on the Sabbath he entered the synagogue and was teaching." This seemingly arcane issue of Greek grammar is of interest to scholars because it is one of the arguments used to claim that Mark wrote his account first. I came across this example from a Reddit discussion board at: https://www.reddit.com/r/AcademicBiblical/comments/3lv3ic/what _is_the_significance_of_the_historical/. For a full discussion of the issues regarding Mark's allegedly poor grammar and its bearing on the priority

of Markan authorship, see Daniel Wallace, "The Synoptic Problem," Bible.org, June 2, 2004, https://bible.org/article/synoptic-problem.

21. It should be said that many reputable scholars, both liberal and conservative, believe that no such "sayings source" like Q ever existed—despite the discovery of the Gospel of Thomas, made up entirely of sayings of Jesus, in 1945. For one thing, no copy of Q has ever been found. In addition, there are other possible explanations for the close agreement in the wording of some of Jesus' sayings in Matthew and Luke—for example, the Farrer hypothesis, which proposes that Mark wrote first, Matthew used Mark, and then Luke used Matthew. See Mark Goodacre, *The Synoptic Problem: A Way Through the Maze* (London: Bloomsbury T&T Clark, 2004), 163.

PART I: THE ROAD TO JERUSALEM

1. According to the second-century Christian writer Irenaeus (AD 130–202), this lost saying of Jesus was communicated personally to the Christian author Papias (ca. AD 70–163) by none other than John the ~~No~~ Evangelist, author of the fourth gospel. It is one of the very few examples of *agrapha*, possibly authentic sayings of Jesus not found in the New Testament. Irenaeus wrote originally in Greek, but his work is known only in Latin translation. Irenaeus, *Against Heresies* 5.33.3–4, trans. Alexander Roberts and William Rambaut, eds. Alexander Roberts, James Donaldson, and A. Cleveland Coxe, *Ante-Nicene Fathers*, vol. 1 (Buffalo, NY: Christian Literature, 1885). Revised and edited for use online by Kevin Knight for newadvent.org, http://www.newadvent.org/fathers /0103.htm.

CHAPTER 1: FISHERS OF MEN

1. We know about Jesus' clothing from John 19:23 and Mark 6:56: "And wherever he came, in villages, cities, or countryside, they laid the sick in the marketplaces and implored him that they might touch even the fringe of his garment." Experts say that the "fringe" almost certainly refers to the *tzitzit* fringe, traditionally affixed to the Jewish prayer shawl or cloak known as a *tallit* and worn by Jewish males to this day.

2. If Jesus was born, as many experts believe, a year or two before Herod the Great's death (Matt. 2:13–21) in 4 BC, and died, as this book will argue,

in AD 30, then he would have been thirty-five years old at the time of his death. The alternative year often proposed for Jesus' death is AD 33. If that were the case, then Jesus would have been around thirty-eight years old when he died.

3. Richard A. Horsley and Neil Asher Silberman, *The Message and the Kingdom* (New York: Grosset/Putnam, 1997), 57.

4. This account of the calling of the first disciples is based on Luke 5:1–10.

CHAPTER 2: THE KINGDOM OF GOD

1. Rodney Stark, *The Rise of Christianity* (New York: HarperCollins, 1996), 7.

2. Ibid.

3. Josephus recounts how Aristobulus, the reigning king of the bickering dynasty, sent to the Roman general Pompey, camped near Damascus, a gift of a golden vine worth five hundred talents. At the time, Aristobulus and his brother Hyrcannus were locked in a deadly conflict over who should be king. Emissaries from both sides arrived to plead the causes of their respective masters and urged the Roman general to intervene— which, eventually, he did, by invading the country and conquering Jerusalem. Josephus, *Antiquities of the Jews* 14.3.1 (34), trans. William Whiston, in *The Works of Josephus: Complete and Unabridged* (Peabody, MA: Hendrickson, 1987).

4. Josephus says that Cleopatra attempted to seduce Herod while she was visiting him, but that he rejected her advances. "When Cleopatra . . . had accompanied Antony in his expedition to Armenia as far as Euphrates, she . . . passed on to Judea, where Herod met her. . . . When she was there, and was very often with Herod, she endeavored to have criminal conversation with the king; nor did she affect secrecy in the indulgence of such sort of pleasures; and perhaps she had in some measure a passion of love to him; or rather, what is most probable, she laid a treacherous snare for him, by aiming to obtain such adulterous conversation from him: however, upon the whole, she seemed overcome with love to him. Now Herod had a great while borne no good-will to Cleopatra, as knowing that she was a woman irksome to all; and at that time he thought her particularly worthy of his hatred, if this attempt proceeded out of lust; he had also thought of preventing her intrigues, by putting her to

death, if such were her endeavors. However, he refused to comply with her proposals, and called a counsel of his friends to consult with them whether he should not kill her, now he had her in his power; for that he should thereby deliver all those from a multitude of evils to whom she was already become irksome . . . and that this very thing would be much for the advantage of Antony himself, since she would certainly not be faithful to him. . . . But when he thought to follow this advice, his friends would not let him . . . and begged of him to undertake nothing rashly, for that Antony would never bear it . . . [Their] considerations made it very plain that in so doing he would find his government filled with mischief, . . . whereas it was still in his power to reject that wickedness she would persuade him to, and to come off honorably at the same time. So by thus affrighting Herod . . . they restrained him from it. So he treated Cleopatra kindly, and made her presents, and conducted her on her way to Egypt." Josephus, *Antiquities* 15.4.2.

5. Brian Handwerk, "Underground Tunnels Found in Israel Used in Ancient Jewish Revolt," *National Geographic News*, March 15, 2006, http://news.nationalgeographic.com/news/2006/03/0315_060315_jewish _revolt.html.

6. The Galilee area and the Jordan River valley south to Perea, just north of the Dead Sea, were given to Herod Antipas (whom Jesus was to call "that fox" in Luke 13:32, and who eventually wanted Jesus killed). To the north and east of the Sea of Galilee, the regions known as Ituraea and Trachonitis were given to Herod the Great's son Philip. In AD 6, the Romans annexed Judea, where the capital city of Jerusalem was located, as well as Samaria to the north and Idumea to the south, and ruled these territories directly under a governor, or prefect, appointed by Caesar.

7. See James D. Tabor, *The Jesus Dynasty* (New York: Simon & Schuster, 2006), 195.

8. K. C. Hanson and Douglas E. Oakman, *Palestine in the Time of Jesus* (Minneapolis: Augsburg Fortress Press, 1998), 114.

9. Tabor, *The Jesus Dynasty*, 195.

10. A Roman talent was roughly 71 pounds, so 400 talents would be the equivalent of 454,400 ounces of gold. At a price of $1,200 an ounce, 400 talents would be equal to roughly $545 million.

11. Josephus, *Antiquities* 17.306–08, trans. William Whiston, *The Works of Josephus: Complete and Unabridged* (Peabody, MA: Hendrickson Publishers, 1987), quoted in Hanson and Oakman, *Palestine in the Time of Jesus*, 115.

12. I generally follow the chronology outlined in John Meier's classic, *A Marginal Jew: Rethinking the Historical Jesus* (New York: Doubleday, 1994).

13. Dale Allison is the author of a classic and scholarly exposition of the apocalyptic prophet scenario, *Jesus of Nazareth: Millenarian Prophet* (Minneapolis: Augsburg Fortress Press, 1998). However, in recent years Allison appears to have moved away somewhat from his original position, expressing a greater humility about what scholars can and cannot know about Jesus' inner thoughts. "Speaking for myself, although I have written a book with the title *Jesus of Nazareth: Millenarian Prophet*, I am no millenarian prophet; and a Jesus without eschatological error would certainly make my life easier," he wrote in a more recent book. "I might, for instance, be able to tell some of my relatives, without them shuddering aghast, what I really do for a living." Dale C. Allison, *Resurrecting Jesus: The Earliest Christian Tradition and Its Interpreters* (Edinburgh: T&T Clark, 2005), 133.

14. For a brief but thorough summary of Ehrman's argument for Jesus as an apocalyptic prophet who mistakenly believed the world would end in his own lifetime, see Bart Ehrman, *Did Jesus Exist?* (New York: HarperOne, 2012), 297–331.

15. Interested readers can investigate all of the Q sayings themselves, those sayings found in Matthew and Luke but not in Mark, in Robert J. Miller, ed., *The Complete Gospels: Annotated Scholars Version* (San Francisco: HarperSanFrancisco, 1992), 249–300. The one text from Q that Ehrman cites in support of his thesis (that Jesus thought the end of the world was coming in his lifetime) is Q:17–37 (= Luke 17:34 = Matt. 24:26–41). This one text does indeed describe an end-times scenario that comes suddenly, when two are in a bed and "one will be taken and the other left," yet there is nothing in the text that indicates this event is *imminent*. In fact, the text says just the opposite. Jesus predicts a future of hardship and suffering when his followers will "yearn to see" the coming of the Son of Man and yet "you won't see it." For an introduction to the debate over whether Jesus was an "apocalyptic prophet," see Robert J. Miller, ed., *The Apocalyptic Jesus: A Debate* (Santa Rosa, CA: Polebridge Press, 2001). One of the best

refutations of the apocalyptic Jesus theory is Richard Horsley, *The Prophet Jesus and the Renewal of Israel* (Grand Rapids: Wm B. Eerdmans, 2012).

CHAPTER 3: BRINGING THE DEAD TO LIFE

1. Shimon Gibson, *The Final Days of Jesus: The Archaeological Evidence* (New York: HarperOne, 2009), 19.

2. Jerome Murphy-O'Connor, *The Holy Land: An Oxford Archaeological Guide* (Oxford: Oxford University Press, 2008), Kindle edition, loc. 2895.

3. John J. Rousseau and Rami Arav, *Jesus and His World* (Minneapolis: Augsburg Fortress Press, 1995), 16.

4. Gibson, *Final Days of Jesus*, 30.

5. Georgina Stubbs, "Buried Alive: 6 Shocking Times People Have 'Woke from the Dead' Terrifying Friends and Family," *Daily Record*, September 27, 2014, http://www.dailyrecord.co.uk/news/weird-news/buried-alive -6-shocking-times-4332522.

6. Jewish New Testament scholar Paula Fredriksen concedes that it's quite possible that the high priest Caiaphas "was the one who decided that Jesus' death was the only effective way to deflate the wild hopes growing among the city's pilgrims." Paula Fredriksen, *Jesus of Nazareth: King of the Jews* (New York: Random House, 1999), 254.

7. Jesus "fought Roman paganism and persecution of the Jewish people, and was killed by Pontius Pilate for his rebellion against Rome, the Jews having had nothing whatsoever to do with his murder," writes Rabbi Shmuley Boteach in "The Ferocious Battle over 'Kosher Jesus,'" *Jerusalem Post*, January 16, 2012, http://www.jpost.com/Opinion/Columnists/The -ferocious-battle-over-Kosher-Jesus.

CHAPTER 4: KING OF THE JEWS

1. The prediction Jesus makes of his death is Mark 8:31–33 = Matt. 16:21– 23 = Luke 9:21–22. The second prediction is found in Mark 9:30–32 = Matt. 17:22–23 = Luke 9:43–45. The third prediction is Mark 10:32–34 = Matt. 20:17–19 = Luke 18:31–34. In John, too, Jesus predicts his coming death; see John 12:7–8.

2. The Israeli biblical scholar Israel Knohl, an Orthodox Jew, argues that the messianic interpretation of Isaiah 53—that is, of a messianic figure

who would suffer and, through his suffering, redeem the people—was not invented by the Christian community but was already "in the air" during the first century among groups such as the Essenes. "In view of these facts," Knohl writes, "we should consider the possibility that the depiction of Jesus as a combination of the 'son of man' and the 'suffering servant' was not a later invention of the Church." Israel Knohl, *The Messiah Before Jesus: The Suffering Servant of the Dead Sea Scrolls* (Berkeley: University of California Press, 2000), 26.

3. Author's transliteration from Hebrew.

4. In addition to Luke's account of Jesus visiting the temple as a young boy, John depicts Jesus visiting the holy city on four separate occasions: twice at Passover (2:13, 12:12), once during an unnamed festival (5:1), and once during Hanukkah (10:22).

5. "Now the towers that were upon it were twenty cubits in breadth, and twenty cubits in height; they were square and solid, as was the wall itself, wherein the niceness of the joints, and the beauty of the stones, were no way inferior to those of the holy house itself. Above this solid altitude of the towers, which was twenty cubits, there were rooms of great magnificence, and over them upper rooms, and cisterns to receive rain-water. They were many in number, and the steps by which you ascended up to them were every one broad: of these towers then the third wall had ninety, and the spaces between them were each two hundred cubits; but in the middle wall were forty towers, and the old wall was parted into sixty, while the whole compass of the city was thirty-three furlongs." Josephus, *The Wars of the Jews* 5.4.3, trans. William Whiston, in *The Works of Josephus* (Peabody, MA: Hendrickson, 1987), 704. In Jesus' day, only the first two walls were built; the third wall, which would have ninety towers and which would encompass the rock quarry that was Calvary, was begun by Herod Agrippa I around AD 44 and only finished during the Jewish Revolt that began in AD 66.

6. James H. Charlesworth, quoted in Thomas H. Maugh II, "Biblical Pool Uncovered in Jerusalem," *Los Angeles Times*, August 9, 2005, http://articles .latimes.com/2005/aug/09/science/sci-siloam9.

7. "Now the outward face of the temple in its front wanted nothing that was likely to surprise either men's minds or their eyes; for it was covered all over with plates of gold of great weight: and at the first rising of the

sun reflected back a very fiery splendor, and made those who forced themselves to look upon it, to turn their eyes away: just as they would have done at the sun's own rays. But this temple appeared to strangers, when they were coming to it at a distance, like a mountain covered with snow." Josephus, *Wars of the Jews* 5.5.6.

8. Historians dispute the extent to which the ancient Romans had an organized system of domestic surveillance. By the second century AD, there was an internal intelligence service, known as the *frumentarii*—originally meaning "wheat collectors"—which gathered information about potential troublemakers. Some experts claim that while the Roman army did utilize spies and informants, it was not done in an organized, systematic way.

9. The term *skekinah*, which means "presence," is a postbiblical term for what is often called the "glory" (*kavod*) of God in the Hebrew Bible. The glory of God dwells in the temple. "And when the priests came out of the Holy Place, a cloud filled the house of the LORD, so that the priests could not stand to minister because of the cloud, for the glory of the LORD filled the house of the LORD" (1 Kings 8:10–11).

10. James King, *Recent Discoveries on the Temple Hill at Jerusalem* (Oxford: Religious Tract Society, 1884), 23.

11. W. Harold Mare, *The Archaeology of the Jerusalem Area* (Eugene, OR: Wipf and Stock, 1987), 158.

CHAPTER 5: A DEMONSTRATION ON THE TEMPLE MOUNT

1. Watson E. Mills, ed. et al., *Mercer Dictionary of the Bible* (Macon, GA: Mercer University Press, 2001), 443.

2. "The present Haram esh-Sharif platform, basically identical with Herod's platform, has outside dimensions of 1,041 ft. (north), 1,556 ft. (east), 929 ft. (south) and 1,596 ft. (west)." Mills et al., *Mercer Dictionary of the Bible*, 443. The *Anchor Bible Dictionary* estimates the total area as 172,000 square yards, which is equal to almost 1.5 million square feet or 35.5 acres. With a typical American football field equaling 57,600 square feet (100 yards long and 160 feet wide), the Temple Mount's total area is the equivalent of twenty-six football fields. See David Noel Freedman, ed., *The Anchor Bible Dictionary*, vol. 6 (New York: Doubleday, 1992), s.v. "Temple, Jerusalem," 365.

3. "At all events, criminal causes were tried before a commission of twenty-three members (in urgent cases any twenty-three members might do) assembled under the presidency of the *Ab Beth-Din*; two other boards, also of twenty-three members each, studied the questions to be submitted to plenary meetings. These three sections had their separate places of meeting in the Temple buildings; the criminal section met originally in the famous 'Hall of the Hewn Stone' (Mishna, *Peah*, ii, 6; *Eduyoth*, vii, 4) which was on the south side of the court (*Middoth*, v, 4) and served also for the sittings of the 'Great Sanhedrin,' or plenary meetings; about AD 30, that same section was transferred to another building closer to the outer wall; they had also another meeting place in a property called *khanyioth*, 'trade-halls,' belonging to the family of Hanan (cf. John 18:13)." Charles Souvay, *The Catholic Encyclopedia*, vol. 13 (New York: Robert Appleton, 1912), s.v. "Sanhedrin." Accessed October 1, 2016, http://www.newadvent.org/cathen/13444a.htm.

4. "When you go through these [first] cloisters, unto the second [court of the] temple, there was a partition made of stone all round, whose height was three cubits: its construction was very elegant; upon it stood pillars, at equal distances from one another, declaring the law of purity, some in Greek, and some in Roman letters, that 'no foreigner should go within that sanctuary' for that second [court of the] temple was called 'the Sanctuary,' and was ascended to by fourteen steps from the first court." Josephus, *Wars of the Jews* 5.5.3.

5. James H. Charlesworth, ed., *Jesus and Temple: Textual and Archaeological Explorations* (Minneapolis: Augsburg Fortress Press, 2014), 10.

6. Josephus even says that "John the Essene" was one of the first military leaders of the revolt and that the Essenes showed amazing endurance and courage under torture by the Romans. See Josephus, *Wars of the Jews* 2.20.4 (566). This reference comes from the noted New Testament scholar Robert Eisenman, author of *James the Brother of Jesus* (New York: Penguin, 1997), in a private e-mail to the author.

7. "But what about the poor or those who could scarcely afford the trip to Jerusalem, much less the inflated charges for these required sacrifices? Maybe Jesus had been told the story growing up of how his mother Mary and his adoptive father Joseph had not even been able to afford a lamb for an offering at his birth. They had managed to purchase two doves. And

somewhere they had to come up with the five Tyrian silver shekels to fulfill the commandment of 'redeeming the first born.'" James D. Tabor, *The Jesus Dynasty* (New York: Simon & Schuster, 2006), 195.

8. "The action of Jesus in the Temple, when taken together with his mockery of the kingly arrogance of Antipas, can thus be understood as a dramatic prophetic performance of the divine action he believed was imminent . . . Jesus was acting as a prophet to help the People of Israel regain control over their lives and livelihoods. He was coming to Jerusalem to announce the coming of God's Kingdom and to pronounce God's verdict against all those who remained part of the problem and refused to dedicate themselves to the solution." Richard A. Horsley and Neil Asher Silberman, *The Message and the Kingdom* (New York: Grosset/Putnam, 1997), 77–78.

CHAPTER 6: PROCLAIMING LIBERTY TO THE CAPTIVES

1. This parable is part of the hypothetical source material unique to Matthew that scholars call "M." Like the hypothetical sayings source Q, a copy of the proposed M source has never been found. Nevertheless, there are debates and sayings of Jesus recorded in the gospel of Matthew that are not found in any other New Testament writing and that many scholars believe constituted a separate body of tradition, or even a written document, that Matthew used when he composed his gospel.

2. "Jesus' arguments about healing on the Sabbath lead to an opposite conclusion: he was a devoted Pharisee rabbi learned in Pharisaic sources." Shmuley Boteach, *Kosher Jesus* (Jerusalem: Gefen, 2012), 96.

3. "Why do your disciples break the tradition of the elders? For they do not wash their hands when they eat" (Matt. 15:2).

4. Josephus, *Antiquities* 17.42.

5. "The Jewish population of Israel, though sometimes put as high as 2,500,000, in addition to a Gentile population of a few hundred thousand, is more reliably estimated as being less than a million, possibly only about half that (depending upon the estimate of the non-Jewish population)." E. P. Sanders, *Judaism: Practice and Belief, 63 BCE–66 CE* (Harrisburg, PA: Trinity Press International, 1992), 210.

6. "This concerns the Wicked Priest who was called by the name of truth when he first arose. But when he ruled over Israel his heart became

proud, and he forsook God and betrayed the precepts for the sake of riches. He robbed and amassed the riches of the men of violence who rebelled against God, and he took the wealth of the people, heaping sinful iniquity upon himself. And he lived in the ways of abominations amidst every unclean defilement." Géza Vermes, "Commentary on Habakkuk (1QpHab)," in Géza Vermes, trans., *The Complete Dead Sea Scrolls in English* (New York: Allen Lane/Penguin Press, 1962, 1965, 1968, 1975, 1987, 1995, 1997), 482. I found this text by consulting Craig A. Evans, "Opposition to the Temple: Jesus and the Dead Sea Scrolls," in James H. Charlesworth, ed., *Jesus and the Dead Sea Scrolls* (New York: Doubleday, 1995), 242. For more about the immense wealth of the priestly ruling classes in first-century Jerusalem, see John J. Rousseau and Rami Arav, *Jesus and His World* (Minneapolis: Augsburg Fortress Press, 1995), 170–71.

7. "They [the Men of the Great Assembly] said three things: Be deliberate in judgment; develop many disciples; and make a fence for the Torah." Pirkei Avot 1.1. *Pirkei Avot: Ethics of the Fathers* (Brooklyn: Mesorah Publications, 1984), 9.

8. The Mishnah, or summary of debates about the oral law that constitutes the earliest part of the Talmud, lists thirty-nine categories of labor that are forbidden on the Sabbath, including sowing, plowing and reaping, kindling a fire, and transferring objects from a private to a public domain (Sabbath 7.2).

9. According to Josephus, the Pharisees (along with the priests and other Jewish leaders) tried desperately to persuade the people not to rebel against Rome in the late 60s following a massacre of Jews in the Roman city of Caesarea Maritima, but they were tragically unsuccessful. "Hereupon the men of power got together, and conferred with the high priests, as did also the principal of the Pharisees; and thinking all was at stake, and that their calamities were becoming incurable, took counsel what was to be done. Accordingly, they determined to try what they could do with the seditious by words, and assembled the people before the brazen gate, which was the gate of the inner temple which looked towards the sunrising. And, in the first place, they showed the great indignation they had at this attempt for a revolt, and for their bringing so great a war upon their country." Josephus, *Wars of the Jews* 2.17.3.

10. "You shall therefore lay up these words of mine in your heart and in your soul, and you shall bind them as a sign on your hand, and they shall be as frontlets between your eyes" (Deut. 11:18).

11. Amy-Jill Levine and Marc Zvi Brettler, eds., *The Jewish Annotated New Testament* (New York: Oxford University Press, 2011), 42.

12. Josephus, *Wars of the Jews* 2:175–77; *Antiquities* 18:60–62.

CHAPTER 7: AN ANOINTING IN BETHANY

1. As noted in the introduction, the criterion of multiple attestation—the presence of a saying or deed of Jesus in a variety of independent sources—is one that skeptical modern scholars use to evaluate historicity. See Matt. 26:6–13 = Mark 14:3–9 = Luke 7:36–50 = John 12:1–8.

2. Estimating equivalences between ancient times and today is always a tricky business. However, according to the US Bureau of Labor Statistics, the average daily wage in the United States is currently around $173. Thus, a flask of ointment that cost three hundred days' labor would be the equivalent of approximately $51,900.

3. See also John 12:8 and Mark 14:7.

CHAPTER 8: "DO THIS IN MEMORY OF ME"

1. Matt. 26:17–30 = Mark 14:12–25 = Luke 22:7–20.

2. While some believe Jesus would have known about or arranged for the man carrying the water jar through supernatural means, there is nothing in the text itself to indicate this. "It appears that, as in the case of the donkey, Jesus had already arranged with a friend or follower to lend the room that would be needed. There is nothing supernatural here, any more than there was in Peter's boat or Joseph's tomb, both borrowed by Jesus." G. J. Wenham, et al., eds., *New Bible Commentary: 21st Century Edition* (Downers Grove, IL: InterVarsity Press, 1994), 971.

3. A. G. Sertillanges, *What Jesus Saw from the Cross* (Bedford, NH: Sophia Institute Press, 1996), 51. See also Richard R. Losch, *All the Places in the Bible: An A–Z Guide to the Countries, Cities, Villages, and Other Places Mentioned in Scripture* (Bloomington, IN: Xlibris, 2013).

4. According to Acts 1:13, Jesus' followers stayed in the upper room in the days immediately after Jesus' resurrection. Both Mark 14:15 and

Luke 22:12 use similar language when describing the "large upper room furnished and ready" where Jesus ate his final meal with his followers. Since ancient times, Christians have assumed that these passages refer to the same "upper room," perhaps the home of the mysterious figure John Mark and his mother, mentioned in Acts 12:12, where "where many were gathered together and were praying" following the arrest of Simon Peter (RSV). One early Christian writer, Epiphanius of Salamis (c. 310–403), claimed that when the Emperor Hadrian came to Jerusalem in AD 130, he found the "upper room," which was now a house church, where the disciples went after Jesus' ascension on the Mount of Olives. See W. Harold Mare, *The Archaeology of the Jerusalem Area* (Grand Rapids: Baker, 1987), 234.

5. Jerome Murphy-O'Connor, *The Holy Land: An Oxford Archaeological Guide*, 5th ed. (Oxford: Oxford University Press, 2008), 117.

6. Ibid.

7. Adding to the confusion, the synoptic writers use imprecise language when speaking about the Passover: "And on the first day of Unleavened Bread, when they sacrificed the Passover lamb, his disciples said to him, 'Where will you have us go and prepare for you to eat the Passover?'" (Mark 14:12 = Matt. 26:17 = Luke 22:9). Technically, the day when the priests in the temple sacrificed the Passover lambs was called the Day of Preparation. Like all Jewish feasts, Passover began at sundown the evening before.

8. See Craig S. Keener, "John and the Synoptics on Passover Chronology," in *The Historical Jesus of the Gospels* (Minneapolis: Wm. B. Eerdmans, 2012), 372.

9. Another attempt to resolve this puzzle is the claim that the Pharisees and the temple authorities observed different customs when the first day of Passover happened to fall on the Sabbath—as would have occurred if John was correct and Jesus was crucified on the Day of Preparation. The Pharisees supposedly were willing to move the calendar forward one day to avoid having the Passover meal occur on the Sabbath, while the more liberal Sadducees, in charge of the temple, simply ignored the prohibitions against working on the Sabbath in order to observe the Passover rites. See Joel B. Green, Scot McKnight, and I. Howard Marshall, eds., *Dictionary of Jesus and the Gospels* (Downers Grove, IL:

IVP Academic, 1992), 177. See also Colin J. Humphreys, *The Mystery of the Last Supper: Reconstructing the Final Days of Jesus* (Cambridge: Cambridge University Press, 2011), 95.

10. Ibid.

11. See Jonathan Klawans, "Was Jesus' Last Supper a Seder?" *Bible Review,* October 2001. Some historians believe that the seder ritual of today was not formalized until after the fall of Jerusalem in AD 70. However, the basic elements of the meal were probably already widely followed even in Jesus' day.

12. Matt. 26:26 = Mark 14:22 = Luke 22:19.

13. Matt. 26:21–25 = Mark 14:18–21 = John 13:21–30.

CHAPTER 9: BETRAYAL

1. Matt. 26:33 = Luke 22:33.

2. The present site venerated as the garden of Gethsemane is located adjacent to the Church of All Nations, built in 1924 on the ruins of a church mentioned by the pilgrim Egeria and constructed between AD 379 and 384. See Jerome Murphy-O'Connor, *The Holy Land: An Oxford Archaeological Guide*, 5th ed. (Oxford: Oxford University Press, 2008), 146.

3. Mark 14:32 = Matt. 26:36 = Luke 22:41.

4. William D. Edwards, Wesley J. Gabel, and Floyd E. Hosmer, "On the Physical Death of Jesus Christ," *Journal of the American Medical Association (JAMA)* 255, no. 11 (March 21, 1986): 1455.

5. Mark 14:32–42 = Matt. 26:36–46.

6. Mark 14:36 = Matt. 26:39 = Luke 22:42.

7. Mark 14:43–52 = Matt. 26:47–56 = Luke 22:47–53. See also John 18:2–12.

8. Matt. 26:3–4 = Luke 22:2.

9. Mark 14:10–11 = Matt. 26:14–16 = Luke 22:3–6.

10. Mark 14:45 = Matt. 26:49 = Luke 22:47.

11. Josephus, *Antiquities* 18.95–97.

12. Ronny Reich, "Caiaphas Name Inscribed on Bone Boxes," *Biblical Archaeology Review* 18:05, Sep/Oct 1992, http://members.bib-arch.org /publication.asp?PubID=BSBA&Volume=18&Issue=5&ArticleID=2.

13. Michelle Morris, "2,000-Year-Old Ossuary Authentic, Say Researchers," *Jerusalem Post*, June 29, 2011, http://www.jpost.com/Video-Articles/Video /2000-year-old-ossuary-authentic-say-researchers.

14. John J. Rousseau and Rami Arav, *Jesus and His World* (Minneapolis: Augsburg Fortress Press, 1995), 170.

15. Bargil Pixner, *Paths of the Messiah and Sites of the Early Church from Galilee to Jerusalem* (San Francisco: Ignatius Press, 2010), 254.

16. Murphy-O'Connor, *Holy Land*, 119. Pixner concludes that "if we consider the most ancient reports, it is clear that today's Church of St. Peter in Gallicantu, on the eastern slope of Mount Zion, most likely represents the correct location of Caiaphas's house." Pixner, *Paths of the Messiah*, 257.

17. Pixner quotes Theodosius (c. 530), who said that "from holy Zion to the house of Caiaphas, which is now the Church of Saint Peter, it is more or less 50 (double) steps." Pixner, *Paths of the Messiah*, 264.

18. Mark 14:53–65 = Matt. 26:57–68 = Luke 22:54–71. See also John 18:13–24.

19. Mark 14:53 says "*all* the chief priests and the elders and the scribes" were assembled. Matthew 26:57 says "the scribes and the elders" were there. Luke 22:66 reports that when day came, "the assembly of the elders of the people gathered together, both chief priests and scribes; and they led him away to their council" (RSV).

20. Mark 14:55 = Matt. 26:59–60.

21. Mark 14:62 = Matt. 26:64 = Luke 22:69–70.

22. Mark 15:1 = Matt. 27:1 = Luke 22:66.

23. John 18:20.

CHAPTER 10: ON TRIAL

1. See "Praetorium," *Anchor Bible Dictionary*, vol. 5, 447.

2. "The entire structure resembled that of a tower, it contained also four other distinct towers at its four corners; whereof the others were but fifty cubits high; whereas that which lay upon the southeast corner was seventy cubits high, that from thence the whole temple might be viewed." Josephus, *Wars of the Jews* 5.5.8.

3. John J. Rousseau and Rami Arav, *Jesus and His World* (Minneapolis: Augsburg Fortress Press, 1995), 13.

4. Mark 15:16.

5. Ruth Eglash, "Archaeologists Find Possible Site of Jesus's Trial in Jerusalem," *Washington Post*, January 4, 2015, https://www.washingtonpost .com/world/middle_east/archaeologists-find-possible-site-of-jesuss-trial -in-jerusalem/2015/01/04/6d0ce098–7f9a–45de–9639-b7922855bfdb _story.html.

6. In the early first century of the Common Era, Jerusalem was surrounded by two main walls—the First Wall, built by the Jewish Hasmonean dynasty around 130 BC, which surrounded the Upper City and the Lower City and, to the north, extended from Herod's Palace in the west to about midway up the western wall of the Temple Mount; and a Second Wall, built in the first century BC perhaps by Herod the Great, which surrounded the northern section of the city abutting the rest of the Temple Mount.

7. John 18:29–38.

8. Josephus, *Antiquities* 18.3.1.2.

9. Philo, *On the Embassy to Gaius* 40.302, trans. Charles Duke Yonge (London: H. G. Bohn, 1854–1890), *Early Christian Writings*. Copyright © 2001–2015 Peter Kirby, available online: http://www.earlychristianwritings .com/yonge/book40.html.

10. Josephus, *Antiquities* 18.3.1.

11. Ibid.

12. Philo, *Embassy to Gaius* 38.299–305.

13. Josephus, *Antiquities* 18.3.1. See also James S. Jeffers, *The Greco-Roman World of the New Testament Era* (Downers Grove, IL: IVP Press, 1999), 130.

14. Ibid.

15. Josephus, *Antiquities* 18.88.

16. Eusebius, *Ecclesiastical History* 2.7, trans. C. F. Cruse (Peabody, MA: Hendrickson, 1998), 58.

17. Matt. 27:11 = Mark 15:2 = Luke 23:3 = John 18:33.

18. Matt. 27:11 = Mark 15:2 = Luke 23:3.

19. This is one of skeptic Bart Ehrman's favorite objections about many gospel conversations: who could have heard them? "Accounts of Jesus's

trial before the Sanhedrin appear in the Gospels, but little there can be trusted as historically reliable. The only ones present were the Jewish leaders and Jesus, none of his followers and no one was taking notes. It seems unlikely that the leaders themselves would tell later Christians what happened at the time." Bart D. Ehrman, *Did Jesus Exist?* (San Francisco: HarperOne, 2012), 330.

20. "[Jesus] fought Roman paganism and persecution of the Jewish people, and was killed by Pontius Pilate for his rebellion against Rome, the Jews having had nothing whatsoever to do with his murder." Shmuley Boteach, "The Ferocious Battle over 'Kosher Jesus,'" *Jerusalem Post*, January 16, 2012, http://www.jpost.com/Opinion/Columnists/The-ferocious-battle -over-Kosher-Jesus.

21. "Thus, a story concocted by Mark strictly for evangelistic purposes to shift the blame for Jesus's death away from Rome is stretched with the passage of time to the point of absurdity, becoming in the process the basis for two thousand years of Christian anti-Semitism." Reza Aslan, *Zealot: The Life and Times of Jesus of Nazareth* (New York: Random House, 2013), 152.

22. "It is generally agreed today that the author of the Fourth Gospel was *Jewish*. The author accurately understands Jewish customs, is steeped in the Old Testament, is aware of finer points of distinctions among pre-70 Jewish sects, and is concerned to demonstrate Jesus as the true fulfillment of the Law and of numerous rituals and institutions of Judaism." Craig L. Blomberg, *The Historical Reliability of John's Gospel: Issues and Commentary* (Downers Grove, IL: IVP Academic, 2011), 27.

23. Philo, *Embassy to Gaius* 38.305.

24. Luke 23:22 = John 18:38.

25. Mark 15:4 = Matt. 27:13 = Luke 23:4 = John 18:38.

26. Géza Vermes, *The Authentic Gospel of Jesus* (New York: Penguin Books, 2005), 337.

27. "[Pilate] ordered Jesus to be crucified. The whole trial may have lasted no more than a couple of minutes. And the order was carried out immediately." Ehrman, *Did Jesus Exist?*, 330.

28. "[Pilate] feared least they might in reality go on an embassy to the emperor, and might impeach him with respect to other particulars of his

government, in respect of his corruption, and his acts of insolence." Philo, *Embassy to Gaius*, 38.

29. Mark 15:6–14 = Matt. 27:15–23 = Luke 23:17–23 = John 18:39–40.

30. Mark 15:9 = Matt. 27:17 = Luke 23:17–23 = John 18:39.

31. Matt. 27:17 = Mark 15:9 = John 18:39, paraphrased.

32. Mark 15:14 = Matt. 27:23 = Luke 23:22.

33. An early example is the French critical scholar Alfred Loisy (1857–1912), who wrote of the Barabbas scene: "Whatever may be the source of this fiction, which defies all probability, the aim of it is to relieve Pilate's responsibility, while establishing the innocence of Jesus." Alfred Loisy, *The Origins of the New Testament* (New York: Colliers Books, 1962), 120. A more recent example is John Dominic Crossan, a cofounder of the Jesus Seminar: "I judge the narrative [about Barabbas] to be absolutely unhistorical, a creation most likely of Mark himself," John Dominic Crossan, *Who Killed Jesus?* (San Francisco: Harper San Francisco, 1996), 111.

34. "Is the hostile crowd solely the (apologetic) invention of the evangelists? We cannot know for certain, but logically it need not be. The presence in the city during the holiday of a crowd violently opposed to Jesus, as well as a crowd energetically enthused, in fact sharpens Pilate's decision: by one act, he can appease one while simultaneously deflating the other. Other reconstructions are less plausible." Paula Fredriksen, *Jesus of Nazareth: King of the Jews* (New York: Random House, 1999), 256.

35. What makes this delicate, of course, is that the account in the Gospels of the crowds yelling, "Let his blood be upon us!" has been used for centuries as an excuse for Christian anti-Semitism.

36. Philo, *Embassy to Gaius*, 38.

CHAPTER 11: THE CRUCIFIXION

1. Mark 15:6–14 = Matt. 27:15–23 = Luke 23:17–23 = John 18:39–40.

2. Matt. 27:37.

3. Dry wood weighs approximately forty-five pounds per cubic foot, so an eight-foot crossbeam a half foot thick would likely weigh about ninety pounds or more.

4. Mark 15:20–21 = Matt. 27:31–32 = Luke 23:26.

5. Tom Powers, "Treasures in the Storeroom: The Family Tomb of Simon of Cyrene," *Biblical Archaeology Review,* July/August 2003.

6. Josephus, *Wars of the Jews* 5.11.1.

7. "A reasonable estimate would be something like 350,000 deaths all told, which would be around one-third if the original population was one million, or one-half if it was 700,000, or one-fourth if it was 1.4 million." Matthew White, *The Great Big Book of Horrible Things* (New York: W. W. Norton, 2012), 52.

8. Mark 15:22 = Matt. 27:33 = Luke 23:33 = John 19:17.

9. Jerome Murphy-O'Connor, *The Holy Land: An Oxford Archaeological Guide* (Oxford: Oxford University Press, 2008), 57–58.

10. Shimon Gibson, *The Final Days of Jesus: The Archaeological Evidence* (New York: HarperOne, 2009), 105.

11. Murphy-O'Conner, *Holy Land,* 66.

12. Bargil Pixner, *Paths of the Messiah and Sites of the Early Church from Galilee to Jerusalem* (San Francisco: Ignatius Press, 2010), 304–8.

13. Mark 15:23. According to an article in *Science Daily,* when researchers applied extracts from the myrrh plant (*Commiphora myrrha*) to a human breast tumor cell line (MCF-7) known to be resistant to anticancer drugs, the myrrh extract killed all of the cancer cells in the laboratory dishes. See "'Gift of the Magi' Bears Anti-Cancer Agents, Researchers Suggest," *Science Daily,* December 5, 2001, https:www.sciencedaily.com/releases /2001/12/011205070038.htm.

14. "It should be noted that in Roman times it was the rule to nail the victim by both hands and feet." Martin Hengel, *Crucifixion* (Minneapolis: Augsburg Fortress Press, 1977), 31.

15. Matt. 27:35 = Mark 15:25 = Luke 23:33 = John 19:18.

16. Frederick T. Zugibe, *The Crucifixion of Jesus: A Forensic Inquiry* (New York: M. Evans, 2005), 57.

17. Matt. 27:37 = Mark 15:26 = Luke 23:38 = John 19:19.

18. Mark 15:24 = Matt. 27:35 = Luke 23:34 = John 19:23–24.

19. "My view now is that we do not know, and cannot know, what actually happened to Jesus' body. But it is absolutely true that as far as we can tell

from all the surviving evidence, what normally happened to a criminal's body is that it was left to decompose and serve as food for scavenging animals." Bart D. Ehrman, *How Jesus Became God* (San Francisco: HarperOne, 2014), 156. See also John Dominic Crossan, *Who Killed Jesus?* (San Francisco: Harper San Francisco, 1995), 160–88.

20. Richard A. Horsley and Neil Asher Silberman, *The Message and the Kingdom* (New York: Grosset/Putnam, 1997), 86.

21. See John 19:25. Some scholars and Christian traditions assert that Clopas and Cleopas, one of the men who encountered the risen Jesus on the road to Emmaus, are the same person, brother of Jesus' father, Joseph. "Exactly who Cleopas was we cannot say. Following Hegesippus, Eusebius believed Clopas to be a brother of Joseph, Jesus' father, thus making him Jesus' uncle. . . . Older scholars also identified Cleopas with Clopas." James R. Edwards, *The Gospel According to Luke* (Grand Rapids: Wm. B. Eerdmans, 2015), 717.

22. For a summary of the arguments for and against the Fourth Gospel having been written by "the beloved disciple," see Andreas J. Köstenberger, *A Theology of John's Gospel and Letters* (Grand Rapids: Zondervan, 2009), 73–79.

23. William D. Edwards, Wesley J. Gabel, and Floyd E. Hosmer, "On the Physical Death of Jesus Christ," *Journal of the American Medical Association (JAMA)* 255, no. 11 (March 21, 1986): 1455–63.

24. The early reformers, including Martin Luther, John Calvin, Huldrych Zwingli, and early Anglican leaders, largely accepted the traditional Christian teaching that Jesus' mother remained a virgin her entire life. The Lutheran Schmalkaldic Articles refer to Mary as "ever virgin." Later, however, many Protestant denominations came to believe that Mary had normal sexual relations with her husband, Joseph, after Jesus was born. See Ted Campbell, *Christian Confessions: A Historical Introduction* (Louisville: Westminster/John Knox Press, 1996), 150.

25. Mark 15:33–34 = Matt. 27:45–46 = Luke 23:44.

26. Mark 15:34 = Matt. 27:46.

27. Mark 15:36 = Matt. 27:48 = Luke 23:36. See also John 19:29.

28. Brant Pitre, *Jesus and the Jewish Roots of the Eucharist* (New York: Doubleday, 2011), 169.

29. If Jesus was born before Herod the Great died in 4 BC, as Matthew 2:3 says, and Jesus died in AD 30, then he would have been around thirty-five at the time of his death.

CHAPTER 12: A HASTY BURIAL

1. Mark 15:39 = Matt. 27:54 = Luke 23:47.

2. Matt. 27:51–52.

3. Mark 15:38 = Matt. 27:51.

4. John 19:31–37.

5. Philo, *Embassy to Gaius*, 38.

6. Mark 15:42–47 = Matt. 27:57–61 = Luke 23:50–56.

7. Shimon Gibson, *The Final Days of Jesus: The Archaeological Evidence* (New York: HarperOne, 2009), 155.

8. Ibid., 152.

9. Mark 15:40–41 = Matt. 27:55–56 = Luke 23:49.

10. Gibson, *Final Days of Jesus*, 136.

11. Mark 15:42–47 = Matt. 27:57–61 = Luke 23:50–56 = John 19:38–42.

12. Read by early Christians such as Clement, but never accepted into the Christian canon due to the presence of Gnostic elements, the Gospel of Peter was lost until a ninth-century partial manuscript of the text was discovered in an Egyptian village in 1886. The text is available in translation in Robert J. Miller, ed., *The Complete Gospels* (San Francisco: Harper San Francisco, 1992), 399–407. See also Gibson, *Final Days of Jesus*, 157.

CHAPTER 13: A GLIMMER OF HOPE

1. Mark 16:2 says that the sun had already risen; John 20:1 says it was still dark outside. It was likely right around dawn and thus light enough to see.

2. In Mark's version, the women see a young man as soon as they enter the tomb for the first time (16:5). In Luke, they enter the tomb, see there is no body, and then two men in dazzling clothes suddenly stand by them (24:4). In Matthew, as the women are approaching the tomb, the angel descends from heaven, causing an earthquake, and then he rolls back the stone and sits upon it (28:2).

3. Matt. 28:8 = Luke 24:9.

4. Tacitus, *Annals* 15.44, retrieved November 2, 2016, http://classics.mit .edu/Tacitus/annals.11.xv.html.

5. Mark 16:14–18 = Luke 24:36–43 = John 20:19–23.

6. New Testament scholar Barbara Thiering is well-known for arguing that Jesus survived the crucifixion and lived for many years with his disciples after his crucifixion. See Barbara Thiering, *Jesus the Man: Decoding the Real Story of Jesus and Mary Magdalene* (New York: Atria Books, 2006). For a discussion of Thiering's theory, see Michael R. Licona, *The Resurrection of Jesus: A New Historiographical Approach* (Downers Grove, IL: IVP Academic, 2010), 633.

7. Mark 16:1–8 = Matt. 28:1–8 = Luke 24:1–12 = John 20:1–8.

8. See, for example, Gerd Lüdemann, *What Really Happened to Jesus* (Louisville: Westminster John Knox Press, 1995); John Dominic Crossan, *Who Killed Jesus?* (San Francisco: Harper San Francisco, 1995), and Bart D. Ehrman, *How Jesus Became God* (New York: HarperOne, 2014).

CHAPTER 14: THE FIRST REPORTS

1. See N. T. Wright, "The Surprise of the Resurrection" in Craig A. Evans and N. T. Wright, *Jesus, The Final Days: What Really Happened* (Louisville, KY: Westminster John Knox Press, 2009), 98–99.

CHAPTER 15: "I AM WITH YOU ALWAYS"

1. Joel B. Green, Scot McKnight, and I. Howard Marshall, eds., *Dictionary of Jesus and the Gospels* (Downers Grove, IL: IVP Academic, 1992), 47.

2. Christian tradition has long accepted that the author of the third gospel and Acts was Luke, the companion of Paul named in three of his letters. Recent scholarship is more skeptical of this identification, however, because of differences between what Paul says in his own letters and what the author of Acts reports. But these differences—whether Paul saw many of the apostles in Jerusalem during his first post-conversion visit (as in Acts) or only Peter and James (as in Paul's letter to the Galatians)—do not seem so significant that they rule out direct contact between the author of Acts and Paul, whether or not the author was Luke. In any event, the parallels between Acts and different details in Paul's letters are

significant in their own right and tend to support, rather than undermine, the basic outline of the events.

3. Jerome Murphy-O'Connor, *The Holy Land: An Oxford Archaeological Guide*, 5th ed. (Oxford: Oxford University Press, 2008), Kindle edition, loc. 2723.

CHAPTER 16: THE RETURN OF THE SPIRIT

1. Num. 28:26.

CHAPTER 17: "NEITHER GOLD NOR SILVER"

1. Known in the Talmud as Nicanor's Gate, Josephus refers to it as the "Corinthian" gate, and Luke calls it "the Beautiful Gate" (Acts 3:2).

2. Matt. 8:5–13 = Luke 7:1–10.

3. Examples of serious disease healings include accounts in Luke 13:10–13 and John 4:47.

CHAPTER 18: THE TRIAL BEFORE THE SANHEDRIN

1. Bart D. Ehrman, *Lost Scriptures: Books that Did Not Make It into the New Testament* (Oxford: Oxford University Press, 2005), 114.

2. J. Gresham Machen, *The Origin of Paul's Religion* (Eugene, OR: Wipf and Stock, 2002), 54.

3. Ronald F. Hock, *The Social Context of Paul's Ministry* (Minneapolis: Augsberg Press, 1995), 21.

CHAPTER 19: THE MARTYRDOM OF STEPHEN

1. The frescoes can be viewed online at the Sacred Destinations website: http://www.sacred-destinations.com/syria/dura-europos.

2. In a letter to the Jesus community in Rome, the apostle Paul commended to them "our sister Phoebe, a deacon of the church in Cenchreae" (Rom. 16:1 NIV). The Greek text uses the female form of the word for deacon (*ousan diakonon*), or deaconess.

3. John J. Rousseau and Rami Arav, *Jesus and His World* (Minneapolis: Augsburg Fortress Press, 1995), 269.

4. Tacitus, *Annals* 2.85.

5. Suzanne Richard, ed., *Near Eastern Archaeology: A Reader* (Warsaw, IN: Eisenbrauns, 2003), 455.

6. One of the earliest Christian martyrs, Ignatius of Antioch (AD 35–108), wrote letters to his fellow Christians on the way to his death in the Colosseum in Rome. In his letter to the community in Ephesus, Ignatius begged his friends not to retaliate against their persecutors. "Meet their animosity with gentleness, their high words with humility, and their abuse with your prayers," he wrote. "And if they grow violent, be gentle instead of wanting to pay them back with their own coin." Andrew Louth, ed., *Early Christian Writings: The Apostolic Fathers* (London: Penguin Books, 1987), 64.

CHAPTER 20: PROTECTING THE GOSPEL

1. Peidong Shen, et al., "Reconstruction of Patrilineages and Matrilineages of Samaritans and Other Israeli Populations from Y-Chromosome and Mitochondrial DNA Sequence Variation," *Human Mutation* 24, no. 3 (September 2004): 248–60.

2. Genetic testing of modern-day Samaritans supports both Samaritan claims of ancient Israelite heritage and Jewish claims of outside intermarriage. "Principal component analysis suggests a common ancestry of Samaritan and Jewish patrilineages. Most of the former may be traced back to a common ancestor in the paternally-inherited Jewish high priesthood (Cohanim) at the time of the Assyrian conquest of the kingdom of Israel." Ibid.

3. Modern experts sometimes date the schism between the Jews and the Samaritans much later, after the time of Alexander the Great or even during the age of the Maccabees, after 160 BC. For a detailed discussion of the Samaritan Schism, see Everett Ferguson, *Backgrounds of Early Christianity* (Grand Rapids: Wm. B. Eerdmans, 2003), 402.

4. Pheme Perkins, *Gnosticism and the New Testament* (Minneapolis: Augsburg Fortress Press, 1993), 9–10.

5. Luke Timothy Johnson, *The Writings of the New Testament: Third Edition* (Minneapolis: Fortress, 2010), 534–35.

6. The texts of all of the extant Gnostic Gospels can be read in Robert J. Miller,

The Complete Gospels: Annotated Scholars Version (San Francisco: Harper San Francisco, 1992). For an introduction to the Gnostic Gospels and their relationship to the canonical Gospels, see Joel B. Green, Scot McKnight, and I. Howard Marshall, eds., *Dictionary of Jesus and the Gospels* (Downers Grove, IL: IVP Academic, 1992), s.v. "Gospel (Apocryphal)," 286–91.

7. F. F. Bruce, *The Book of Acts* (Grand Rapids: Wm. B. Eerdmans, 1988), 175. See also Darrell L. Bock and Buist M. Fanning, eds., *Interpreting the New Testament Text* (Wheaton, IL: Crossway, 2006), 363.

8. The standard work on literacy in Israel during New Testament times is Catherine Heszer, *Jewish Literacy in Roman Israel* (London: Mohr Siebeck, 2001). Heszer claims that in the time of Jesus, only 3 percent of the Jews in Israel were literate. However, in recent years this viewpoint has been challenged by new discoveries that seem to indicate that even members of the lower classes in ancient Israel had a rudimentary knowledge of reading and writing. See Isabel Kershner, "New Evidence on When Bible Was Written: Ancient Shopping Lists," *New York Times*, April 11, 2016, http://www.nytimes.com/2016/04/12/world/middleeast/new-evidence-onwhen-bible-was-written-ancient-shopping-lists.html.

9. A famous example is the Wadi Qelt, which extends south from Jerusalem to Jericho, near the Dead Sea. As you leave the ancient village of Hebron, south of Jerusalem, and head west toward Gaza, there are numerous wadis and hidden wells in the rough mountains and valleys toward the ancient settlement of Lachish, now an Israeli *moshav*, or agricultural village.

CHAPTER 21: THE ROAD TO DAMASCUS

1. A. J. Hultgren, "Paul's Pre-Christian Persecutions of the Church: Their Purpose, Locale, and Nature," *Journal of Biblical Literature* 95, no. 1 (1976): 97–111.

2. Larry W. Hurtado, *How on Earth Did Jesus Become a God?: Historical Questions about Earliest Devotion to Jesus* (Grand Rapids: Wm. B. Eerdmans, 2005), 94.

3. Sherman E. Johnson, *Paul the Apostle and His Cities* (Wilmington, DE: Michael Glazier, 1987), 39.

4. Archaeologists have actually discovered a section of the Roman road, made up of small basalt stones, to the west of Caesarea Philippi, as well as

the remains of ancient Roman bridges. It was likely along this route, as the Roman road curved near Damascus, that Saul of Tarsus had his vision.

5. Some translations resolve this apparent discrepancy by translating the Greek verb *akouō* as "understand," which it can mean, so that in the second passage the men did not "understand" the voice. In his own letters, Paul says simply that Jesus "appeared" to him.

6. F. F. Bruce, *Paul: Apostle of the Heart Set Free* (Grand Rapids: Wm. B. Eerdmans, 2000), 77.

7. There is a tremendous amount of discussion and theological debate about how to describe what happened to Paul on the road to Damascus and whether it should be considered a "vision" or another physical appearance of Jesus like the ones described in the Gospels. Even many conservative Christian scholars view it as a "vision" in some sense, different from the appearances of Jesus to Mary Magdalene and the apostles. The German New Testament scholar Martin Hengel refers to it as a "visionary 'seeing of the Kyrios' . . . a real, 'objective' seeing of a supernatural reality in divine splendour of light, which makes itself known as the 'Lord' and is recognized by [Paul] as such." Martin Hengel and Anna Maria Schwemer, *Paul Between Damascus and Antioch: The Unknown Years* (Louisville: Westminster John Knox Press, 1997), 39. N. T. Wright, in his magisterial study of the resurrection, refers to the appearance of the risen Jesus to Paul as Paul's "inaugural vision": "The context of Saul coming to believe that Jesus was the Messiah was a vision which seemed to him at the time much like the biblical theophanies." N. T. Wright, *The Resurrection of the Son of God* (Minneapolis: Augsburg Fortress Press, 1994), 397. However, Norman Geisler argues that the resurrection appearance of Jesus to Paul on the road to Damascus should be called an "appearance" and not a "vision." Norman Geisler, *The Battle for the Resurrection: Updated Edition* (Eugene, OR: Wipf and Stock, 2004), 114. The Christian philosopher William Lane Craig says that the appearance to Paul on the road to Damascus had "visionary elements," such as a light and a voice from heaven, but that the appearance should not be reduced to "just" a vision. It was not, Craig says, merely something in Paul's mind but was actually "out there," in that the phenomena were experienced in some way by Paul's fellow travelers as well. William Lane Craig, *The Son Rises: Historical Evidence for the Resurrection of Jesus* (Eugene, OR: Wipf and Stock, 2000), 109.

CHAPTER 22: THE HEALING MINISTRY OF PETER

1. Josephus, *Antiquities* 18.85–89.

2. James A. Montgomery, *The Samaritans, the Earliest Jewish Sect: Their History, Theology, and Literature* (Eugene, OR: Wipf and Stock, 2006), 250.

3. Mark 6:45 = Matt. 11:21 = Luke 9:10 = John 1:44. See also the discussion of Hellenistic culture in the Galilee region in G. Scott Gleaves, *Did Jesus Speak Greek?: The Emerging Evidence of Greek Dominance in First-Century Palestine* (Eugene, OR: Pickwick Publications, 2015), 90.

4. John J. Rousseau and Rami Arav, *Jesus and His World* (Minneapolis: Augsburg Fortress Press, 1995), 40. The authors state that the conclusion that archaeologists have indeed located the remains of Peter's actual house is "widely accepted today."

5. Josephus, *Wars of the Jews* 3.9.3.

CHAPTER 23: THE BAPTISM OF CORNELIUS

1. Eckart Köhne and Cornelia Ewigleben, *Gladiators and Caesars: The Power of Spectacle in Ancient Rome* (London: British Museum Press, 2000), 20. Trying to calculate the value of ancient money is very difficult, but Natalie Haynes makes an attempt in her book *The Ancient Guide to Modern Life* (New York: Overlook Press, 2012). She reports that a Roman *sesterce* could buy two decent loaves of bread and thus calculates its worth as being around £1.50. If we assume a *sesterce* is worth about one US dollar, then Caligula spent a considerable amount of money very quickly.

2. James G. Crossley, *The Date of Mark's Gospel* (London: T&T Clark International, 2004), 22–24.

3. Josephus, *Antiquities* 18.8.8.

4. The Roman legion was a unit of about five thousand, roughly ten cohorts each made up of five hundred men. Archaeological inscriptions indicate that there were at least two Cohorts Italica in Syria around this time made up primarily of Roman (Italian) citizens. See Laurie Brink, *Soldiers in Luke-Acts* (Tübingen: Mohr Siebeck, 2014), 153.

5. Acts 11:26.

NOTES

CHAPTER 24: PERSECUTION RESUMES

1. Josephus, *Antiquities* 19.4.1.

2. Josephus, *Antiquities* 19.3.4.

3. "When the king [Herod Agrippa I] had settled the high priesthood after this manner, he returned the kindness which the inhabitants of Jerusalem had showed him; for he released them from the tax upon houses, every one of which paid it before, thinking it a good thing to requite the tender affection of those that loved him." Josephus, *Antiquities* 19.6.3. In the Talmud, Agrippa is praised for his reverence for the Torah: "King Agrippa stood and received it [the Torah scroll] and read standing for which act the sages praised him." Sotah 41a.

4. Achille Camerlynck, "St. James the Greater," in *The Catholic Encyclopedia* (New York: Robert Appleton, 1910). Accessed October 15, 2016, http://www.newadvent.org/cathen/08279b.htm.

5. For a summary and discussion of the patristic or early Christian evidence, see Sean McDowell, *The Fate of the Apostles: Examining the Martyrdom Accounts of the Closest Followers of Jesus* (London: Routledge, 2016).

6. This is the first reference in the New Testament to James the Just, the brother or male relative of Jesus, as a leader of the Jesus community.

7. Josephus, *Antiquities* 19.8.2 (343–52).

8. Ibid., 20.7.3.

CHAPTER 25: SPREADING THE WORD

1. Alan F. Segal, *Paul the Convert: The Apostolate and Apostasy of Saul the Pharisee* (New Haven, CT: Yale University Press, 1990), 231.

2. The Book of Jubilees 22:16–17, trans. R. H. Charles, revised by C. Rabin, in Hedley Frederick Davis Sparks, *The Apocryphal Old Testament* (Oxford: Oxford University Press, 1985), 72.

3. Eusebius, *Ecclesiastical History*, trans. C. F. Cruse (Peabody, MA: Hendrickson Publishers, 1998), 105–6. Eusebius quotes extensive passages from a lost book of Papias's called *The Interpretations of the Sayings of the Lord.*

4. Henry B. Culver, *The Book of Old Ships: From Egyptian Galleys to Clipper Ships* (Mineola, NY: Dover Publications, 1992), 41–47.

5. For more information, see Norman Geisler and Joseph M. Holden, *The Popular Handbook of Archaeology and the Bible* (Eugene, OR: Harvest House, 2013), 352–53.

CHAPTER 26: WELCOMING PAGANS

1. Later in Acts, Luke reports that the makers of idols, in particular, saw clearly the threat posed by this new movement: "About that time there arose no little disturbance concerning the Way. For a man named Demetrius, a silversmith, who made silver shrines of Artemis, brought no little business to the craftsmen. These he gathered together, with the workmen in similar trades, and said, 'Men, you know that from this business we have our wealth. And you see and hear that not only in Ephesus but in almost all of Asia this Paul has persuaded and turned away a great many people, saying that gods made with hands are not gods. And there is danger not only that this trade of ours may come into disrepute but also that the temple of the great goddess Artemis may be counted as nothing, and that she may even be deposed from her magnificence, she whom all Asia and the world worship.' When they heard this they were enraged and were crying out, 'Great is Artemis of the Ephesians!' So the city was filled with the confusion, and they rushed together into the theater, dragging with them Gaius and Aristarchus, Macedonians who were Paul's companions in travel" (Acts 19:23–29).

2. How Galatians coincides with Acts 15 is part of the historical problem. In the missionary journeys in Acts, Paul is persecuted for the message about Jesus generally, not specifically circumcision or the cultural divisions between Jews and Gentiles. I owe this point to Greg Jenks, PhD.

3. Ignatius, *Epistle to the Smyrnaeans*, 4, in Andrew Louth, ed., *Early Christian Writings: The Apostolic Fathers* (London: Penguin Books, 1987), 102.

4. "Calculating the Time and Cost of Paul's Missionary Journeys," Open Bible blog, July 2012, https://www.openbible.info/blog/2012/07/calculating-the-time-and-cost-of-pauls-missionary-journeys/. You can use the program itself at: http://orbis.stanford.edu.

5. This assumes a minimum wage of $10 an hour, or $80 a day, multiplied by 237 days or $18,960.

NOTES

CHAPTER 27: THE COUNCIL OF JERUSALEM

1. See also Mark 6:3.

2. Eusebius, *Ecclesiastical History,* 3.20.

3. In Mark 15:40, three women witness the crucifixion of Jesus—Mary Magdalene, a woman named Salome, and "Mary the mother of the younger James and of Joses" (NABRE). Mark adds that these three women followed Jesus when he was in Galilee and took care of him. These are the same three women who, according to Mark, brought spices to cleanse Jesus' body and saw the empty tomb. Yet there is a slightly different account in the gospel of of John: the three women were Mary the mother of Jesus, his mother's sister, Mary [the wife] of Clopas, and Mary Magdalene. If Clopas is the same as Alphaeus, this would mean that Jesus' mother had a sister, also named Mary, who was married to a man named Alphaeus/Clopas and had a son named James (making him Jesus' cousin). Another alternative is that by "sister" was meant "sister-in-law" or even cousin. Some propose that "Mary the wife of Clopas" and Mary the mother of Jesus are one and the same, that, after Joseph died, Mary remarried a man named Clopas (making James Jesus' brother)—but this seems to contradict what John reports in his gospel. See "Clopas," in David Noel Freedman, ed., *Anchor Bible Dictionary,* vol. 1 (New York: Doubleday, 1992), 1066.

4. Josephus, *Antiquities* 20.9.

5. Eusebius, *Ecclesiastical History* 2.23.4.

6. Ibid.

7. Ibid., 2.23.10.

8. Ibid., 2.23.13. This is also what Jesus prophesied about himself in Mark 14:62: "You will see the Son of Man seated at the right hand of Power, and coming with the clouds of heaven."

9. Ibid., 2.23.12, 16.

10. Ibid., 2.23.16.

11. Josephus, *Antiquities* 20.9.

12. "So [Ananus] assembled the sanhedrin of judges, and brought before them the brother of Jesus, who was called Christ, whose name was James, and some others; and when he had formed an accusation against them as

breakers of the law, he delivered them to be stoned." Josephus, *Antiquities* 20.9.1.

13. "King Agrippa took the high priesthood from [Ananus], when he had ruled but three months, and made Jesus, the son of Damneus, high priest." Josephus, *Antiquities* 20.9.1.

14. The evangelical scholar Ben Witherington III believes the James Ossuary is likely genuine. Along with Herschel Shanks, the founder and editor of the *Biblical Archaeology Review*, Witherington wrote *The Brother of Jesus: The Dramatic Story and Meaning of the First Archaeological Link to Jesus and His Family* (San Francisco: HarperSanFrancisco, 2003).

15. Jerome Murphy-O'Connor, *The Holy Land: An Oxford Archaeological Guide* (Oxford: Oxford University Press, 2008), 115–16.

16. Eusebius, *Ecclesiastical History* 2.23.18.

17. Sanhedrin 59a.

APPENDIX II: WHO'S WHO IN THE EARLY JESUS MOVEMENT

1. "Is not this the carpenter, the son of Mary and brother of James and Joses and Judas and Simon?" (Mark 6:3).

2. In the New Testament, the Greek word *adelphoi*, translated as brothers or brethren, can be used in the narrow physical sense of biological brothers or in a broader sense to include male relations generally or even members of the same religious community.

3. "And are not his sisters here with us?" (Mark 6:3).

4. "And going on a little farther, he saw James the son of Zebedee and John his brother, who were in their boat mending the nets" (Mark 1:19).

5. The identification of Salome as the mother of James and John and the wife of Zebedee comes from two passages in the New Testament. Mark 15:40 describes the women witnesses to the crucifixion of Jesus: "There were also women looking on from a distance, among whom were Mary Magdalene, and Mary the mother of James the younger and of Joses, and Salome." The parallel passage in Matthew, however, doesn't refer to Salome but to the "the mother of the sons of Zebedee" (27:56). Salome is again mentioned in Mark when the women go to the tomb to anoint the body of Jesus with spices: "When the Sabbath was past, Mary

Magdalene, Mary the mother of James, and Salome bought spices, so that they might go and anoint him" (Mark 16:1).

6. In Greek, *Iacobos ho mikros* (Mark 15:40).

7. "There were also women looking on from a distance, among whom were Mary Magdalene, and Mary the mother of James the younger and of Joses, and Salome" (Mark 15:40).

8. "And James the son of Alphaeus, and Thaddaeus" (Mark 3:18).

9. "When the Sabbath was past, Mary Magdalene, Mary the mother of James, and Salome bought spices, so that they might go and anoint him" (Mark 16:1).

10. "He appointed the twelve: Simon (to whom he gave the name Peter); James the son of Zebedee and John the brother of James (to whom he gave the name Boanerges, that is, Sons of Thunder); Andrew, and Philip, and Bartholomew, and Matthew, and Thomas, and James the son of Alphaeus, and Thaddaeus, and Simon the Zealot, and Judas Iscariot, who betrayed him" (Mark 3:16–19).

Further Reading

Arav, Rami, and John J. Rousseau. *Jesus and His World: An Archaeological and Cultural Dictionary.* Minneapolis: Augsburg Fortress Press, 1995.

Barnett, Paul. *Jesus and the Rise of Early Christianity: A History of New Testament Times.* Downers Grove, IL: InterVarsity Press, 1999.

Bauckham, Richard. *Jesus and the Eyewitnesses: The Gospels as Eyewitness Testimony.* Grand Rapids, MI: Wm B. Eerdmans, 2006.

Bird, Michael F., Craig A. Evans, Simon J. Gathercole, Charles E. Hill, and Chris Tilling. *How God Became Jesus: The Real Origins of Belief in Jesus' Divine Nature.* Grand Rapids, MI: Zondervan, 2014.

Blomberg, Craig. L. *The Historical Reliability of the Gospels*, 2nd ed. Downers Grove, IL: IVP Academic, 2007.

Bock, Darrell L. *A Theology of Luke and Acts: God's Promised Program, Realized for All Nations.* Grand Rapids, MI: Zondervan, 2012.

Borg, Marcus J. *Jesus: The Life, Teachings, and Relevance of a Religious Revolutionary.* New York: HarperOne, 2006.

———and John Dominic Crossan. *The Last Week: A Day-by-Day Account of Jesus's Final Week in Jerusalem.* San Francisco: Harper San Francisco, 2006.

Brown, Raymond E. *An Introduction to New Testament Christology.* Mahwah, NJ: Paulist Press, 1994.

———. *The Death of the Messiah: From Gethsemane to the Grave.* New York: Doubleday, 1994.

Bruce, F. F. *Paul: Apostle of the Heart Set Free.* Grand Rapids, MI: Wm B. Eerdmans, 1977.

Conzelmann, Hans. *History of Primitive Christianity.* New York: Abingdon Press, 1973.

Crossan, John Dominic, and Jonathan L. Reed. *Excavating Jesus: Beneath the Stones, Behind the Texts.* San Francisco: Harper San Francisco, 2001.

Crossan, John Dominic. *Jesus: A Revolutionary Biography*. New York: HarperCollins, 2009.

———. *The Historical Jesus: The Life of a Mediterranean Jewish Peasant*. San Francisco: Harper San Francisco, 1991.

———. *The Birth of Christianity: Discovering What Happened in the Years Immediately After the Execution of Jesus*. San Francisco: Harper San Francisco, 1998.

———. *Who Killed Jesus? Exposing the Roots of Anti-Semitism in the Gospel Story of the Death of Jesus*. San Francisco: Harper San Francisco, 1996.

Crossley, James G. *Why Christianity Happened: A Sociohistorical Account of Christian Origins 26–50 CE*. Louisville, KY: Westminster John Knox Press, 2006.

Daniel-Rops, Henri. *Daily Life in the Time of Jesus*. Ann Arbor, MI: Servant Books, 1962.

Dunn, James D. G. *Jesus Remembered*. Grand Rapids: Wm B. Eerdmans, 2003.

Ehrman, Bart D. *How Jesus Became God: The Exaltation of a Jewish Preacher from Galilee*. New York: HarperOne, 2014.

———. *Did Jesus Exist? The Historical Argument for Jesus of Nazareth*. New York: HarperOne, 2012.

Eusebius. *Eusebius' Ecclesiastical History: Complete and Unabridged*. Translated by Christian Frederic Crusé, Peabody, MA: Hendrickson, 1998. Print.

Evans, Craig A. *From Jesus to the Church: The First Christian Generation*. Louisville, KY: Westminster John Knox Press, 2014.

———. *Jesus and His World: The Archaeological Evidence*. Louisville, KY: Westminster John Knox Press, 2012.

Evans, Craig A., and N. T. Wright. *Jesus, the Final Days: What Really Happened*. Edited by Troy Miller, Louisville, KY: Westminster John Knox Press, 2009.

Gibson, Shimon. *The Final Days of Jesus: The Archaeological Evidence*. New York: HarperOne, 2010.

Grant, Michael. *An Historian's Review of the Gospels*. New York: Charles Scribner's Sons, 1977.

Hanson, K. C., and Douglas E. Oakman. *Palestine in the Time of Jesus: Social Structures and Social Conflicts*. Minneapolis: Augsburg Fortress Press, 1998.

Hengel, Martin. *Between Jesus and Paul*. Minneapolis: Augsburg Fortress Press, 1983.

Hengel, Martin, and Anna Maria Schwemer. *Paul: Between Damascus and Antioch*. Louisville, KY: Westminster/John Knox Press, 1997.

Horsley, Richard A., and Neil Asher Silberman. *The Message and the Kingdom: How Jesus and Paul Ignited a Revolution and Transformed the Ancient World*. New York: Putnam, 1997.

Hurtado, Larry W. *How on Earth Did Jesus Become a God?* Grand Rapids: Wm B. Eerdmans, 2005.

Jeffers, James S. *The Greco-Roman World of the New Testament Era*. Downers Grove, IL: IVP Academic, 1999.

Josephus, Flavius. *The Works of Josephus: Complete and Unabridged*. Translated by William Whiston, Peabody, MA: Hendrickson Publishers, 1988.

Lohfink, Gerhard. *Jesus of Nazareth: What He Wanted, Who He Was*. Collegeville, MN: Liturgical Press, 2012.

Lüdemann, Gerd. *What Really Happened to Jesus: A Historical Approach to the Resurrection*. Louisville, KY: Westminster/John Knox Press, 1995.

Magness, Jodi. *Stone and Dung, Oil and Spit: Jewish Daily Life in the Time of Jesus*. Grand Rapids: Wm B. Eerdmans, 2011.

Malina, Bruce J. *Windows on the World of Jesus: Time Travel to Ancient Judea*. Louisville, KY: Westminster/John Knox Press, 1993.

Mason, Steve. *Josephus and the New Testament*. Peabody, MA: Hendrickson Publishers, 2003.

Meier, John P. *A Marginal Jew: Rethinking the Historical Jesus*. New York: Doubleday, 1994.

Miller, Robert J., ed. *The Complete Gospels: Annotated Scholars Version*. San Francisco: Harper San Francisco, 1992.

Murphy-O'Connor, Jerome. *The Holy Land: An Oxford Archaeological Guide*, 5th ed. Oxford: Oxford University Press, 2008.

Pitre, Brant. *Jesus and the Jewish Roots of the Eucharist: Unlocking the Secrets of the Last Supper*. New York: Doubleday, 2011.

Pixner, Bargil. *Paths of the Messiah and Sites of the Early Church from Galilee to Jerusalem: Jesus and Jewish Christianity in Light of Archaeological Discoveries*. San Francisco: Ignatius Press, 2010.

Robinson, James M., ed., *The Nag Hammadi Library in English*. San Francisco: Harper and Row, 1978.

Sanders, E. P. *The Historical Figure of Jesus*. New York: Penguin Books, 1993.

Stark, Rodney. *The Rise of Christianity: How the Obscure, Marginal Jesus Movement Became the Dominant Religious Force in the Western World in a Few Centuries.* New York: HarperCollins, 1996.

Theissen, Gerd, and Annette Merz. *The Historical Jesus: A Comprehensive Guide.* Minneapolis: Augsburg Fortress Press, 1998.

Vermes, Géza. *The Religion of Jesus the Jew.* Minneapolis: Augsburg Fortress Press, 1993.

Witherington III, Ben. *New Testament History: A Narrative Account.* Grand Rapids: Baker Academic, 2001.

Wright, N. T. *Jesus and the Victory of God.* Minneapolis: Augsburg Fortress Press, 1996.

———. *The Resurrection of the Son of God.* Minneapolis: Augsburg Fortress Press, 2003.

INDEX

Note: page numbers in *italics* refer to photos

Joses, 250

Journal of the American
Medical Association, 106

Jubilees, 217

Judah, 175

Judah of Galilee, 12–13, 232

Judas Iscariot, 73
betrayal of Jesus, 61–62
and Jesus' arrest, 78–79

Judas (relative of Jesus), 250

Judas the Galilean, 163

Judas (Yehuda), 9, 250

Jude, xviii

Jude (Thaddeus), 9

Jude (Yehuda), 250

Judea, 197

Junia, 255–256

K

kashrut (kosher dietary laws), 203, 217

Kepha (the Rock), 9. See also Simon
Peter (Simon bar Jonah)

Kfar Cana, 13

kiddush (blessing), 71

Kidron Valley, 32, 33, 34, 97–98

king of the Jews, Jesus
(Yeshu'a) as, 27–36

kingdom movement, xv. See
also the Way (hodos; ha-
derech); Jesus movement
cells of, 10–11
growth, 11

kingdom of God, xiv, 9–19
Jesus on, 5, 19
as open to all, 48–51

Klausner, Joseph, xvi

kokhim (burial niches), 22

L

L (source material unique to Luke), 153

Lamb of God, Jesus as, 67

language, on Pentecost, 143

Last Supper, 72
timing of, 67–68

laying on of hands, 194, 219

Lazarus (Eleazar), 10, 59, 251
death of, 21
tomb of, 21, 23

The Life and Times of Jesus the
Messiah (Edersheim), xvi

Life of Christ, xvi

limestone (even Yerushelaim;
Jerusalem stone), 141

literacy, in first century, xxviii, 285n8

lithostratos (Roman flagstones), 88

Lod (Lydda), 194

Loisy, Alfred, 278n33

Lucceius Albinus, 236

Lucius of Cyrene, 205, 256

Lucius Sergius Paulus, 254

Lucius Vitellius, 90, 191

Luke, 282n2
knowledge of Jewish holy books, 154

Lydda (Lod), 194

Lystra, 227, 229

M

Maccabees, 12, 146

Magdala, 3, 212
synagogue, 167

About the Author

Robert Hutchinson studied philosophy as an undergraduate, moved to Israel to learn Hebrew, and earned a graduate degree in New Testament from Fuller Theological Seminary. He has been a professional writer his entire adult life, over the years writing both for Christian publications, such as *Christianity Today*, and for secular magazines and newspapers. Hutchinson's first paid article, in 1978, was about the children of the Hare Krishnas living in Seattle, and he has had a lifelong interest in non-Christian religions. His 2015 book *Searching for Jesus: New Discoveries in the Quest for Jesus of Nazareth—and How They Support the Gospel Accounts* was widely praised by both Christian and secular scholars. Hutchinson's classic travelogue about the inner workings of the Vatican, *When in Rome: A Journal of Life in Vatican City*, was called a "*tour de force* that manages the rare and difficult feat of being at once ribald and reverent, informative and outrageous and, not least, very funny." Hutchinson lives with his wife and children in a small seaside town on the West Coast. He blogs at www.RobertHutchinson.com.

STAY IN TOUCH

For more information about Robert Hutchinson and his upcoming books and presentations, visit his website, www.RobertHutchinson.com.

You'll find free resources that include these and more:

- Book excerpts
- Exclusive features
- Downloads of audio and video presentations
- Special reports
- Free e-mail updates

Robert J. Hutchinson
27525 Puerta Real #100–340
Mission Viejo, CA 92691

www.RobertHutchinson.com